DONATION :

Best wishes,

# LITIGATION

*as*

*Spiritual Practice*

# LITIGATION

## *as*

## *Spiritual Practice*

George J. Felos

BLUE DOLPHIN

Published by
Blue Dolphin Publishing, Inc.
P.O. Box 8, Nevada City, CA 95959
Orders: 1-800-643-0765
Web: www.bluedolphinpublishing.com

ISBN: 1-57733-104-4


Library of Congress Cataloging-in-Publication Data

Felos, George J., 1952-
    Litigation as spiritual practice / George J. Felos.
       p. cm.
    ISBN 1-57733-104-4
       1. Felos, George J., 1952- 2. Lawyers—United States—
Biography.  3. Practice of law—United States.  4. Trials—United
States.  5. Spiritual life.  I. Title.

    KF373.F39 A3 2001
    340'.092—dc21

                                                        2001035696


Cover / Jacket Design by: Jeannie A. Casnellie © 2002
(727) 772-8315
P.O. Box 761, Palm Harbor, FL 34682

Printed in the United States of America

5    4    3    2    1

# Contents

# *Preface*

WE CRAVE SPIRITUAL FULFILLMENT. If you doubt this, just survey the bestseller list, now replete with road maps to inner peace. But you don't have to look that far. Dissatisfaction runs rampant. At home and at work, many are experiencing levels of frustration, anger, and futility described as unprecedented. This dissatisfaction, while appearing negative or destructive, actually signifies the positive. Despair often reveals the source from which spiritual yearning springs.

We believe that this endemic feeling of deep frustration causes increasing intolerance of each other, rising levels of incivility, random acts of violence, and portends, no less, the dissolution of society as we know it. This rings true—but only half true. This futility and dissatisfaction *is* the harbinger of a dead end, but the dead end doesn't have to be a crash onto the rocks and flaming wreckage. I believe what we sense as our "end" actually heralds a transformation of profound and evolutionary dimensions.

Pundits predict that this new fire of spiritual transformation will first ignite in the United States and then spread across the planet. We often begin the spiritual journey only after we experience for ourselves that material wealth doesn't, in and of itself, provide the joy and fulfillment we hunger for on a deeper level. Unfortunately, the abstract concept that materialism doesn't result in happiness has little meaning for us. Sometimes it takes feeding and gorging ourselves to near oblivion for us to realize that the path we have chosen carries our death. Thus, the place in this world where material prosperity reigns—where tangible needs are not only satisfied, but also serve as justification for extreme indulgence—marks the place where conditions for spiritual awakening are most ripe. I guess we still remain world leaders!

Amidst this play of our unraveling social fabric, we view litigation and lawyers as a prominent sign of our coming demise. Lawyers seem to be a lightning rod for what we feel is most wrong with us. The perceived aggression, avarice, intractableness, intolerance, and purposeful manipulation of the simple into the complex to suit their own needs, elevates lawyers to the top of our hate list. We see the litigation process as a pus-filled boil that needs to be lanced from the societal body. Political desire to modify the civil justice system is more intense now than in recent memory.

As an attorney, a trial attorney, I confess a different view. But it's not my purpose to explain how lawyers see themselves, or to analyze whose perceptions may be more accurate. (Interestingly, a recent survey of lawyers revealed that twenty percent saw themselves as somewhat aggressive and obnoxious, while these same lawyers thought seventy percent of *other* lawyers possessed these dubious characteristics!) However we may think of lawyers, the fact remains that litigation, trial in the courtroom, still bears great resemblance to its historical predecessor, trial by combat.

Most of my friends seem amazed that I work and perform rather successfully in this arena. As a spiritual aspirant for close to twenty-five years with definite monastic tendencies, my friends don't understand how I survive within the aggressive and often highly negative energies of the courtroom. They view spiritual inclinations as incompatible with practicing law, let alone being a trial attorney. But a true seeker of God has no spiritual focus. There is no duality separating your work and your spiritual life. The universe does not discriminate. It serves up life, *all* of life, all the time, as a continual lesson to wake us from our spiritual ignorance. The purpose of life, the real job we have, is to be open to this lesson, to receive life and be transformed by it, whether we happen to like it or not.

My work in court has proved stimulating, challenging, and professionally fulfilling. But more than that, it has been spiritually rich. This book describes the excitement of the courtroom, the thrill and agony of the case, and the pain and ecstasy of the inner unfoldment this work catalyzes. If the seemingly barren and war-strewn field of litigation can be the playground where spirit dances, it can revel anywhere.

The urge behind this book is to encourage and impel you to utilize your life's endeavor, whatever it may be, to its highest purpose—to move from making a living from your work, to having your work make you more alive. Along the way I hope this book will entertain, fascinate, generate some laughter, and perhaps even inspire!

# Acknowledgments

U PON JOINING THE FELLOWSHIP OF AUTHORS, I was pleasantly surprised to learn that countless preceding writers had encountered the same process-describing metaphors I had discovered. Seven years ago, driven to compose, I planted myself down with barely a blueprint for my intended effort. Writing the first third of the book felt like traversing a winding road. All I could see before me was the immediate curve of highway—just the next few paragraphs in view at any time. After a while the road started to straighten, and as I approached the midpoint, I easily surveyed how the rest of the book would fall into place. About two-thirds of the way I began to feel distinctly pregnant. The book I was carrying had taken on its own life force, and as my literary child-to-be increased in measure, so did my urge to birth it.

As I have also discovered, the formation of a book into a published work involves passage through many cycles, some particularly challenging for a first-time author. Along the way I often received assistance at what seemed to be just the right moment. I am grateful to Rev. Pat Palmer for her review of my initial efforts and her continuing support and encouragement. The suggestions of Constance Felos for simplifying the book's structure proved helpful, as did the proofreading of Cynthia Gay. Agent John White graciously provided help even though I am not his client. Author Stephen Spignesi's validation of this enterprise was particularly helpful, coming at a time of self-doubt. Many thanks to Laurie

Rosin whose gentle and keen editorial skills taught me much about writing and greatly contributed to the book's final form. I am very grateful to Jeannie Casnellie for her cover design, and to author and teacher Alan Cohen for his endorsement, the first I received. I thank all the people at Blue Dolphin Publishing, especially Linda Maxwell for her work on the format and the index, and Paul Clemens, who believed enough in this book to publish it. Finally, I am very grateful to my family for their unceasing love and support.

I have strived for accuracy, though that effort, arguably, can be better judged in the book's legal expositions than in its metaphysics. Quoted references to documents such as pleadings, motions, discovery requests, court orders, and correspondence are verbatim. All quoted deposition testimony is also verbatim, as the subject depositions were transcribed. Trial testimony and proceedings that were not transcribed are quoted upon firm recollection.

Attributing sources in spiritual writing is another matter. Anyone who has been exposed to numerous spiritual teachers and teachings knows that core truths and concepts are often similarly expressed, even among disparate traditions. And as most spiritual instructors freely admit, there is, in essence, nothing in their message that has not been said before. Thus, many of the concepts, analogies and stories used to describe spiritual principles are generalized, though we might recall where we first heard one or another. Much of what I have written, while I hope distinctive in presentation, germinated from my exposure to many different teachers and sources. I learned much about yogic philosophy and practice at the Kripalu Center for Yoga and Health. The idea for my exposition of the scriptural phrase, "As a man thinketh in his heart, so is he," was generated from *You Are the Power*, by Rev. J. Kennedy Shultz. I recall first hearing the story of the Zen master grieving the death of his child in Charlotte Joko Beck's, *Everyday Zen*. Analogizing to motion pictures the process by which mental projection can create personal reality was first encountered in the writings of Paramahansa Yogananda.

In reviewing the manuscript I did discover that certain expressions resemble particular passages or phrases remembered from a book read or lecture heard years before (and doubtlessly, there are many such similarities I do not recall). For instance, about intimate relationships I wrote, "it is hard to be open-hearted but harder to be closed-hearted." Stephen Levine in *A Gradual Awakening*, writing about the Buddhist practice of loving-kindness, offers "…it's hard to be loving all the time. But it's harder not to be loving." The two passages seem sufficiently different not to warrant ascription to the prior work, yet their similarity might suggest that the later effort is not purely original. I therefore decided to preface my phrase with, "A wise man once said," and use such clarifiers elsewhere to denote the possibility of connection to an unnamed or unknown source. I am grateful to all those who have walked this path before me, from whom I have received so much.

My manuscript reviews also evidenced my discomfort with certain exposures of my private life, many of which are divorce related. Writing about your tribulations is often purgative, but however well-crafted or personally meaningful the prose, it does not necessarily mean the product should be shared or will interest others. In my review I asked myself, *Is this passage useful in elucidating a larger idea or principle?…Would someone benefit from reading this?* An affirmative answer to either was sufficient to retain the passage (overcoming but not eliminating my feeling of vulnerability).

Finally, I feel as optimistic about our collective future as I did seven years ago. While we continue to struggle with the ever-increasing pace of change, some of which feels so wrenching, we also are accessing the changeless and eternal with greater frequency and ability. This evolution of consciousness, our ultimate salvation, has even begun to be felt in small ways in the legal system. I hope this book plays some small part in that evolution.

George J. Felos
April, 2002

CHAPTER ONE

# The Big Case Arrives

C ASES ARRIVE IN DIFFERENT WAYS. This one entered on a
forklift. Six cardboard file cartons, each over three feet
long, now occupied my ten-by-twelve foot screened-in
porch. On the Saturday morning of Labor Day weekend 1992, I
turned out of bed and in my underwear stumbled towards the lanai.
I opened the sliding glass door and stared at the twenty-or-so linear
feet of paper that would probably consume just about every minute
of the three-day holiday weekend. My stupor was eventually
interrupted by a self-pity that cried that every *other* inhabitant of
Tampa Bay would be spending the next three days boating, beach-
ing, barbecuing, or just goofing off. With all this simply too much
to bear in a fully vertical position, I plopped into a chair luckily
placed nearby.

I sat immobile for a few moments until a sailboat caught my eye
as it glided through the channel behind my house and into the open
bay. One or two small white sails already glistened in the distance.
The blue sky and unimpeded sunshine made this a perfect day for
everyone else to stretch into. I noticed a neighbor bringing some
gear down to his dock in anticipation of a day on the boat. A pair
of gray pelicans flew in formation over the channel, and a snow-
white egret strutted the back lawn, perhaps stalking breakfast. As it
hunted, its head remained rock-steady while its long neck undu-
lated as it moved. An egret's concentration is good enough to snag
a lizard now and then, always exciting to see—apart from the
lizard's point of view.

1

Even though it wasn't mine, I loved that house—1960s concrete block, small, two bedroom, with original appliances of medium sky-blue. Thank God it was built before Florida slipped into the dark ages of avocado and gold. The house obviously wasn't much, apart from its prime location on a small peninsula in St. Joseph Sound. Looking west I enjoyed a gorgeous view of the open Sound and the thin green line on the horizon that was Caladesi Island. This natural barrier island and state park lies north of its concretized counterpart, Clearwater Beach. My backyard ended with a sea wall at Curlew Creek, a natural waterway that flowed into the Sound. The Creek's two hundred-foot breadth cushioned me from the backyards of the homes to the south. From my living room window looking northwest past the cul-de-sac and vacant lot beyond, the water eventually passed under the Dunedin Causeway drawbridge out into the Gulf of Mexico.

I felt soothed and protected by the surrounding water. That's what drew me to the house. I had moved in eighteen months before, in March 1991, leaving my marital home, my wife, and my son about two miles to the north. A month and a half before separating, I was shown the house by a realtor who told me the owners insisted on a yearly lease. Only wanting a month-to-month tenancy, I asked the realtor to convey my transient-sounding offer. She stressed there was no way this would be accepted.

While standing in the house with the realtor, I knew I would live there, as improbable as the circumstances made it seem. Believing that something will happen is not foresight. Rather, it is the *actual* experience in the present of something that will occur in the future. The paradox with this form of intuition is that the future is no longer the future because it becomes for that moment the present. When I entered that house for the first time, I knew I would live there because, through foresight, I realized I was *already* living there.

Most times this "knowing" for me is sensed as a feeling. Sometimes I hear it, and sometimes I see it. This is not to say that I go around every day intuiting tomorrow's events. I'm stuck in my head a good portion of the time, like most of us in our mentally over-developed culture. This means that most of our energy is tied up intellectually, engaged in thought and reacting to thought. And much of the time our reactive thought process drives our emotions. How we feel depends upon whether we happen to be attracted to, averse to or indifferent to what we are thinking.

Intuition does not lie in the rational mind. Sometimes it is "seen" through other centers of the body, such as the heart or solar plexus. Everybody has had that "gut feeling." For me, the experience of intuition through sight is like seeing two different realities at the same time. To use a *Star Trek* analogy, it's dimensionally multi-phasic. (I wondered whether I could write this book without referring to *Star Trek*, and didn't get past page three!)

The crew of the Enterprise, beset in one episode by all types of strange maladies, discovered that they were infected by invisible parasitic creatures attached to their bodies. The creatures were unseeable because they existed in another phasic dimension. They occupied the same space and time, but at a different vibrational level. With the benefit of a hand-held "multi-phasic viewing device" constructed by our heroes, they could press a button and observe the creatures on their skin. Release the button and they were gone. Intuitive seeing is somewhat like that for me. A transparent image exists and is there, and then it's not. While extremely subtle, it is also undeniably real.

Unfortunately, while sitting on the lanai that morning, my mind wasn't occupied with fascinating intricacies of metaphysics; it was filled with the ponderous reality of twenty file feet of *Fellouzis vs. United States of America*. The case had disaster painted all over it. This was a tax dispute, more precisely a tax refund case, a subject I knew nothing about. Litigators don't have to have a background in the particular area of law of every case they try. It sure helps though. Of all specialties in the law, tax practice is probably the least known and most dreaded by general practitioners. Luckily I awoke without hunger, because the prospect of going through reams of unintelligible sections of the Internal Revenue Code was enough, by itself, to start my stomach turning.

And it got worse from there. This case had a long—very long—checkered past. My potential clients unhappily had just surmised that the attorney they hired in the early eighties stole $50,000 of their money that was intended for the I.R.S.; was disintegrating from illegal drug use; had the law on his heels; and had neglected the case to the point where court dismissal was a danger. The distressed clients, hoping to at least retrieve their file, couldn't even reach the lawyer. The papers they eventually garnered came from other attorneys loosely associated with the miscreant, and these files were in a state of organization roughly resembling that of the fallen attorney's state of affairs.

Why was I going to waste my Labor Day weekend on this mess? Two reasons. Although my personal and professional lives were not quite the disaster this case was, they were pretty close. My marital separation had cut me to the bone. So much so that in July 1991, after four months on my own, I had left town for a two-month residence at a yoga center where I lived and worked essentially as a monk. For me my retreat was a matter of emotional and spiritual survival. For my law office, however, which consisted of me, my father, and our long-time secretary, my absence brought the opposite. In 1990 I had argued in the Florida Supreme Court the state's landmark right-to-die case, was in all the newspapers and on TV, and generated over $160,000. In 1991 my paycheck was about $35,000. In 1992, although I was starting to come around personally, (which means I was no longer crying in places not of my choosing), my income was about the same as the previous year. I was near broke. Which gives rise to the second reason for expending my holiday weekend on this case: it was worth over a million dollars.

Manny Fellouzis used to import and wholesale oriental antiquities and collectibles. He was my father's best friend and a client for many years. Never wanting for an opportunity to chatter about his affairs, he often storied about the vast sums he would garner when his case was finally settled or won by the sterling tax expert he had retained. In his heyday, Manny and his wife Mary had donated Chinese antiques and some American art glass to the Carnegie Museum and from 1979 to 1981 deducted over $600,000 from their taxable income for these contributions. By the time the I.R.S. got through with them, they had paid over $350,000 in additional tax and another $430,000 in interest and penalties assessed against them. This took a sizable cut out of their net worth and made the difference between an upper middle class and upper crust retirement. Manny and Mary were seeking a new knight to raise their banner, and I became their prime candidate.

One of the first lessons I learned as a lawyer was that businesses and their insurers don't just hand over money, and governmental entities are even more belligerent to the suggestion that a citizen could possibly present a legitimate monetary claim. I knew the I.R.S., after battling this case for ten years, was not about to fork over $780,000 plus interest thereon that had been compounding daily for eons. My second lesson was that a client's estimation of his own case was usually two or three times that which a dispassionate examination of the facts would reveal. The third and most important instruction to a plaintiff's lawyer is to investigate thoroughly a contingency fee case before you take it. If you lose you not only don't get paid, you often incur the costs of the suit, and forfeit hundreds and sometimes thousands of hours of effort over what can be many years.

So after a shower, some breakfast, and a little Bach on the piano, I picked a file carton—it really didn't matter which one—hunkered down at the lanai table, and with a couple of legal pads and pen or two started in. When facing a huge task, I often find it difficult to overcome my initial resistance to beginning. But this time I found it relatively painless falling into a rhythm: an hour in the files, ten minutes up to stretch a bit, another hour in the files, a walk around the house and an apple and something to drink, two hours on the case and twenty minutes at the piano—*hey, is the afternoon really about over!*

Absorption elicits a type of serenity. When one so completely engages in what one is doing, the doer seems to drop away and the only thing left is the doing. With our constant mental judging, evaluating, commenting upon, and dissecting of our own experience, it's a joy when the judge, evaluator, commentator and dissector take a temporary leave of absence. Entering the Fellouzis case was like passing through a portal into a different world. Names, places, events, confrontations, explanations, charges, countercharges, all combined to bring this new realty into greater focus in my mind. Jade, nephrite, Ch'ien-Lung, Yung-Cheng, K'ang-Hsi, ivory, carryover, depreciation, Ch'ing Dynasty, Weissman, Horowitz, Chung, Lee, Chen, Nathan Ivory, *koro*, table screen, amberina, assessment, deficiency, claim for refund, all became the symbolic inhabitants of this world.

A great fascination occurs when the seemingly inert come alive. This magic can happen upon entering a house as the estate representative after an individual's death. From each of the tangible objects and papers examined (in order to inventory the estate and determine its value), a picture of another's life emerges. As each drawer is opened you see what was kept, what was kept close, and what held meaning for this person. You sometimes even smell what his tastes drove him to purchase the last time he went to the supermarket. But words on a file page and objects in a home are not really inert. Though our minds give them life, our mental images are also shaped by the elemental vibrations with which those words and objects are imbued.

Day turned into night, and night along with some sleep turned into day. The rhythm and silence deepened, and I began to feel as if I existed in an interior realm. As I continued in and out of the files I began to recall images of my "weekend from hell," as I fondly referred to it. I had also spent Memorial Day weekend 1991, just two months after my marital separation, in this house inside a world of my own. That weekend I experienced rage. Savage, unadulterated, and murderous rage. For the first time in my life I, who rarely became angry, who would barely express irritation where others would be out of control, found myself taken to the farthest edge.

I had been a platinum husband and father. I worked, shopped, cooked, cleaned, and primarily looked after our son who was born in 1986. I assisted and encouraged my spouse as she entered the career of her dreams. I faithfully stood by through her years of confusion and occasional destructive impulses, some of which were scarily intense. I cared for her and our son the many times she was too stressed out or incapable of attending to herself. I didn't drink, squander money, or lack fidelity. I considered myself reasonably attractive and carried few major bad habits. I loved her. And I was dumped! Not even for another man. Had I been a lout or had she enamored herself with someone else, perhaps the rejection would have been easier.

To her, I seemed unattractive, sexually unexciting, balding, boring, and just not enough fun to be with. Now that she had been nurtured, provided for, loved, and given a safe and supportive environment within which to build her confidence and sense of self, she didn't need me anymore. And she was not the least reluctant to repeatedly hurl this fact in my face along with her intense hatred. For her, marriage to me inflicted a fate worse than death. Three months before we separated I was flying home from a trip and had the feeling that my spouse, who was safe at home, wanted the airplane to crash. When I arrived I shared my intuition with her. She admitted that for the past year or so she had wished for my death, and whenever I flew (assuming she wasn't with me) hoped the plane would crash, as she had just done that day.

Throughout the process of our breaking apart, the pain and torment I suffered was tempered, no, made more bearable, by the first principle of spiritual life: we are the creators of our own reality; what we experience we have attracted to ourselves; our perception of the outer world is a reflection of our inner self. This principle of responsibility recognizes that blaming, whether it be another person, a situation, an event, the world, fate, God, or ourselves, is an avoidance of what is really happening. Blame is a convenient opportunity not to see and experience what is painful, uncomfortable, and true.

Every situation of distress carries possibilities for greater awareness. Adversity offers insight into how our ideas and beliefs limit us and obscure our experience of who we really are. I undeniably knew that my spousal relationship was self-induced. She reflected back to me my inner torment of self-rejection and lack of self-worth. My long-held negative patterns, beliefs, and feelings about myself grew progressively more difficult to tolerate. There were times *I* wished I were dead, it felt so unbearable being with myself. We're not given these experiences to be tortured; they make us move, change, and expand. The more resistant we are to afflictions the harder they come.

When my wife told me that day she had wished me dead, I felt a dagger piercing my heart. Usually impassive to these rips, this time I found myself on the bed, sobbing into the pillow. After a minute or two I had a vision. I beheld my spouse as the expression of my inner reality. I recognized her as the instrument the material world had provided, at my behest, to push and lead me towards the greater awareness within which I needed to start living. I am not talking about an intellectual experience. With a feeling as if someone had pushed an arm through the center of my body, I saw and felt her soul in karmic interplay with my own and realized her role of *service* to me, and in her service, her own suffering as she played out her own karma. In that moment my pain was transmuted to deep compassion and love for her and for myself.

In the world of spirit every moment holds the possibility of transcendence. Understanding of the truth is helpful. While mental knowledge doesn't, by itself, bring us in touch with spirit, it can lead the way. Right knowledge helps to foster right intention, which helps in developing right attitude and action. For me, transcendence is a matter of Grace. It is not gained or earned, it is bestowed. What we can do is prepare a fertile field, be receptive, and when we are the recipients of Grace, be grateful. I don't mean to say that some divine entity parsimoniously parcels out transcendence. What I mean is that spiritual unfoldment is something you can't force. You open like a flower. Self-emanation is not something you achieve but that which you relax into. Our natural state is Grace. You can't make it happen, you let it happen.

By late Sunday night, while unfortunately not grace-illumined, I had slogged through enough of the file to detect some emerging light. While there were still major holes in the record before me, some issues seemed pretty well defined. The foremost question seemed to be how much these donated art objects were really worth. This made it a valuation case. Such controversies usually end up as a courtroom battle of experts. Manny and Mary had relied on two appraisers at the time of donation. Of the items donated, three constituted the lion's share of the $630,000 total appraised value. The big ticket was a contemporary carved ivory model boat, meant to resemble the royal yacht of a first-century Chinese emperor. Not particularly unusual, you say? Well, this model yacht happened to be six feet long, seven feet tall, and intricately carved from four hundred pounds of ivory. The appraisal said $380,000, and that's what the clients had deducted from their taxable income.

The second item was a ceremonial incense burner known as a *koro,* approximately eight inches long and six inches high. This magnificently detailed piece was carved from spinach-green jade, or more precisely nephrite. Nephrite and jadeite are the two minerals recognized as true jade, as distinguished from many lesser stones also called jade. The koro was valued at $90,000, primarily because it was reputedly fashioned during the reign of Emperor Yung-Cheng, 1712-1732. The third item was a jade "table screen" said to be worth $95,000. Undeniably gorgeous, the fourteen-inch-diameter disc carved from white nephrite was displayed on a beautifully crafted wood stand. One side of the disc depicted two exotic birds on a flowered branch etched into the jade and painted with gold. The reverse presented an aviary scene created by the inlay of brilliant precious and semi-precious stones. I crackled just imagining how splendid it would appear in my living room.

Obviously the government's appraiser took a less glowing view of these items, but how much dimmer brought a shock to me. The I.R.S. valued *all* the donated items at a grand sum of $54,000, just a slight variance from the taxpayers' $630,000 point of view. The government's "expert" appraised the ivory boat at $35,000, the koro at $5,000 and the table screen at the princely sum of $1,200. Something seemed very wrong here. I had handled many cases disputing the value of an object. If an item is claimed to be worth $90,000, it may be worth $60,000 or $80,000 or even $30,000, but $1,200! I had never come across such a disparity, especially in a case that had gotten this far. Either someone had been grossly incompetent or purposely disregarded market value in rendering his opinion. I hoped it wasn't my clients or their crew.

In a valuation contest, credibility of experts is often the decisive factor. Here the government seemed to have a one-up. Its expert was the erudite-sounding James B. Godfrey, graduate of the University of Virginia in oriental studies, former manager of the Chinese Arts department at Christie's auction house in New York, lecturer, author, internationally recognized dealer in oriental antiquities, and consultant to rich and famous collectors, at least according to the autobiographical sketch preceding his appraisal. From what I could tell, the appraisers my client had relied on didn't even reach high school. They plied the trade as wholesalers, as did my clients. Lack of education isn't necessarily a handicap in the courtroom. Juries sometimes relate more to common sense from an untutored expert than to the often convoluted and at times condescending testimony of highly educated experts. The respective credentials provided a plus for the I.R.S., but not a big worry.

What presented a problem, a major problem, was the relationship my clients had with their appraisers. While perhaps not in bed together, it sure looked like heavy petting. The first, Matthew Weissman, had toiled in the general antique wholesale trade for over forty years and specialized in American cut glass. Weissman had been selected, my clients proclaimed, because being in the trade for so long, "no one was more qualified." He was also, unfortunately from my perspective, one of Manny and Mary's largest customers, purchasing over $400,000 of goods the year before the appraisal. *Why are clients so stupid,* I repeatedly thought.

The apparent conflict of interest with the other appraiser looked even worse. Eric "Makana" Lee, a native of Hong Kong, conducted a significant oriental export operation from that Asian city and had been my clients' primary business agent before their retirement. Oh, and a slight detail to add—Lee had purchased Mary and Manny's company for over $800,000 around the time of his appraisal and owed my clients over $400,000 on the business mortgage! I imagined the fun I could have as opposing counsel "exploring" this issue on cross-examination.

The "intimacy" between the taxpayers and their appraisers had been seized on by the initial I.R.S. auditor and promptly ballooned into a full-fledged criminal investigation. "Tax fraud" had an awful-sounding ring—at best, massive fines and penalties, at worst, incarceration as an example to deter others. If you could imagine an alleged white-collar criminal least suited to jail, it was Manny, with his soft physique, nervous personality, and need for comfort and control. After he had been slowly put through the wringer, the investigation was terminated for lack of evidence of criminal intent.

The records revealed summaries of I.R.S. interviews taken with Weissman and Lee. As a plus, the appraisers declared that the values placed on the donated items were their own and were not provided by the taxpayers. They also stated, to my chagrin, that the description and dating of the objects were Manny's. This was a salient factor, as a high portion of the value attributed to many of the items appeared to be due to their status as antiques. Since Manny apparently didn't put the actual numbers on the appraisals, I guessed this had stymied the criminal investigators. But the coziness in the procuring and performance of the appraisals didn't fly with the I.R.S. money men. They heaped on penalties for "substantial negligence" and "substantial underpayment." Manny righteously insisted the criminal investigation had been undertaken solely for harassment and the civil penalties purposely assessed for the same reason.

Righteousness, it seemed, was not only confined to my client. I was beginning to have an opinion about everything. While I followed my intention to look at this case with an objective eye, I noticed I was far from feeling dispassionate. I seemed to become irritated and slightly indignant at each misstep of my clients that the record revealed. Finding the weak spots in the case and anticipating how the opposition can exploit them is my job. The emotional reaction to my work revealed my agenda, my stuff, my stake in the action. This case was my ticket out of an economic desert and a professional drought. How dare my clients blow it by acting irresponsibly, imprudently, and in an unthinking manner? In other words, how dare they act like human beings? How inconsiderate of them not to have realized twelve years ago how much I would need this case and how their actions would impact on me in the future!

A master once said that meditation is the practice of awareness without judgment. I found attentiveness much easier to develop than nonjudgment. I had become fairly adept over the years in cultivating awareness of my thoughts and feelings. I even started to get the hang of diving beneath my emotions to the place of insight where one sees how and why these emotions arise. My self-judgment increased, however, as I became more aware of how my thoughts, actions, and feelings were being driven by underlying fears, insecurities, and limiting beliefs. *I can't believe how arrested I am, I should be able to do a lot better.* Obviously this was not exactly what the master had in mind in describing meditation.

A meditation practice without self-compassion confines one to a truly hard and painful path. In meditation, and I don't mean just sitting on a pillow, who you are is slowly revealed to you, as who you are not (but who you thought you were) unravels bit by bit. A lot of this we don't care or like to see. Our selfishness, greed, callousness, hatred, envy, superiority, and insensitivity all stare us in the face. You can't make them go away, you can't avoid them, and most of all, you can't fight them. Becoming angry or irritated or reactive to our darker aspects only empowers them. Self-rejection or disgust over my lack of progress just fuels the object of my contempt even more. Paradoxically it is our acceptance of what ails us that frees us. If you want to be straight, allow yourself to be crooked—so the scriptures say.

One of the hardest things I have ever found doing is, in essence, the non-doing of meditation. Meditative awareness is also profound beyond description. Tremendous joy emerges when watching without judgment, without reaction, the thoughts and feelings that previously would have sparked negative or critical judgments. When I goof, if the thought *you're not good enough* arises, I experience great freedom when it passes by without perturbation. Without disturbance in the mental field, there is nothing with which to cause a follow-up negative thought or feeling to arise. The thought floats by like a cloud against the sky—just thought. This non-doing, non-fighting, disempowers the thought. When we decline to invest energy in what we don't want and refrain from resisting what we want to release, the thought-energy exhausts itself and withers away. For me, the process of reaching this state has been very long and gradual. One approach that has helped me a lot is humor. Often for me, laughing at the absurdity of reacting to the world from my egotistical construct shifts my energy from self-criticism to self-acceptance, from self-judgment to compassion.

As I laughed at myself and my clients' "inconsiderate" behavior, I focused on another aspect of the valuation battle, what my clients had paid for the objects they later donated. Acquisition cost furnishes one of the best indicators of fair market value. As you by now probably imagine, Manny and Mary purchased many of these items for a song, at least in comparison to the appraised values. Yes, some of these items were acquired ten-to-fifteen years prior to donation, which in a market driven by inflation could account for the disparity between cost and donated value. The koro, however, was bought for $10,000 and the table screen for $12,000, both within three to four years of donation. Even though the taxpayers were dealers and likely snatched wholesale buying opportunities, convincing the jury to accept donated values of $95,000 and $90,000 for these items was going to take lots of explaining.

The ivory boat imparted a story unto itself. Unbelievably, this work of art supposedly worth $380,000 was acquired for $17,000 less than three years prior to donation. Where could I find buys like that? The piece had been made by and purchased from the Nathan Ivory Factory, named for its location on Nathan Road in Hong Kong, that city's counterpart of Rodeo Drive. This story was revealed through exotic-looking documents containing the seals and signatures of various Hong Kong officials who took the attestations of Mr. Au and Mr. Ng, respectively the owner and general manager of Nathan Ivory. Apparently, the yacht sold to Manny was the last of a series of seven huge ivory model boats produced by Nathan Ivory over a period of five years. Each of the prior six pieces sold for over $100,000 wholesale. Nathan stopped making the model vessels for two supposed reasons: first, the escalating price of ivory made them too expensive to produce; and second, the craftsman in charge of the carving had died, leaving this specialized art form to expire with him. Manny's boat was the only one imported into the United States, and therefore he touted it as a one-of-a-kind item.

Nathan Ivory was at that time one of the largest producers of carved ivory products in the world. The ivory-carving trade was centered in Hong Kong, Japan, and China, with Hong Kong the principal venue. Companies fashioned their wares primarily for export. From what I could tell, Nathan Ivory imported tons of raw ivory from Africa each year, kept a portion for its own use, and resold the balance to other producers. This started reading like a movie script, and I was intrigued.

Manny purchased the boat in January 1978. A little less than a year before, a bill had been introduced in the United States Congress to ban the import of ivory into the United States. Such a prohibition, likely to become worldwide, would have spelled doom to Nathan Ivory's business. So enter into the United States Mr. Au and Mr. Ng to fight this prospective legislation. And whom do they enlist? Why, Manny, of course, one of their largest customers in this country. After introducing his colleagues to his Congressman and pleading their cause, Manny sent Mr. Au and Mr. Ng to Washington with the suggestion they hire a professional lobbyist. The maneuver must have worked, because the bill that eventually passed was significantly watered down. Ivory products could still be imported into the United States, but only if the importer can document that the raw ivory originated from an African country with an approved elephant conservation program. As a result there was no ban on ivory, the supply of raw ivory for legal use immediately shrank, the price of raw ivory rocketed through the roof, and the tons of ivory in the Nathan Ivory warehouse tripled in value within a few months, putting millions of dollars into the pockets of Mr. Au and Mr. Ng!

Therefore—yes we've finally gotten here—on his next trip to Hong Kong, Manny received a boat worth over $100,000 wholesale for $17,000 as an expression of Mr. Au's and Mr. Ng's profound gratitude. Can you believe it? Will the jury believe it? And even if they do, how were we going to leap from the wholesale Hong Kong value to a U.S. fair market value of $380,000 less than three years later? I really didn't care at that moment. The story was so much fun and such a stretch, maybe my client would have to send me to Hong Kong to check it out!

Proving market value was obviously going to present a challenge in this case. It also became clear, however, that we had a major hoop to jump through before we could even start talking about market value. The law seemed pretty straightforward: if a dealer makes a charitable contribution from his business inventory, he can only deduct from his income the acquisition cost of the items. Undisputedly, Manny was a dealer in the types of goods he donated. To no one's surprise, the government claimed that the donations were made from Manny's business inventory and his deduction thus limited to his purchase price. If the I.R.S. prevailed on this point, the case was *finis,* judgment for the government.

But there's an out for the taxpayers. If they can prove they maintained a personal collection apart from their business inventory and can show the donated items were part of the personal collection rather than part of the business, they are entitled to deduct fair market value and are not limited to acquisition cost. The trick here apparently is to physically segregate the personal collection from the business, maintain clear and separate records for each, and keep the item in your personal collection a sufficient time before donation. I couldn't induce from the record how the facts on this issue squared up with this legal standard, but for some reason, perhaps fatigue or just foolishness, I wasn't particularly concerned about it.

What I was concerned about, and what remained very muddled, were numerous technical defenses raised by the I.R.S. The government's bottom line proclaimed that the statute of limitations barred the bulk of the taxpayers' claims for refund. According to the I.R.S., the claims had not been correctly presented to the agency or filed in a timely fashion with the court. This is a fancy way of saying, "you lose because, somewhere along the way, your lawyer screwed up royally." I read and reread the volumes of correspondence between the I.R.S. and my clients' former attorney, pondered the official documents generated by the I.R.S., and tried to divine what the applicable portions of the tax code meant. The statute of limitations issue still didn't make much sense. I remembered a skit from a show put on in law school. Somebody posed as a stand-up comic, and the only lines he delivered were portions of the Internal Revenue Code. I can't recall how much was in the delivery and how much was the Code, but it sounded like he was talking a Martian dialect!

The quagmire of I.R.S. technicality wasn't going to be traversed tonight. It was late and quiet when I finally shut off the lanai light. I felt the sensation of darkness flooding in. The sky still showed some moon, and I watched the reflections on the ripples of water. After staring into the dark silence for a while, I realized I hadn't talked to anyone and probably hadn't even uttered a sound for close to three days. After being so focused on the work for so long, I continued to sit and unharnessed my mind, letting it stretch and fly and do what it wanted without suggestion. My breath deepened as I relaxed; images floated by. Here and there I noticed glimpses of my "weekend from hell." These weren't just memories, though. The images held something more tangible. Perhaps the similarity of spending a holiday weekend in this house, alone, without a sound, made the memories of that Memorial Day weekend more real.

Solitude and silence can generate immense power. Unless you have refrained from speech and interaction with others, it is difficult to realize how much energy is expended in that pursuit. I once took a week-long meditation retreat that was conducted in silence. By consciously not speaking, I had an opportunity to examine the constantly arising urge to talk. I was surprised that much of what I wanted to say was truly unnecessary, strictly habitual, and subtly calculated to obtain recognition or validation from others. When your energy is not dissipated through unmindful speech, it builds and remains available for inner reflection. It provides a light with which to see yourself with greater clarity. That is why many of the great spiritual masters practice silence, some for years at a time. As I eventually got to bed the memories of my Memorial Day weekend continued, infused with a sense of realness, and as I lay in bed in the darkness, I realized these images must hold some message for me.

CHAPTER TWO

# The Weekend from Hell

A FEW DAYS BEFORE that hellish 1991 Memorial Day weekend, I had noticed, not unexpectedly, escalating feelings of anger directed towards my wife. Just two months before, I had most reluctantly left my home, coaxed out with the suggestion this was a trial separation. The reality that my marriage was over had barely begun to sink in. Divorce has the effect on one's emotional body like a cuisinart has on vegetables—puree. During those two months post-separation, I had endured intense emotional catharses, and to an outsider glancing in I probably looked as if I were just plain cracking up. As painful and exhausting as it was, in moments of respite I felt a deep joy and appreciation for the sacredness of the process.

Catharsis provides a way for our unprocessed experience, our blocks, our unconsciousness to be brought into awareness and released. Those areas of darkness within us, seemingly dead zones, hold the memories of past events, whether from childhood, infancy, or past lives (if that suits your persuasion), which we were unable to consciously encounter when they occurred. Instead of fully experiencing the fear or terror of some traumatic episode when it happens, the part of the episode we don't process becomes lodged in ourselves. I am not speaking metaphorically. I mean that our physical as well as our emotional and mental bodies are the repositories of these unintegrated events.

In the physical body, these areas are characterized by lack of sensation, or conversely by extreme sensitivity, and are the places

17

where energy is locked. When these zones of unconsciousness are probed, perhaps physically by a bodyworker or mentally by a therapist, strong defensive reactions in the form of fear or pain may arise. The closer one comes to touching what was too difficult to bear in the past, the greater the fear or pain.

For instance, if a young child were attacked by a dog and bitten in the leg, the adult may feel pain in that limb even though the physical wound healed many years before. That pain guards the terror the person could not consciously experience and thus suppressed as a child. If that area of the body is worked and the pain consciously met, the adult can face the previously unexperienced terror from the past. The adult, during or after this process, may actually remember the suppressed incident, but it doesn't make any difference. Once the residue of the past is cleared, the related bodily pain disappears. Also commonly released are emotional or mental fears that arose as a response to the repressed event. Catharsis is not about working out a sore muscle, it's about coming into consciousness.

While we may purposefully intend to approach and liberate these dark areas by ourselves or with facilitation, the universe does this on its own by presenting us with situations that resemble or remind us of our unprocessed past. And because we are not conscious of these past events, we don't know why we experience disproportionate fear or unease in certain situations. If, for instance, in another life you were killed, whenever you now encounter a person who resembles your past murderer, unexplained feelings of fear or discomfort may arise. The unintegrated experiences we carry with us act as magnets, attracting to us that which is needed to move them from darkness into light. We don't have to do anything; this process is propelled by the evolutionary urge to become free, to become whole, to become closer to the Divine.

Without a doubt, was my process being propelled! During those initial months of separation I seemed to be shrieking so often I was lucky the neighbors hadn't called the police. I used pillows as situations permitted. Divorce, like any other life-shaking event, catalyzes the release of deeply held blocks—as if God takes your psychic body by the shoulders and shakes and shakes, and the stuck stuff gets dislodged and starts to move. You feel you are being flushed out by the Divine roto-rooter. The harder the shaking, the more that comes loose.

I was shaken pretty hard. My divorce felt like a death, not only the death of my marriage, but more painfully, the death of my dreams, beliefs, and concepts of who I was and how my life would be. I was a one-marriage person for better or worse, my son would *not* be the product of a divorced family, and that old and gray trustworthy loyal George would end his life hand in hand with his lifelong mate. All such beliefs were shattered on the rocks.

The emotional pain we suffer usually results from damage to who we *think* we are. When we fasten to our self-concepts, the more we suffer when those concepts are threatened or destroyed. Excessive identification with the roles we play doesn't leave much room to experience who we are beyond those scripts. Such attachment limits our choices, our expression and our creativity.

For me, I closely identified with the role of "George the father." Having felt myself betrayed as a child, a part of me swore I would always be there for my son, as if being the perfect father would somehow purge the misdeeds of my parents. And I was there, sometimes too much, as children need space to grow. I suffered tremendously leaving Alexander. Being a semi-absentee dad did not coincide with "George the father." My prior-role attachment impeded my ability to adjust to this new reality. For me, being a father and my concept of what a father should be were almost one and the same. I felt like a tremendous failure, and in some way believed I had betrayed my son as I swore I would never do.

The path to spiritual understanding is often described as a process of elimination— we discover that we are not this, not this, not this. Realizing that I was not "George the father" was very painful, but also a step toward liberation, both for my son and me. Letting go of my role attachment, at least partially, allowed me to love Alexander more from my heart and relate less from the confining space of who I thought I should be or what I believed a "good" father was required to be. The trick, when a concept or belief is shattered, is to be aware of our propensity to replace it with another we identify with. The new concept may feel good and work better than the old, but to the extent we become attached to it, it still limits us. Freedom is having such deep trust in our inherent goodness and deep faith that God is the ultimate source of our expression, that we live and act from our true being, which is spontaneous, always appropriate, always for the higher good, and creatively unlimited.

While my separation was bringing up enough of its own related issues, I recognized that most of my cathartic releases had nothing to do with the divorce. A lot of very old stuff was moving through the pipeline. Fortunately, I had experienced this process of releasing blocks as a result of doing spiritual work for the past few years. The catharsis, as harrowing as it could be, was made easier by my knowledge of what was really happening. I knew that growing sensations of unease and dread usually preceded a release. Sometimes these feelings would build over a few hours, other times they would come on very quickly. Often a sinking feeling in the pit of my stomach would accompany the dread and unease; sometimes I felt downright nauseous.

The dislodged blocks of my unconscious past were like large cells floating in psychic space that I could almost see. As they emerged from my dark craggy recesses, they rose upward through my body from the midsection to the chest area and ultimately through my throat into release. I felt like some sort of alchemical bottle with no bottom, large bulbous sides, a thin short neck, and no top. I perceived these cells as black and sometimes huge, extending laterally out of my body. As the cells emerged and rose, they had to pass through the tiny neck of the bottle, my throat, in order to be discharged. Here the fear and panic seemed greatest, the terror most intense. Here also I confronted the greatest urge to push what was coming up back down.

As these unprocessed experiences entered my throat, I often felt absolute, unimaginable terror—like I was being murdered, hacked to bits. One time I could actually feel a long blade plunging into my chest; another time I could smell the dank, putrid odor of an attacker. Other dark cells brought on indescribably intense grief and its accompanying pain, as if a beloved child of mine were dying in my arms.

In the narrow confines of the bottleneck, one feels that the searingly close repressed event is being experienced for the first time. Paradoxically, cathartic release *is* the experience of the past event, and at the same time it is not. My shrieks of terror or the sobbing from the pit of my soul reflected the occurrence suppressed so long ago, yet some part of me somewhere (and believe me, that place was sometimes very hard to find) always knew that this was me, now, coming into greater consciousness.

Although the passage of a cell through the throat seemed to take an eternity, in relative time, the process usually elapsed in less than fifteen minutes. Once the block was experienced and discharged, I often noticed a feeling of lightness, as if a dead weight had been lifted. I also sensed an interior spaciousness, sometimes so vast, I felt as if I could rise like a helium balloon. Sometimes after a release I would feel a joy and peace, a homecoming, like the prodigal son returning to the abode of the Father after a long, wayward journey. This experience of integration, bringing into awareness that part of me previously excluded, was also occasionally followed by a period of insight. Here, the truth of why the past event occurred and how its suppression had shaped my personality (sometimes over numerous lifetimes), was revealed to me.

In the period after my separation, though, it seemed the blocks arose in a torrent without the luxury of much time for insight. Unlike my previous experiences where a major block might be released every few months, here the cells were just lined up one after another. I had days in which, for hours at a time, they kept coming like waves in succession. After catharting in the bedroom I would, during what seemed to be a brief respite, start walking toward the kitchen and literally be "seized" in the hallway, dropping to the floor as another cell broke on shore.

My inability to control this process scared me. The waves hit a lot while I was driving. I usually held on until I could ditch the road for some vacant parking lot. During some less intense episodes, I managed to keep driving. I imagined, if I got into an accident, how

I might explain my condition to a traffic magistrate. I've resided in traffic court waiting to defend clients and have heard the judge retort to some ludicrous explanation for a motor violation with, "I've been on this bench ten years and have heard every excuse under the sun." Well, not this one, judge!

These recurring cathartic episodes left me physically exhausted and emotionally wrung. At times it wouldn't have taken much to convince me I was going off the deep end. An enlightened counselor and a couple of close friends provided help. They encouraged me to stay with the process, which of course contradicted the probable conventional medical advice to "medicate," a nice-sounding name in this case for pharmacological suppression. As difficult as the path was for me, in my faith I knew it led to a sacred gift for my purification. I trusted deeply that I would not be given more than I could bear.

Little did I know that this trust would be taken to its farthest edge during that 1991 Memorial Day weekend. As the anger towards my wife was intensifying prior to that weekend, I purposely did not return her phone calls, knowing that I would probably erupt just hearing her voice. On Thursday while she worked, I left a message on her home phone that it was best not to call or see me until I contacted her. On late Friday afternoon she showed up at my door.

At first, knowing it was her, I resolved not to answer. But since she knew I was there, she kept ringing the doorbell until I reluctantly let her in. We ended up seated across the lanai table. I listened to how she was "concerned" about me and how she wondered what was going on. I knew if I began to speak it would be difficult to constrain myself—pretty uncomfortable for a master of self-control. After being pressured to talk, with an intensity of anger I had never experienced before, I started to express how ill-used and ill-treated I felt by her. This was not an explosion of anger, but a narrow, intense beam, the steam starting to whistle from a boiling teapot. My anger, amplified to rage by the content of my own words, could barely be contained. As I continued to talk, I pounded my fist on the wooden table, at first in a measured rhythm. The next one or two smashes were less controlled. By this time my wife was more than frightened. In the sixteen years she had known me, she had seen me expressively angry perhaps less than a handful of occasions, and in that time probably couldn't have conceived of me in rage or on the brink of violence. Recognizing her fear I mustered my will power to resist striking the table, and in doing so noticed for the first time how much my hand ached. A ceramic pot decorated the table and the thought of grabbing and throwing it at her flashed before me. At that she lurched back and blurted, "You just thought of hitting me with that pot." (Yes, we both at times were able to read each other's thoughts.) After a momentary pause, she leapt from her chair in terror exclaiming, "I've got to get out of here," to which I replied, "I told you not to come in the first place." With that she was gone and I was left in searing rage.

For the first time in my life I felt lost. The energy inside my body pulsed so strong I felt if I didn't "do" something, I would explode into pieces. I was on fire, fueled by thoughts of bludgeoning and tearing her apart. If she were there at that moment I thought I would kill her—happily destroy her. No wonder rage plus alcohol often equals murder or mayhem. Thank God I didn't drink.

All of a sudden the rage shifted into intense pain. I could not bear the thought that I had almost attacked and wanted to kill my wife, whose love and acceptance I desperately wanted. I felt shock I was acting in a way so contrary to how I believed I should be, and horrified I was capable of acting this way. When the pain became unbearable I somehow shifted back into the energy of uncontrolled, destructive rage. I didn't know what to do. Rational thought was gone. Something told me not to leave the house. I was blind.

One of the hardest things to do is *experience* emotion we deem to be negative or simply don't want to have at that moment. "Emotion" is, as is often said, energy-in-motion. This energy causes a physical sensation in the body and also has color. Anger feels hot and beats red, fear feels cold and is yellow. Envy is green. Experiencing emotion means neither suppressing it nor expressing it, neither blaming yourself nor someone else for it, and neither fleeing nor fighting. What else is there? What's there is the edge between these opposites, these polarities. What's left is the experience of this energy as it moves through your body. The energy of emotion, like electricity, is neutral. What makes this energy hard to take is that the "electric" current of intense emotion can be physically uncomfortable, even downright shocking. Is it any wonder then that we choose not to remain in these experiences?

Avoidance catapults us into a host of "negative" emotions, one being anger, which are usually unconscious defensive mechanisms. Something happens and our initial response is fear or pain or some other uncomfortable feeling. Because we've conditioned ourselves not to encounter this fear or pain or discomfort, we automatically and instantaneously shift into a defensive emotion. For example, say I'm handling a major business closing for a new client and the other attorney promises to prepare and bring certain of the documents for signature. At the closing, the other attorney saunters in and instead of delivering the papers, announces that he thought I was going to draft them. Everyone at the closing table stares at me as if I were responsible for the mishap, and I become angry. I storm back into my office to prepare the needed documents.

Suppressing this anger would mean trying to convince myself that I'm not really angry, which of course I am, or shoving it away. That's flight. Expressing this anger might run the gamut from telling the other attorney off, to mentally blaming him for his incompetence or purposeful neglect, or perhaps blaming myself for not effectively communicating with this person. That's fight. Either is easy, and we do them habitually. Both put us in our head and take us out of our body. And whatever the path to our head, once there, our minds will reinforce for us the premise we've concocted.

If blaming someone else is where I am, I'll soon think that, *this other attorney has had it in for me ever since I beat him in court last year . . . he's making me look bad in front of my clients to try to steal their business . . . he's of low moral character, a real slime,* and so on. The mind, like a mercenary, will take on any battle you want to fight. This reinforcing exercise in your head adds more fuel to the anger. We all know how easy it is to pump ourselves up when we get going. Now we can really get angry!

Alternatively, back in my office I can pause a moment, recognize I'm angry (this is the easy part), and draw my attention into my body. What does this emotion feel like? For me now it's hot and red, centered in my chest, and swirling around like a thousand ants crawling over my skin. That feels intolerable, so my attention shoots back into my head and I start manufacturing anger-reinforcing thoughts. Aha! I recognize I've returned to the blame game and bring my awareness back down into my chest. The sensations are still there, but less intense. The red is not as bright or dense, I'm not as hot, and the crawling feeling is more bearable. I might oscillate a bit more between my head and body, and suddenly—the anger is gone.

Once the emotion is processed, I realize that, although I've successfully handled numerous closings like this before, I feel insecure about my competency. Beneath that insecurity I feel a fear fed from a voice that whispers, *You're not good enough.* I finally see that my anger deflected my awareness from my underlying insecurity and fear, which on some level I chose not to experience consciously at that moment.

Let us remember a couple of things. First, awareness and insight do not obviate the need for appropriate action. After preparing the documents I can calmly explain to my clients the miscommunication and apologize for any delay or inconvenience. The next time dealing with this attorney I may request papers in advance to give myself adequate time to draft them if they're not received. I can take an honest and critical look at my skills to assess whether any areas need improvement or brushing up. I can go back to the place inside where the feeling of not being good enough resides and determine what I need to heal this area.

Second, experiencing emotion does not necessarily mean you are standing still, looking inward. The energy may lead you in various ways to assist in its release. If I'm angry I may feel the urge to run or shout or cry or pound a pillow. Your body in each situation can tell you what it needs to do. That is staying with the energy. Shouting at the person you think has made you angry is not staying with the energy, but merely dumps or transfers your energy somewhere else. You may enjoy the rush of temporary relief, but what you have displaced from yourself will come back to you multifold. The underlying feeling you have temporarily avoided has not gone away; in fact it has assumed greater psychic "importance" by virtue of the resources expended in keeping it hidden. Thus, you will keep on attracting to yourself the same anger-producing situations in increasing intensity until you reclaim for yourself what this anger conceals.

Also, there are times that don't practically permit the full experience of some emotions. If something comes up when you're in the middle of a presentation at work, or operating heavy machinery perhaps, make a note of it and deal with it later. The whole focus here, when an emotion arises that you're having difficulty experiencing, is to immediately ask yourself, *What's really happening here? Why have I attracted this situation to me? What do I need to learn?* You may not be able to fully experience the emotion or answer any of these questions, but just asking them is a quantum leap into self-responsibility.

Experiencing uncomfortable emotions takes much practice. Usually, the more intense the emotion, the more fearful or painful any underlying issue and the greater our propensity to react unconsciously. We often lose awareness when we need it the most. That is why practice and a consistent attitude and intention are so important. If you start to dig the well when the house is burning down, you'll never get water when it's needed.

No amount of water could douse the fire of the rage I was experiencing—rage at my wife, rage built up over years held tightly in control, rage of lifetimes of human suffering. I was burning and felt as if my flesh were being consumed by fire. I thought I would soon burst. I also felt a crazed urge to make this go away, to relieve this unbearable feeling. Unlikely as it may seem, I noticed my yoga mat on the lanai floor, half sat and half fell on it, and heard my mind mockingly laugh, saying there was no way I could meditate now. I crossed my legs, closed my eyes, and saw myself sitting where I was, as if my eyes weren't closed, only now, the lanai was in conflagration and my body was actually on fire. The image resembled the movie scenes of someone being in hell, with flames and brimstone engulfing the unfortunate character. You know the picture—the person, usually feeling very guilty for committing some transgression, shrieks in torment until he wakes up in a sweat realizing it was a dream.

For me though, this was no dream. I sat and burned as if being roasted in an oven. After what seemed to be a very long time, the rage with its heat and fire disappeared, only to be replaced by excruciating pain. A different form of torture was not exactly an improvement in my situation. This pain arose in the pit of my gut and doubled me over in its intensity. Mental images and feelings of utter worthlessness and rejection accompanied the agony. For what felt like an eternity, I moaned and sobbed amidst the sharp spasms, with my mind helpfully interspersing fleeting images of self-destruction. At least that offered one way to make it all go away.

At some point, I know not how, the state of pain vanished, replaced instantaneously with the searing rage—rage now so enormous I could dismember armies, destroy cities, chew and spit out planets. The only way to sit with this rage, to experience it, was by meditating. The fury was too consuming to suppress, and had I acted it out—well, I'd probably still be in prison. I sat in the fire, apparently for hours and then, as before, shifted into the pain and back to the rage again as this pattern kept repeating itself. I felt like a coin balanced on its edge, on one face the rage and on the other the pain. Every so often an invisible finger would rotate the coin 180 degrees, and I would move from one to the other.

From day to night, night to day; time made no difference. I think I slept Friday night, but if I did, it consisted mostly of dreams of being tormented in some inferno. On Saturday I remember something about going to a beach, perhaps in an attempt to cool myself off. Oddly, I didn't go into the water, thinking that I saw it boil or bubble.

By Saturday night the process reached its climax, and it seemed the fire was consuming me, whether my eyes were open or closed. The episodes of pain had also reached their greatest intensity. In the blackness of the night I lay on the mat, doubled over in excruciating pain, with a picture in my mind clearer than reality. I saw myself on the cold terrazzo floor of the kitchen with the side of my throat cut and blood gushing from my carotid artery. I watched the hot red blood darken as it adjusted to the cool of the terrazzo. The knife fell away from my palm, now too weak to grasp it, but subtle body twitches proved I was still alive—barely. I retained enough consciousness to know I was near-dead, coupled with the terror of realizing there was no escape, no way to summon help. As I drifted off I joyfully imagined the torment and grief of those later discovering my body. Could I make it to the kitchen? What knife would I use? Could I really do it? The suffering was unendurable. I could—and then the coin turned, and I fell into rage. When the rage eventually shifted to pain again, there I was back on the terrazzo. Death's siren beckoned. I wondered whether I dare go to kitchen, get the knife, and just lie on the floor to entertain what would happen. Each time the tormenting pain brought me a step closer—it could all be over so soon—and each time at the farthest edge I was rescued by the rage. Somehow, sometime, somewhere in that black night I collapsed into sleep.

CHAPTER THREE

# Choosing the Right Road—
# Taking the Case

B LUE. The light blue of the sky was the first thing that entered
my waking consciousness. Before I quite realized where I
lay, my body signaled it was sore, spent, and wasted. If this
were a hangover, I had just had a two-day bender to end all benders.
The fever of rage had broken. As I started to move around, I felt as
if I had exited from a deep dark chasm, a pit I didn't realize I had
fallen into until this emergence. My savior rage. Sweet, blessed
rage. I understood its essential nature: survival. Rage had given me
another place to occupy when the pain became too much to bear.
Healthy rage. As the day progressed, feelings like those of the
previous two days passed through me with much less intensity, like
the aftershocks of a major earthquake. I now felt objective space
around the feelings, which enabled me to process them without too
much difficulty.

Space around a feeling or sensation allows you state, "I am
experiencing . . ." whatever it might be. This declaration acknowl-
edges the reality that you are not what you are experiencing at that
moment. You recognize that the anger or grief or pleasure you feel
is not who you are, but what is passing through you—as if you are
the sky as distinguished from weather phenomena. When clouds
pass by or massive thunderclouds erupt, they can't harm or affect
the sky, the backdrop upon which they manifest.

If an intense emotion arises in me that I can't seem to tolerate, reminding myself I am not the emotion will often immediately lessen its intensity. The sensation remains, but now, surrounded by something greater than itself, it's no longer as large. Without this objective space, this knowing, we fall prey to the illusion that we *are* the feeling or sensation or thought that happens to be occupying our field of awareness. Paradoxically, letting go into the sensation of emotion is the key to experiencing it, yet without the knowing that you are not the emotion, it's awfully difficult to let go. By Sunday night the after-tremors had faded away and I felt progressively more spacious. By Monday morning I had entered a profound state of Grace.

Some say that without evil as a contrast, we would not be able to truly recognize goodness. Perhaps without the experience of hell we wouldn't know heaven if it stared us in the face. What had passed through me that Memorial Day weekend was so massive, it opened internal space of immense proportions. I felt the light pour in and touch places that had been in darkness for eternities. I saw illumined vast interior landscapes and inhaled sweet fragrances like that of the first of all mornings. I experienced with gratitude and unsurpassed joy what the scriptures describe as birthless, eternal, perpetual, primeval—that which weapons do not pierce, fire does not burn, water does not wet nor the wind cause to wither. In this reality, so grounded in the truth that your essence is the eternal unchangeable God, you become the sky. You become the stage upon which the play and dance of creation unfolds, without identifying with the manifestations of creation.

In this state I experience a different relationship with my mind. Instead of controlling me, which it does most of the time, my mind is deprived of its dominion. Like a car with a standard transmission, the mind is like the engine gear that is spinning and spinning, but only has power to move the car, (impel actions, behaviors, and feelings), when it is engaged with the corresponding gear of the drive shaft. Usually the mind, especially with its erratic and unconscious needs, fears and desires, drives us wherever it wants to go. Try some time to impose mental order or quiet your mind; it's next to impossible. Grace feels like your "higher self" stepping on the clutch—the gear of the mind lifts and disengages, and it loses all authority over you.

This detachment doesn't mean your mind stops. You wouldn't want it to. You need your mind. How else would you remember to pay your power bill? In a state of Grace your mind continues to spin, but has lost the power to affect you. Like the Emperor with no clothes, stripped of its false claim of authority, the mind is even a little bit embarrassed that it's been exposed as the impostor that it is.

In this denuded condition your mind, the creator of your ego personality, will feel mighty insecure and may use any weapon at its disposal to reassert control. And of course thoughts are its weapon of first choice. The thoughts generated are those most likely to hook you, to engage you back into response. At these times thoughts with high emotional content may arise, some real tear-jerkers, or perhaps past scenes of anger or pain.

But because I am then so saturated in the truth that I am not the contents of my mind, these thoughts have no power or pull. Sometimes my mind, disappointed that the ploy didn't work, will try another tack. I will notice thoughts portraying situations of intense pleasure, and smile and chuckle at the ingenuity of my mind to get me back on its playing field. Finally, realizing that for now its cause is hopeless, my mind will slow down, actually rest, and helpfully act when called upon.

This autonomy from mental control is characteristic of how events and emotions are encountered during Grace. Whatever occurs also has no pull or control because these events and feelings are merely phenomena playing upon the infinite field of consciousness. As each moment unfolds, it doesn't matter *at that moment* what happens, what is said, what is done, what is felt, what occurs. In the eternal present everything is in the process of arising and then passing away. Nothing holds permanent and immutable except the ocean of God's consciousness from which and upon which the forms of Divine consciousness play. Life in Grace is a succession of these unfolding moments. Whether the next moment brings death or a fortune is irrelevant because nothing that can happen can ever harm or hurt you, or improve or make you better.

In reality you have never been born and never can die. You are the expression of the Divine.

Immersed in this reality we experience no fear and no anxiety, but an indescribable freedom from the calculated and unconscious devices and behaviors we use to control, protect, and defend ourselves from what we falsely perceive threatens us. "Freedom is another word for nothing left to lose," yet how can we lose when we have gained everything? Thou art whole. If we are infinitely large, if the Divine within us, which *is* us, contains all of creation, what can be taken from us and who is there to take it?

Before I get too stratospheric here, let me assure you I obviously don't experience my life predominantly as above described. If anyone did, they'd have no reason to incarnate here other than for our salvation. Times of profound perfection are like standing on the highest mountain peak in the rarefied sky and looking at the sea of clouds below. Sometimes these are fleeting moments or minutes; other such experiences last hours, and on very rare occasions, days. Most times we live and modulate within a continuum having on one end full remembrance of our Divine self, and on the other, complete forgetfulness.

Let us remember that transcendent states are not characterized by passivity or indifference. When I say "it doesn't matter" or is "irrelevant" how life unfolds, an extremely important distinction must be made. In the present, at the moment something occurs, nothing we can do can change it. No matter how much we may dislike what is happening or may want to alter the here and now, changing it is beyond our power. What we do possess is the power to choose. We can choose to accept and receive, or we can fight and resist. The wise say that the essence of suffering is wanting things to be otherwise. If you make life a contest between the universe manifesting as it will at that moment and your personal preference, who do you think is going to win?

But this is critical: your inability to change what is now happening does not mean you are unable to affect what will transpire in the future—even in the next moment. If the present moment is not to your liking, take action; engage and direct your energy to shape the future so it unfolds differently. And as your present, which is the culmination of your past actions, unfolds, accept the result of your action. Find the balance between willfulness and surrender. A bird needs both wings to fly.

And fly I did for a few days after my weekend from hell. During that time something remarkable happened. On Monday I noticed odd thoughts intermittently drop into my mind. Each flashed a small and seemingly unrelated snippet from the history of my marital relationship. Over the next two or three days these thoughts continued to appear out of nowhere, and then I started to recognize a connection. One remembrance or incident, of no particular consequence by itself, when placed with one or two of the other thoughts, together began to take on meaning. As this process continued, I saw many pictures emerge, like a jigsaw puzzle being put together. They seemed related, yet how did they ultimately connect?

As the number of pieces grew and the pictures became larger, the puzzle began to take shape. I was fascinated at this process, particularly as these thoughts or puzzle pieces were not of my making, but were being provided to me. If you have ever assembled a jigsaw puzzle, you know that there are "critical" pieces, those that join two distinct areas of the puzzle. When you find that piece, there's that feeling of "Aha, yes, they do fit." When a "critical" snippet of thought would appear and join two unrelated parts of the puzzle, I felt as if a light bulb had flashed on. After a while I realized that what was being revealed to me was the truth of our marital relationship.

Since our separation, the feeling that something didn't add up between us had troubled me. We shared a very deep spiritual connection; on some level we loved each other; we both dearly loved our son and wanted to do anything we possibly could to keep his home together; we were both good people and shared in common most of our beliefs and our lifestyle. No wonder others thought we fit together so well. I just knew there was something more than her professed reasons for her insistence on ending our marriage. I had prayed deeply during the past two months to discover what that truth was.

Now, before my mind's eye, this truth emerged. When the puzzle was complete I stood in awe. I perceived with clarity who we were in relation to each other and why we chose to take our path of marriage. I saw our souls prior to this incarnation discussing what each needed to learn in this birth, and in compassion and love for each other agree to take this journey. As firmly and unshakably as I have ever known anything, I knew what had been revealed to me was the truth. I lay in bed that night in the darkness drifting towards sleep, marveling at how this tapestry was woven before me the past few days. Then a clear voice softly spoke, saying, "This is your prayer answered."

Lying in the same room waiting for sleep the night before Labor Day over a year later, I realized why those scenes of my weekend from hell were replaying before me. That experience had been a turning point for me, allowing me on a deeper level to begin to accept the death of our marriage, as if my life were a massive book and a page had turned. I don't mean this strictly as a metaphor. On some level there I felt an energetic shift, a sense of closure. I had stopped looking back. Although I knew the road ahead would be very hard, I could begin to move into the rest of my life. This was a great healing for me.

In some way I understood that this case was also a turning point for me. Like another page turning in my life's book, I knew I would take the case and that it held great importance. Mind you, I didn't say I knew whether or not I would win. I simply recognized that it was my next step. Where that step would lead me remained unknown. But knowing the result was not important; it was enough finding what path to take.

Doubt is the destroyer of much we set out to accomplish. The more demanding the challenge, the more debilitating doubt can be. Realizing you are on the right road is of great value during a long and hard journey. In times of struggle you may not even see the road, but knowing it is there can dispel doubt's claim that you have mischosen. We all know on some level whether our present course moves with or against the flow of our life. That night I realized taking the case was, for me, moving with the current. (Little did I then know to what extent that realization would be tested.) The images of my hellish weekend ended, and I settled into sleep. I drifted off feeling that the case came as God's gift.

On Labor Day I awoke appreciating that this gift needed a lot more unwrapping. I could go only so far in unraveling tax procedure without getting to the law library. I did narrow down the issues some. This next section gets a bit technical, so just try your best.

Here goes. If the government concludes you owe more income tax, and you disagree and don't pay, its decision is formally proclaimed in a Notice of Deficiency. Once the Notice is issued you have ninety days to file a petition in tax court. The benefit of going to tax court is that you don't have to pay the deficiency the I.R.S. is claiming in order to have your case heard. The limitation is that your case is decided without a jury by an administrative judge who hears only tax cases.

If you don't want to rest your fate in the hands of one individual, you can take your case to federal district court for a jury trial. But here's the rub: to get to a jury via federal court, you must first pay every penny of what the government claims is owed in taxes, interest, and penalties. You get it back to the extent you win in court. Most people can't afford to pay up front and thus end up in tax court. Very few tax cases make their way to district court, alas explaining the judiciary's apparent ignorance in dealing with these cases. Got it so far? Hold on, there's more.

Getting to district court is a minefield. Once the Notice of Deficiency is issued, if the taxpayer hasn't elected to go to tax court, the government issues its tax assessment. This piece of paper authorizes the I.R.S. to seize your property and take your bed-clothes while you are sleeping. (To the true and loyal operatives of the Service, please forgive me for indulging in a little I.R.S. bashing now and then.) Upon paying the tax and the interest and penalties assessed, you can then file your case in district court—right? Wrong. Next step, once you've paid your money, is to file with the I.R.S. a "claim for refund."

In the refund claim you must explain to the government exactly why you think you're entitled to get your money back and convince them they were wrong to conclude you owed more tax in the first place. Good luck! You've been trying to persuade them for years you don't owe the money, and now magically they're going to agree with your claim for refund?

The story gets worse. Per the tax code, you only have two years from the date you start to pay the tax assessment to file your refund claim. Any monies you paid more than two years before filing your refund claim you can't get back, according to the statute of limitations. This means if the amount the government assessed against you is huge and you need time to pay, you lose off the bat that which you can't pay within a two-year period. After your claim for refund is filed, the I.R.S. has six months to consider it.

Upon receiving a denial of your claim, or after six months if the I.R.S. fails to rule, you then have two years in which to file your suit in district court. If you don't file your action in court within that two-year period, guess what? Of course, your suit is thrown out of court as another ugly Statute of Limitation gleefully digests the taxpayer's petition for justice.

From what I could tell, here is how the facts in Manny and Mary's case played out procedurally. (If you understand this, you might want to consider a career in law.) The I.R.S. assessed approximately $350,000 in additional taxes and $250,000 in penalties and interest in July 1987. Within a few months the clients paid the $350,000 in additional taxes. Shortly thereafter a claim for refund was filed. In July 1988, Manny and Mary received a letter from the government titled "Disallowance of Claim For Refund" stating that the claim could not be processed because the taxpayers had not paid all of the tax due. Correspondence ensued between the parties, and the clients' first attorney finally figured out that the government wouldn't consider the claim for refund until all the interest and penalties were paid.

The taxpayers then requested the I.R.S. to tell them the exact amount necessary to satisfy the assessment. This generated additional letters and notices from the I.R.S. containing contradictory amounts. Finally, the "Problem Resolution Office," (a misnomer for sure in this case), proclaimed in writing that payment to the government of $422,065 on February 1, 1989 would satisfy in full the taxpayers' assessment. Apparently substantial interest had accrued since the July 1987 assessment. Manny and Mary forked over that hefty sum on the specified date and thought they were well on their way to district court. Unbeknownst to them, crossing in the mail with the proclamation from Problem Resolution was a letter from another I.R.S. department stating that it had errone-ously computed the original assessment and that an additional $50,000 was now owed.

Which arm of the mighty government to believe? That took another year to finally decipher. The predictable end result was a beleaguered Manny and Mary paying the extra $50,000 which, by the time they paid it in October 1990, had grown to $68,000. Their attorney mailed an "amended" claim for refund to the I.R.S. on January 31, 1991, which was never formally denied. In September 1991, he filed on behalf of the clients a refund suit in the Federal District Court in Tampa, Florida.

Thank God I don't get headaches. Trying to figure this all out on Labor Day would put anyone's cranial-muscular system in distress. If you've been paying close attention, you realize that I had something to worry about. If you can't understand all this mumbo jumbo don't worry and don't feel bad. (As you will later see, it took a Federal District Court judge over fourteen months to sort out and rule on the statute of limitations issue, and even then, who knows if he got it right?)

Was the 1988 claim for refund valid even though all the tax, penalty, and interest hadn't been paid? If it were valid, all the payments of the taxpayers were timely, but their suit was filed late in district court. The 1988 claim was apparently denied in July 1988, but the September 1991 suit was filed way beyond the two-year period to do so. If the January 31, 1991 refund claim was the valid one, no doubt the suit filed later that year was timely. However, utilizing this claim date meant that any payment made prior to January 31, 1989, two years before the claim date, was not recoverable. This would bar a refund of the $350,000 paid in 1987 and 1988. Were both claims for refund valid? And what about the filing date of the last one?

Our final claim was sent by certified mail on January 31, 1991, just within two years of the February 1, 1989 payment of

$422,065. But, it was received by the I.R.S. on February 2, 1991, one day after that two-year period expired. I guessed that for some reason January 31 was the filing date, since the government, in its answer to the taxpayers' court complaint, admitted that this refund claim was filed with the I.R.S. on January 31, 1991. If the filing date of the last claim for refund actually was February 2, 1991, the February 1, 1989 $422,065 payment would also be barred by the statute of limitations and the case would be a complete bust.

The first attorney was a C.P.A. prior to becoming a lawyer, and was a reputed tax expert. I naively thought that he must have been alert enough to do what was necessary to comply with the limitations statute. Amazingly, we are willing and eager to ascribe to some "expert," knowledge that we feel we lack.

What I was not lacking, as evening fell on Labor Day, was the satisfaction, relief, and fatigue you feel upon returning home after a long demanding journey. What luscious fun actually turning the television on and catching a little baseball. As I wound down, I visualized the next step soon approaching in my new adventure—meeting with Mary and Manny to forge in steel our bargain.

# CHAPTER FOUR

# *Bargaining for the Contingency Fee*

W ANTING. Across the long and impressive table in our cedar-paneled conference room sat Manny and Mary waiting for my verdict. Manny looked clammy and ashen-faced, attributable, I hope, to the condition of his case and not his recent heart problems. Unlike Manny, who tends to react to misfortune with depression, Mary's typical response to the same stimulus is irritation or anger. This situation, however, was grave enough to cast a pallor even over her usually animated countenance. This case had consumed the last ten years of their lives, with endless payments, campaigns, maneuvers, and worry. They were battle weary. Now they waited to hear, from me, whether or not there was anything left to salvage. They desperately wanted it to be better, and most of all, to be over.

For me, I sorely wanted my clients to sign the bottom line of an agreement giving me a hefty percentage of a million-dollar-plus recovery. With a slight vision of sugar plums dancing in my head, I had scooted to the law library earlier that morning and found the Internal Revenue "timely mailing, timely filing" statute. If you mail a document to the Service before a deadline has elapsed, and they receive it after the deadline, that law deems the document to be filed as of the mailing date. The refund claim mailed January 31 and received February 2 was considered by the government to have been filed on January 31, 1991. This reasonably assured me that the $422,065 payment made on February 1, 1989 was within the two-year statute of limitations. I was ready to get on board and sat on my side of the table intending to negotiate for my fee the highest portion of the potential recovery I could garner, fifty percent being the legal maximum.

As I started to relay my estimation of the case, I found myself in one of those ethical dilemmas that are strictly a private matter of conscience. Our relationship that morning bore two distinct facets. First, as an attorney and counselor I was duty bound to advise and act according to the best interests of my potential clients. As independent parties in the process of negotiating the terms of a business transaction, however, we also held adverse interests. I wanted to get the highest allowable fee, while they wanted to pay as little as possible.

While exposing the grimmer details of the case and thoroughly explaining the procedural muck, my conscience asked: *Are you accurately and dispassionately giving an evaluation of this case, or are you using this evaluation as a means to enhance your negotiating position?* Actually, before a question like this arises, a subtle but distinct feeling in the body signals you that something may be amiss, as if the arrow of a magnetic compass in your gut gets pulled slightly off the mark. You often can answer the query of conscience by examining your intention.

Overtly, the words and ideas I was conveying were necessary and appropriate. The clients were entitled to get the whole picture, and parts of the portrait were not looking too pretty. If you read a transcript of what I said, no question of overreaching would appear. But as I listened to what I was saying, I wondered about my choice of words and questioned my inflection. Was I subtly shaping the evaluation for my gain? The harder the case, the greater the risk of losing—which justifies a higher contingency fee.

We find the truth of our expression not so much in what we say, but in what we want. In our interactions with people we project an energy. Some consider it part of our electromagnetic field, others something more exotic, but the label doesn't matter. This energy conveys what we really want, our true intention. The more we are in touch with ourselves, the more conscious we become of this energy. When we interact with others, they come into contact with our projected energy, as we do with theirs, and because this energy doesn't lie, we are always aware energetically of each other's true intention. We may not consciously know, but we are aware nevertheless.

This true intention and inner knowing are often expressed in body language, to which any studious observer of human interaction can attest. All you need do is sit in the park and watch two people converse on a bench outside of hearing range. While you may not discern the content of the conversation, the body cues probably will reveal the interpersonal dynamics of the interchange.

When we are involved with another and we want something from him, we start pulling his energy. Whether it's love or money or a sale or approval, our need, on an energetic level, involves taking. And the takee, knowing on an energetic level that we are endeavoring to take, usually becomes defensive. Instead of the takee's energy being projected outward, it is drawn inward. For example, when a telephone solicitor calls and tells you this is your lucky day, you don't have to listen to the pitch to know that this interchange is not in your best interest. This knowing is not based upon what the person tells you, or your prior experience, but what you feel. The innate capability to know another's true intention is available to us in every situation—it helps in poker too!

The nature of energy is that it moves. When we constrict our energy due to an awareness on some level that another person wants to take from us, we feel drained and eventually negative. The flow of energy is energizing; stop the flow and it is enervating. Contrary to common belief, holding on to what we have doesn't make us feel better. Yet each one of us becomes consumed with getting what we want and correspondingly protecting what we have from others we believe want to take it from us.

This attitude of wanting is not just the overt greed of coveting our neighbor's spouse or lands—it pervades the smallest parts of our daily lives. When we're driving to work in the morning, we want the car in front of us to make that light so we can get through the intersection. We always want a pleasant greeting from the cashier at the check-out counter, even though we fail to spare others from our occasional surliness. Riding the elevator to the fourth floor, we don't want the other passengers to press the buttons for floors two and three because it unduly interrupts our passage.

You get the idea. We want our lives to transpire according to our plans and desires, and we interact with people as if they should labor as our agents in facilitating the smooth course of our day. So here we are, most of us unconscious islands wanting others to be or act a certain way while we protect ourselves from their wants and desires.

Engaging with people and interacting with life from a position of want is called deficiency consciousness, a belief that we are lacking in some way and become *full-filled* by an external source. Deficiency consciousness is also a belief in limited supply, and thus the corollary that wealth for one must come at the expense of another. When we operate from deficiency consciousness, on an energetic level we are like an octopus grabbing and sucking the energy of others with our tentacles. No wonder our presence can bring another to arms.

In contrast, abundance consciousness is the knowing that we are complete in every aspect and that when we give, we are always replenished from an inexhaustible internal supply. When we operate from abundance consciousness, the result is absolutely disarming. Since the nature of energy is to move, abundance consciousness *is* giving. When something is full, movement creates overflow. When our cup is filled to the brim, the substance of life—our energy, our love, our compassion, our humor—cascades over the sides. This gift of ourselves cannot be given discriminately, because when we operate from abundance, we do not choose to give; giving is our essential nature.

No wonder abundance consciousness is so allaying. Everyone you come into contact with instinctively knows that you're a giver and not a taker. On an energetic level other persons do not constrict their field, because there is nothing they need to protect. There is nothing you want from them, nothing you need, and therefore no risk that you will take from them. You are totally non-threatening.

Feeling safe, many people will then allow you to enter their personal energy field, though some people who are out of touch with themselves may not. More than that, when other people let you in, they like what they feel, want to experience more of it, and start to generate it themselves.

Most of us will naturally gravitate toward those who exude the qualities we yearn for on a deeper level. Again, this process of discovering intention through energy often occurs for us on an unconscious level. If I am on line at the supermarket and say to the lady in front of me, "What an attractive hat you have on today," or even, "Isn't the sunshine beautiful today?" the response usually depends upon who I am as I say it, rather than what I say. In situations like this, people are often wary of strangers. If we feel someone wants something from us, that sense may generate thoughts such as, *Who is this person? Why is he talking to me? What's he after. Be careful.* When we innately know the situation poses neither threat nor risk, however, people just naturally open up— which explains why we are so present with children.

Not to be fixated on foodstuffs here, but I have enjoyed such wonderful times waiting on line at the grocery market. When feeling consciously abundant I will say something to the person in front or in back, or perhaps just smile. The person opens. Within a few minutes the five-or-so people waiting, along with the cashier, are joking and laughing and having a good time—such a good time that they really don't want to get off line and miss the fun! How does this happen? I'm not a stand-up comic. The fact is that joy is our fundamental nature. We weren't made in God's image to be glum. We find it a balm and relief to let go of our fear and let loose. With a little encouragement we can pop our lids and naturally effervesce. Getting on a check-out line of insular, preoccupied shoppers and a few minutes later wheeling my groceries away from a warm and expressive group enhances my energy. Shopping and all the other requirements of our day do not have to deplete us.

It is deficiency consciousness that depletes us, not our job, our home, our spouse, our finances, our neighbors, the government, or the world. The mistaken belief in lack results in our incessant and unending striving to obtain what we think we need to become whole. But how can we ever be satisfied with what we achieve or acquire when the hole we are trying to fill is illusory?

Deficiency consciousness creates a black hole in our lives that pulls into itself all that we serve up, whether it be more money, greater recognition, a fancier car, a larger home, or a more attractive spouse. Procurement motivated by the false belief we are deficient results in fear and unhappiness. When we believe our acquisition has filled a deficiency, that deficiency always remains with us as fear, because we also hold the concomitant belief that this deficiency can instantly remanifest in our life if we lose what we used to fill it in the first place. Unhappiness arises from not being able to relax long enough to enjoy our accomplishments and acquisitions. We are too occupied warding off the designs of others or acquiring more to solidify our position. No wonder we are so tired.

This consciousness of need and want so pervades our culture, it has deeply infiltrated our individual minds. If we scrutinize even our most well-intentioned actions, we can usually find the seed of want and desire. Our charitable gift may partly be made to see our name on the donor's list, and to make sure everyone else views it too. Making dinner for our spouse or other helpful conduct may be motivated by the need to satisfy our self-concept of being a good or loving person. Accomplishing at work may satisfy a desire for peer validation. The list is endless.

Please note, I am not advocating that you halt these worthy efforts until every trace of self-want is eradicated from your motivation. We are in a learning process because we don't reside in our purity of heart all the time. Good works are better than no works, even if they are generated in part by selfishness. It is the *practice* of giving that illumines whatever obstructs us from giving unconditionally. So commence doing that which you wish to grow into. What I do advocate is becoming aware of what moves you. Our motivations on various levels are highly complex and sometimes very subtle, yet these innermost intentions are available for us to discover. And discover we must if we desire to evolve from want-based consciousness.

So there I was with Manny and Mary, pondering my motivations as I continued my evaluation of the case, when Manny, in a distressed voice blurted out, "Mary, that's it. I can't take any more. We're dropping the case ... it's over." *Aaaaagh!* Exploring the subtleties of my intentions immediately vanished and was temporarily replaced with survival consciousness, the ultimate need.

*They can't be serious. They would never just walk away from this case after all they've put into it ... would they?* As I thought this, Manny proceeded to explain how all the years of struggle had left him and Mary so emotionally drained and physically unwell, he couldn't see how they could go forward, especially in light of my less-than-glowing assessment of the case. I explained I was duty-bound to point out the difficulties in their suit and was playing devil's advocate to a degree. With that disclosure I proceeded to reemphasize the positive aspects of the case.

Well, by the time we got around to talking about the percentage fee, I had to convince Manny and Mary that a one-third fee would leave enough potential recovery to make the case worthwhile for *them* to pursue. My need to acquire the case was so pressing, it didn't leave enough room for me to fully discern my clients' truest intention.

After the engagement documents were drafted and signed and Manny and Mary departed, I sat semi-dazed, relieved that the case would be proceeding at all and wondering whether I had encountered negotiators with far greater skills than my own. Their professed desire to end the case certainly had me going, and I now suppose Manny, adept in sales as he is, sensed my wanting. I guess I'll never know for certain, but as I got to know my clients better through the course of our marriage, I came to discover how very well they could perform.

It is true that money usually fuels the engine of litigation. Yet, while in most cases the initial engagement between attorney and client is consummated in the flesh of dollars, a rare case does appear in which the parties are wedded through spirit. Let's move back a few years and travel the road to such a union.

# CHAPTER FIVE

# My Death and Resurrection

C ONSCIOUS DYING. What in the world was that, and why would I ever want to buy a book about it? I might have asked myself these questions later, but for now I was pulling books off the shelves at the Kripalu Shop, spending the last hour of my ten-day retreat like the other two hundred-or-so guests readying to depart that Sunday afternoon. I wiggled through the bookstore throng and out onto the front terrace for one last look. The Kripalu Center for Yoga and Health presently inhabited a former Jesuit Novitiate prominently situated on three hundred acres in the Berkshire Mountains, or Hills if you're a purist, in Lenox, Massachusetts. Just the view was worth the thousand dollars I spent to participate in "The Expanded Self"—an apt name for an intensive program designed to facilitate personal transformation utilizing every psychological and spiritual method known to man, plus a few new ones invented for our benefit.

Although spring was approaching, we were treated to a couple of snows and the spectacular sight of Stockbridge Bowl punctuated by traces of white. Kripalu sat on the south side of a foothill facing a horseshoe of distant mountains ringing a basin filled by Lake Mahkeenac. Unseen at the bottom of the hill was Tanglewood, the summer home of the Boston Symphony. I would later discover, to my delight, that orchestral magic filled Kripalu's July and August night air if the wind cooperated. I filled my lungs with mountain purity and saturated every cell with nature's glorious masterpiece, intending to imprint this experience in my being before I pivoted to return to suburbia.

The ride to Bradley airport in Hartford/Springfield took about an hour and a half and was graciously provided by Stanley, my new friend and one of the twenty-five participants in my program. To say we were slightly elevated while traversing the back roads of Massachusetts would be a vast understatement. We left cloistered Kripalu after this, our first visit there, too captivated with the joy and newness of driving to care—or more accurately, to recognize—how radically different we felt.

A diverse set of circumstances had converged in my life, which now birthed a personal transformation of immense and unexpected proportions. I came to the retreat in April, 1988, wanting a change in my life and was returning home with my old life vaporized.

Although I experienced my initial spiritual awakening in my early twenties, I had spent the last few years of my mid-thirties backsliding. My marriage at the best of times was mutually tolerable, work was abundant but very stress-producing, and I felt directionless. This malaise resulted in more escape, which for me meant television-watching, overeating, staying up late, a little drinking and what felt like an ever-present low grade depression. Am I describing the normal American life style? I was running from my life, knew on some level there had to be more, and wanted to change but didn't know where to turn or what to do. While I had knowledge of the tenets of spiritual life and had practiced many over the years with varying degrees of success, I now felt impotent to effect a renaissance. My ripened dissatisfaction provided the first element for transformation.

Even with ripe fruit, it helps to give the tree a good shake. At Kripalu we were sliced, diced, and turned inside out. The yoga center was run by an avowed religious order whose members followed a traditional Indian guru, the center's spiritual director. I had attended some weekend retreats Kripalu conducted in Florida over the years and thus knew of the Massachusetts facility. The center housed two hundred fifty full-time residents. Many possessed traditional skills in Western transformational modalities, and some residents were remarkably adept natural healers.

I had never visited a place quite like Kripalu. What I found most impressive was the palpable energy generated by this large group of people dedicated to personal unfoldment and the spiritual growth of others. In India it is said that you can feel the guru's presence a mile or two from the place he resides. The energy I felt was deeply loving and powerful, and I had little interest in ascribing it to any particular source. A safe and supportive setting and adept facilitators contributed the second element for my transformation.

The third element was my son Alexander who was three months shy of two years old at the time. His resemblance to me was evident even without comparing baby pictures. With my son as catalyst, I felt stirrings of my own early childhood, which was less than idyllic. Whose is? I unconsciously blamed myself for permitting myself to be abused, as I believed I was, as a child. Although long aware intellectually of this common dynamic, I had no idea it applied to me.

A core belief that had shaped my life, of which I had been unaware, was brought into my consciousness during my program. At some point early in my childhood I self-divided into a protector and the inner essence I was protecting. I became so proficient at erecting walls around what I was protecting, I eventually lost sight of my core self. George the protector had lost the treasure entrusted to him, had utterly failed, and deserved to be blamed. With this awareness I understood the underlying basis of my self-rejection and why it was so difficult to change this pattern. I recognized I had believed I was unworthy of love, and now for the first time realized that *I can love myself.*

On a psychological level my healing seemed ordinary. While this psychological dynamic may appear simple and obvious, however, its realization was not. What looked like the fundamental emotional block of a lifetime was lifted with great effort through a complex process, the details of which I will not describe (having recently read a *Wall Street Journal* review claiming that spiritually oriented books are unnecessarily personally dramatic). Suffice it to say that my realization was not and could not have been the product of intellect. My healing occurred on an energetic level with mental knowing an afterthought. For the first time in my cognizant life-experience, my two individuated parts reunited and I was whole.

My body felt as if someone had pulled out a sluice gate somewhere between my navel and the base of the spine—like the metal plate you see a magician thrust in and out of a box during the illusion of sawing someone in half. When this gate was pulled, a rocket of energy exploded up my spine and out of the top of my head. This energy, continuing to surge through me, was so utterly powerful that resistance, had there been anyone there left to resist, was unthinkable. I suppose you could describe this as *kundalini* rising, a superconscious experience, or the fire of the Holy Spirit. Nomenclature, however, was nonexistent for me as I existed, at that moment, beyond distinction, differentiation, or judgment. This is a cup I had sipped from before—but now I was immersed in boundless measure. I was drunk with God.

So drunk that, as our program session ended, the leader asked two fellow participants to lift me to my feet and support me until I got the hang of walking again. As I wove and stumbled about, buttressed by my attendants, it quickly became apparent my verbal abilities were in the same condition as my locomotion. While I could group a few words together, my predominant expression was laughter and a grin just short of it. Nothing was wrong with my musculature or my vocal cords. There was just no one minding the store.

My individual ego identity exited, or temporarily disassembled, or merged into something greater, or I don't know what! Without "someone" in my body to walk or talk, I seemed to have the facility of a newborn. Some doctors suggest that infants possess the physical ability to crawl and walk much earlier than the age at which these skills routinely occur. They posit that these abilities do not develop sooner because the infant lacks a sense of self. Until the baby's consciousness becomes individualized, there is no one to direct the body to move.

My compadres soon conducted me out-of-doors into a world of living wonder. Colors exploded, sounds electrified, and every molecule held the signature of its own distinctive smell. No barrier separated myself and my surroundings. Everything was alive—not just in the physical sense, but all was imbued with Spirit, the intelligent unseen life force that is omnipresent. A flock of birds sitting on the grassy hillside moved into flight, and with an indescribable ecstasy I flew on their wings. I sensed the collective consciousness of the flock and knew when they would turn and dive and ascend. Nothing was inanimate. Everything was vibrating, and all resonated into a symphony of unbounded joy.

The deepest part of me saw, knew, felt, and experienced the miracle of creation. In some way I cannot describe in language, God's omniscient perfection was placed before my eyes. Everything was Spirit in the inexorable process of becoming aware of itself. Like a stamp press forever changing a piece of metal, I had imprinted upon me the purpose of life—God-realization—and in the knowing of this purpose came instant fulfillment.

Although to some I reckon the above sounds like metaphysical gobbledygook, I will attest there exists such a Universal Consciousness that not only can be experienced by us but is us. The expression "we are all one," while perhaps tritely used in pop culture, rings profoundly true. Yet the illusion of separateness remains extremely compelling.

Each leaf of the thousands on a majestic oak is unique. From the vantage point of one leaf, all others appear separate. Imagine you are a small speck on a leaf and you look outward. Another leaf hangs in front of you. The two leaves are distanced in space and appear to be unconnected individual entities. Without a larger vista, it is very difficult to see that both are part of the same living organism. We all walk in this world bound to the universal tree of life as surely as each leaf of a tree is a part of the greater whole. We just don't experience that connection most of the time, or when we do, the sensation is subtle.

"Subtle" is antithetical to any description of my experience. I lost the boundary between the idea of myself and the world around me and gained immeasurably. Subject and object merged, and in some way I experienced the essence of each thing my consciousness touched. I felt the joy of grass as it grew and sensed the genetic code by which it manifested into physical reality. In ecstasy I became the solemn grace and beauty of a tree and knew the freedom of the passing clouds. I don't speak metaphorically:

For ye shall go out with joy, and be led forth with peace: mountains and the hills shall break forth before you into singing, and all the trees of the field shall clap their hands (Isaiah 55: 12).

I'll side with the literal interpretationists on this one. As surely as I know my left arm and right arm are both part of me, in this way also was I bound to each aspect of creation.

As my impromptu custodians and I later moved back inside, I experienced the same sense of perception regarding certain people we encountered. In some way I looked into the person and felt the essence of the individual. At the core radiated a perfect luminescence. I could feel this radiance become filtered and blocked and shaped as it self-emitted, and through this process saw how the personality and ego identity of the person configured into place.

A light bulb partially painted black will cast its light where it remains unpainted. Each light painted with a different design will cast a different pattern. The amount of light that can shine through the bulb and the pattern of its dispersal are perhaps endlessly varied. This is a two-dimensional representation of what I experienced multi-dimensionally.

Perhaps the traditional oriental ivory carving of spheres within a sphere provides a better analogy. From a solid ball of ivory, concentric spheres of declining size are carved, hollow balls within hollow balls, with the surface of the orbs perforated to create beautiful patterns. A space between the spheres allows each one to be rotated independently. Most carvings contain a few balls, while others may contain upwards of twenty. Imagine a bright concentrated light at the core of the spheres. The light seen from outside would depend upon the number of spheres, the amount of open space on the surface of each, and the way in which the spheres are aligned.

Similarly, some souls were radiantly expressed while others less so due to blockage or extensive overlay. When I perceived and felt someone so completely, I often could hear her thoughts and knew what she was going to say before she said it. It was as if the individual before me was transparent and I could see the person's form, yet look through it at the same time. The reactions to me were wildly different. Some spontaneously became joyous, and I saw their light grow brighter. Other people dimmed as they became nervous or insecure in my presence, as if what I had might be contagious. I suppose it depends upon what you want to catch!

As the hours passed, the stream of energy started to lessen in intensity, and with this my ego-self returned in stages with its need to control. The intellect believes it is in control because it thinks it knows what is going on, and based upon that knowledge thinks it can manipulate what transpires to suit its needs. To the extent we identify with our minds, the same can be said about how we live our lives. Unfortunately the intellect's perception of reality is limited, because the finite rational mind exists in an infinite world. No matter how hard you try, you can't get an eight-ounce cup to hold a gallon of water. But we have it all figured out!

By middle age few experiences we encounter prove difficult to rationalize, explain, categorize, or otherwise integrate into our intellectual belief systems. Sometimes our concepts need adjusting in response to some new major life event, but on the whole, most of us have become solidified in who we think we are and what we think the world is about. Even if an event traumatizes our belief system, the immensely able mind can incorporate into itself what is unknown, and thus threatening. Like a spider extending and forming a new web where there was nothing before, so our minds will create structure and pattern from the unknown to make our experience familiar. My experience was so powerful, though, efforts to contain it within my intellectual ambit proved futile, and worse than that, painful.

Standing fast in the river is easy when the current is gentle. Considerable energy must be expended to withstand a greater flow. My effort to explain, categorize, and control this experience—like trying to stand firm against a raging current—rendered me mentally and physically fatigued. Like copper wire resisting surges of electricity, I began to heat up, and at times became feverish. Luckily for me, my "event" occurred at the beginning of my program, which afforded me time to become somewhat accustomed to these high energetic states. I became marginally adept at letting go and allowing the current to sweep me away.

Also, because the energy was so palpable, its absence felt deafening. For some reason, I would suddenly notice that the energy appeared to be gone. Catapulted from the heights of spiritual ecstasy into the ordinary, I instantly knew the anguish described by various saints and masters of the times when the devotee feels separate from God. While not yet flaying myself, I was near desperation over my fall from Grace. And then after a few hours, a touch of a hand on my head or the sound of a spiritual chant would somehow open the energetic floodgates again. As if someone were flipping a light switch on and off, I began to feel like someone's cosmic yo-yo in motion. Again, with the benefit of time and some facilitation, I started to recognize these fluctuating states as a larger process of oscillation, which somewhat lessened my emotional reaction to these shifts.

Still somewhat shaky on the outside, and thoroughly alchemized within, I was wrapped up neatly, given a lollipop, and sent back home with a "good luck," as if that were somehow going to make it easier to integrate this experience into the framework of the life I had just interrupted. On the plane I pulled from my carry-on the book from the Kripalu Shop on conscious dying. Written by a meditation teacher active in hospice work, it described the enormous potential for spiritual awakening, both for the patient and the caregiver, which sometimes is realized during the death process.

Scripture says neither hands, nor feet, nor emotion, nor mind, nor body are we. Our death—the permanent separation of our spirit, our consciousness, from the body—if experienced with awareness, can provide the opportunity to dispel the greatest of illusions: that we are this body. The author goes on to describe how meditation and spiritual practice *is* the process of dying—the means by which we extinguish our ego and body identification and realize we are the expression and manifestation of the Divine.

Pretty heady stuff, especially for one who had just died and been reborn, so to speak. I deeply connected with the message of this book, and as I gazed out the window upon the clouds and surface below, I felt death move a bit closer.

# CHAPTER SIX

# Reentering the World Through the "Right-to-Die"

T ODAY'S APPOINTMENT WAS MY FIRST with Doris F. Herbert since my return from the Kripalu Center two weeks earlier. Leaving for the office that morning had been difficult. My attraction to the secular was about as much as you would expect from a monk on spiritual fire. Except for my family whose practical welfare still somewhat concerned me, I maintained no interest in my prior life. Friends, social occasions, news, current events, sports, television, entertainment, alcohol, sex, planning, the future, law, politics, earning money—they all held little meaning for me.

Mrs. Herbert had first wobbled into my office many months before. Her frail and moderately hunched frame carried average weight, but she appeared thinner as her loose-hanging skin tended to accentuate her bones. Her wavy white hair surrounded smallish facial features. Any inclination to view her as a stereotypical little old lady was immediately punctured by her firm and somewhat coarse New England accent, which I well recognized from my years of law school in Boston.

She had come to tell me about the stroke-impaired condition of her cousin, Estelle M. Browning, now kept alive through artificial feeding. My partner had previously drawn Mrs. Browning's testamentary will. Mrs. Herbert showed me a document her cousin had previously signed declining tube feeding and wanted to know what, if anything, could legally be done to implement it. My opinion was requested because Mrs. Browning's physician and nursing home had already told Mrs. Herbert the feeding tube must remain in place, and that any efforts to remove it would be met by their resistance.

When I first met Mrs. Herbert I had known as much as the average general practitioner about removal of feeding tubes, which means I told her I would have to research the issue before I could give her a reasoned assessment of the matter. My client now entered my office this morning expecting to receive a more detailed opinion.

Baptized as I was in mystical fire, I found clients, at best, an unwelcome distraction from my all-consuming spiritual practice. Each morning I eagerly awoke at four-thirty for three or four hours of yoga and meditation. The office felt painfully mundane to me and for good parts of the day there I would devour scripture. At home, after making dinner and putting my son down for the night, I would consume spiritual books of every sort and persuasion, then practice more yoga and meditation before bed. I considered most talk, other than of God and Spirit, inconsequential.

For anyone living with me this would have been more oppressive had it not been for the deep passion and transformative energy that was expressing itself through me. Intense and genuine spiritual fervor can also be compelling to those in proximity. Putting oppressiveness aside for the moment, my wife and those close to me could fully focus on their primary reaction—fear. They were obviously disturbed by and concerned with my abrupt and radical change and believed I was close to becoming nonfunctional.

More accurately, I had little use or tolerance for the function of convention. By that I mean I witnessed events, activities, and interactions apart from the inherently justifying viewpoint of society. I had ceased being habitual. Each situation I encountered now had a nakedness that allowed me to discern whether it truly served my higher purpose—God-realization—and if I concluded it didn't, I chose not to become engaged with it. I felt like the little boy in the fable "The Emperor's New Clothes," and was fascinated and astonished to see how what we do and say, for the most part, falls within pre-determined cultural channels.

The energy of this consciousness also contributed to the fear response of those around me. A fish doesn't know it lives in water until it is out of water. My family and acquaintances seemed like fish, swimming heedlessly in the ocean, unaware of land or air. Despite this near-total identification with the culture in which we swim, we all realize on some deep inner level that our societal identities are assumed and not organic. We can find it extremely unsettling, however, to discover that the life we believe we have chosen has, in large part, been selected for us. This is why mystics, saints, and great religious figures often are the progenitors of revolution. God-consciousness on that level transcends culture, institutions, and bureaucracies, and can be extremely dangerous to the status quo. And the hazard to the message-bearer, as our grisly history amply shows, usually, in the short run, exceeds that to the bureaucracy.

Never so impolite or pretentious to equate my awareness with that of any master, I was careful not to go around pointing out to people how their behavior was unconsciously culturally driven. Nevertheless, consciousness is felt without words, and somehow without saying or doing anything, I emitted an energy that conventional sensibilities found disquieting.

Again, I want to emphasize that the energy I was experiencing felt as tangible and real as physical matter, with often no distinction between the two. I had not "adopted" some new philosophy nor decided to "operate" under some new belief system. I was part of a process so compelling that my participation wasn't optional. In these first few weeks, yoga provided a refuge, one of the only ways I could begin to integrate this experience—and I plumbed its depths in a way I had never previously imagined.

Performing certain physical postures in coordination with breath, the public's common perception of yoga, is as superficial a definition as calling prayer the act of sitting down with your palms together. "Yoga," as derived from Sanskrit, means "to yoke or harness," like oxen pulling a wagon, their individual wills brought together so they may operate in unison. The ultimate purpose of yoga is God-consciousness, which the aspirant attains through the "yoking" of body, mind, and spirit. In the philosophy and practice of yoga, the confluence and harmony of our various aspects naturally and consistently lead to Self-realization. (See Appendix "A" for a more detailed explanation of yogic theory and practice.)

With little knowledge of esoteric theories, my yoga practice became markedly less self-directed. Instead of thinking or choosing what posture to perform, a seemingly independent energy would start to move my body. As my mind observed with astonishment, my body sometimes naturally flowed into one posture after another according to its own volition. I assumed formal postures, called *asanas,* I had never practiced before, some of which were previously unknown to me. I deeply entered physically demanding postures with an ease and flexibility I had never before possessed. The energy that led me was so compelling that, on occasion, I would awake at night in bed and find myself fully engaged in an asana. I rode the waves of this healing energy with a great and profound joy.

The yoga was also emotionally integrative. I was walking a razor's edge, and without a way to fully feel and release intense emotional energy, I could easily have fallen over the side. My spiritual opening was not a one-way door. This entryway does not discriminate between the dark and the Divine. Infusion with the reality that we are the creation and expression of God will naturally summon for release those acquired parts of ourselves held outside this truth. So my hobgoblins, and repressed experience manifesting as fear, came to say hello. And through the yoga I said good-bye.

While in an energetic flow, my body would sometimes assume a posture that was accompanied by a sense of fear and feeling of pain connected with a physical limitation. In maintaining the posture, often against a strong mental urge to bail out, my body would heat up and start to shake. Sometimes the shaking would progress to an ecstatic eruption of energy and sensation; other times it would gently fade. Whether more dramatic or subtle, the result was the same: the fear vanished, the physical block in the posture evaporated, and I was left with a deep experience of peace and well-being.

On occasion the release was preceded by verbal expression or followed by recollection of an experience previously hidden. But there was nothing I needed to understand, no issue to analyze nor anything to mentally integrate. The yoga provided the process by which the matrix of my fear could energetically dissolve and release. Through this yoga the distinction between mind and body—energy and physical matter—began to feel increasingly tenuous, and I, in turn, experienced more and more the sensation that my body was neither bound in space nor time.

The body is a concept. With that bald-faced assertion, I'm sure a few of you would like to do something to *my* body in an effort to prove the contrary. Well, whatever it truly is, for almost all of us all the time, our body is what we think it is. We know, courtesy of medical science, that our physical form constantly changes. Our cells are always in the process of formation and disintegration, creating for us a completely new cellular identity every seven years or so. The chemical and biological processes of digestion, respiration, and elimination, while repetitive, are never identical from moment to moment. The fingernails we have today are not the ones we had nine months ago, and yes, the mop of hair we sport, or in my case used to display, ends up periodically on the hairdresser's floor.

Yet despite the truth of this impermanence, we neither relate to nor experience our body in that manner. Our relationship with our physical self is more fixed. Why is it you realize one day you've gained ten pounds? How does weight "creep up" on you? The fact is we are so body unaware, unless marked physical pain or sensation intrudes, we are not even conscious of our tangible self in the waking state. What we carry instead is the idea we have a body, and that static idea is vastly different from the reality of a physical form comprised of the ever-changing bundling of atoms and energy.

Said another way, body is condensed energy. Quantum physics has proven that energy and matter, while different manifestations of a unified field, indeed sit on each side of the Einsteinian equation. In the science of spirit, the idea of a unified field is expressed in the statement that all creation is vibratory. The material world consists of lower vibratory states. The world of thought and emotion exists at a higher frequency, and the refined spiritual states at more subtle vibrations. Further, the higher vibratory states control the lower and denser worlds—mind over matter.

Whatever man creates on the physical realm is said to always be preceded by a thought, idea, or intention. In a like way we shape our own bodies, which, when unconsciously sculpted, become frozen mind.

It is not just me saying this. A recent study showed that in long-term marriages, the couples, as time progressed, started looking more and more alike. This is not because sleeping on the same Sealy Posturpedic can somehow "bi-mold" spouses. The researchers also found that as the marriage lengthened, the *thought processes* of the couples started to converge. Think more alike and therefore look more alike.

Certainly the mind/body connection has been sufficiently re-searched and accepted in our society to render the preceding propositions less than radical. We are beginning to understand that, in a general way, rigid minds create stiff bodies, and an openness to life results in physical ease and relaxation.

While the above principles are by now tame in the abstract, the demonstration I was fortunate to receive seemed pretty wild to me. My energetic healing at the Kripalu Center was simultaneously accompanied by a dramatic change in my body. When I eventually took time to notice, I found my entire body markedly more flexible. I am not talking about being able to stretch a bit more. What occurred was not a progression, but a quantum leap.

The core belief, "I am unworthy of love," had shaped and constricted my body. The release of this block instantaneously unlocked my soft tissue, and I was physically reconfigured in a more natural way. I looked like a different person! My posture was automatically uplifted and my face was broader, less wrinkled. A natural smile beamed amidst new facial features. I looked much younger. People I knew came up to me and, without quite realizing why at first, said I looked very different. Hey—sure beats a face-lift.

Again, it's no great surprise that a change in facial musculature will alter countenance. The correlation between the configuration

of underlying soft tissue and outward facial appearance is scientifically proven. Forensic archaeologists have put a face on extinct
hominids by replicating musculature on fossilized skulls and then
fitting a synthetic skin over that frame. Criminologists have utilized the services of these archaeologists, with great success, to
place a face upon the decomposed remains of unnamed murder
victims. Identification of victims and apprehension of criminals
result from these facial replicas.

The real value to me of this physical transformation was not
looking younger or feeling more fit. It was the realization and
demonstration that mind manifests and forms the physical world,
and that a shift in belief can instantaneously and automatically
alter substantial matter. To intellectually understand this principle
is one thing, but it is quite another to actually experience it. The
willful application of this principle is what we commonly call
spiritual thought.

The mystics have said that this world, this universe, is nothing
but the thought-form of God. In Genesis, God intended that there
be light and there was light. Christ fed the multitudes with only a
handful of fish, not because he was a sushi master, but because he
had the deepest realization that matter is an expression of mind and
spirit. This creative power is not exclusive to the Divine, but comes
as part of our birthright.

We are made in the image of God. This does not refer to having
two arms, two legs, and a head. It means that in some way we
naturally possess the attributes and qualities of the Universal
Consciousness. I believe Christ intended his life on Earth to be an
example—a testament of what is possible for *us*. We are not only
instructed to worship God, but to "*become* sons of God" (John 1:
12).

Well, for better or worse, whether spiritually infused or infected with incipient megalomania, there I sat talking with Mrs.
Herbert. Eureka. To my astonishment, here was something practical, something secular, something *legal* that seized my attention. I
actually enjoyed using my left brain again as I entered the rational
realm of legal analysis. We now discussed my preliminary research,

(which is reviewed at length in the next chapter), and the latest in her cousin's medical condition.

After she departed it seemed evident to me that the case, given my recently acquired fascination with death and dying, was a blessing rather than a coincidence. As I worked the case in the following days and weeks and met and talked frequently with Mrs. Herbert, I found my engagement in the practical world to be grounding and stabilizing.

Equanimity is the hallmark of spiritual life. Equanimity is being able to openly engage each situation life offers, not with judgment, attachment, despair, or blame, but with an underlying joy of living. It is knowing that who you are and what you experience is a function of your inner state and not dependent on external circumstances. Equanimity is neither eating too much nor eating too little, neither oversleeping nor depriving oneself of slumber, neither desiring pleasure nor avoiding pain. It is practicing moderation in your expression and habit. It is the ability to function in any situation with ease and humor. A true yogi is said to experience life the same way whether residing in a palace of gold or sitting on a dung heap.

No one, including myself, doubted that my energetic experience left me unbalanced. In a way, my spiritual opening was vertical. This opening was very deep and ascended to great heights. Any structure, no matter how magnificently tall, will tend to wobble and tip over unless anchored horizontally. The process of integrating this spiritual experience into my life, building the horizontal, took almost three years. Much of this work was painstaking.

People have spiritual breakthroughs of different intensity. If the opportunity is not nurtured, if we don't take practical steps to align our lives and habits with the realized truth of who we are, the opening effectively closes, although never completely. For me, my opening wasn't just a course correction, but a nuclear event. I didn't have the luxury of choosing to close it by inaction; either I would integrate it or flip out.

Through this case I began to reenter and re-create the structure of my professional life as a new person. I knew this was not just another legal matter to handle, but a means for me to serve and grow spiritually. After completing my research and advising Mrs. Herbert of the result, she instructed me to take court action to remove the feeding tube. I told her I would have to meet Mrs. Browning before I could commit to take the case. I procrastinated. We would never absolutely know if Mrs. Browning indeed retained, underneath that impaired exterior, cognizance of her dilemma. Did I want the responsibility of implementing a choice that perhaps was no longer hers? With these thoughts I eventually came to her bedside.

# CHAPTER SEVEN

# A Client Fights for Death

S UCH A DEEP, DARK, SILENT BLUE. I stared as far into her eyes as I could, hoping to sense some glimmer of understanding, some hint of awareness. The deeper I dove, the darker became the blue, until the blue became the black of some bottomless lake. "Mrs. Browning, do you want to die? . . . Do you want to die?"—I near shouted as I continued to peer into her pools of strikingly beautiful but incognizant blue. It felt so eerie. Her eyes were wide open and crystal clear, but instead of the warmth of lucidity, they burned with the ice of expressionlessness.

Before me lay Estelle M. Browning, fetally curled on her side in a nursing home bed. Her head was propped by a pillow upon which her still ample white-gray hair scattered. She was incontinent of bladder and bowel as evidenced by the numerous tubes exiting from under the sheet unto other places discreetly hidden. A victim of a major stroke in 1986, she had been in this condition, more or less, for the past year and a half. Her limbs looked frozen and in fact had become forever locked from the paralysis secondary to the stroke.

Mrs. Browning was a total-care patient, and as her body atrophied from lack of use, the intervention to keep her functioning necessarily increased. Bedsores, despite efforts to prevent them, were a constant problem. Discharges and infections involving almost every body orifice were routine. Even the simplest tasks like trimming her toenails required a podiatrist's debridement of necrotic tissue. And all this was made possible by a simple device that stood before me: Mrs. Browning's nasogastric feeding tube.

A plastic sack half filled with sickly beige-looking fluid hung from a metal I.V. pole attached to her bed. From the bottom of the sack a plastic tube snaked down into Mrs. Browning's nose, up through her nasal passage, down through her throat and into her stomach. However uncomfortable you might imagine this to be, the reality is much worse. Mentally competent patients fed through nasogastric tubes on a temporary basis uniformly describe the discomfort as unbearable. Incompetent patients often end up with their wrists tied to the sides of their beds due to their repeated removal of the tube.

There was nothing mechanical about the device at her bed-side—just the pull of gravity causing a constant drip, drip, drip from the bag into the tube, regulated by a simple knob which adjusted the size of the aperture at the bottom of the sack. While "assisted feeding" might evoke images of Mom and apple pie, the contents of the sack bore little resemblance to food. This wasn't a homogenized ham sandwich Mrs. Browning was having for lunch, but an amalgam of chemicals in a fluid delivery system registered as a drug with the F.D.A. And as with many drugs, this one causes unwelcome side effects, most notably a whole range of digestive and excretory problems. At the other end, frequent vomiting clogs the tube and requires its removal, cleaning and reinsertion. I surmised that Mrs. Browning's tube was performing its function, as its recipient was more amply fleshed than I had quite expected.

Whatever your opinion about tube feeding, the hard fact was, it now stood between Mrs. Browning and her death. As is common with a major stroke, Mrs. Browning had lost the ability to swallow. The swallowing reflex is physiologically complex, requiring numerous muscular acts to occur in precise coordination. Damage from a stroke interrupts messages from the brain to the body, and thus many stroke victims have to "relearn" how to swallow in the same way that speech and movement are retaught. Depending upon your opinion, those may be the lucky ones. For Mrs. Browning, the stroke was so massive that attempts at rehabilitative therapies proved fruitless and were terminated after a few months.

Medical prognosis at the onset of an acute cerebrovascular accident, (a CVA), is highly problematic. The extent of the patient's damage and the likelihood, if any, of recovery are extremely difficult to determine during the initial weeks after an acute CVA. After major strokes, some people make astounding and near complete recoveries; others don't improve at all, and many decline rapidly and die.

Due to this variability and the uncertainty of predicting which outcome may occur, artificial provision of nutrition and hydration is routinely instituted post-CVA. And for some it definitely is a lifesaver. Many patients would not have the opportunity to recover and lead successful and happy lives were it not for nasogastric and gastric feeding. A gastric feeding tube is surgically inserted directly into the stomach, thus bypassing the nose and throat. Otherwise the delivery system is the same. Medicine prefers gastric tubes for longer-term use, as degrading nasal tissue becomes a problem after a few months of nasogastric feeding.

For Mrs. Browning, as well as for countless Floridians like her, the feeding tube was not a chance for hope, but, as seen from the eyes of most others, an instrument to cruelly perpetuate, a painful, degrading, and horrific existence. While medically appropriate when first inserted, Mrs. Browning's feeding tube became, once her prognosis was known, an unwelcome agent artificially prolonging the natural process of her death.

Distaste for Mrs. Browning's forced feeding was more than a matter of general consensus. A year or two before her stroke, Mrs. Browning had signed a "living will." In it, she specifically refused artificial provision of nutrition, should she develop a condition she could not recover from which made her death imminent. Her living will was unusual because most documents of that time did not address the issue of artificial feeding.

The "right-to-die" issue had burst into the public consciousness through the Karen Ann Quinlan case, which involved the use of a respirator. The 1970s proved to be the legal battleground regarding use of that device upon the terminally ill, and by the early 1980s most jurists and ethicists concurred that the mere existence of medical technology did not necessarily mandate its use. Feeding tubes were different. When patients and their families started to assert the same rationale and legal precedent in the mid-1980s in attempts to refuse or terminate artificial feeding, they were met with stiff legal opposition and moral outrage. By the time Mrs. Browning had suffered her stroke, the procedure for removing a respirator had become commonplace; but terminating artificial feeding remained a monumental task. Once inserted, the feeding tube assumed a life of its own, and as we later would grimly joke, the tube appeared to have more rights than the patient.

Courts throughout the country were all over the place on this issue and decidedly reluctant, if not unhappy, to be the societal arbiters of this conflict. Deciding whether artificial provision of nutrition could be terminated, and if so under what circumstances and procedure, involved the weighing of complex moral, ethical, medical, and legal concerns. Making this decision was much better suited to the deliberative process of a legislative body. There, fact-finding and discussion, which can include all interested parties, could hopefully result in a consensus for applicable legislation.

The courts acknowledged that the adversary system at the heart of our jurisprudence, with its strict adherence to rules of evidence, was a poor way to formulate public policy regarding right-to-die. Unfortunately for the courts, "pulling the plug" on the terminally ill, especially when that "plug" provided nutrition, was a political hot potato most legislators were delighted to toss back to the judges. As a result, policy was being set piecemeal on a case by case basis. Next time you complain about courts legislating, vent your frustration on your elected representatives!

The methodology for deciding pre-feeding tube cases was varied. Some courts permitted withdrawal of life support when the medical procedure was deemed to be "heroic" as opposed to "routine." Other courts ruled that "invasive" rather than "non-invasive" procedures were permissibly terminated. Of course these judicially provided labels did little to guide other patients, their families, or health care providers. What might be considered heroic or invasive in one situation might prove to be non-invasive in another case, depending upon the prognosis of the particular patient and other subjective conditions. Other courts were not as concerned with the type of medical treatment in question, but focused more on determining the treatment preferences of the patient. Since most treatment decisions in these situations involve those who are mentally incapacitated or physically unable to communicate, determining patient intent is problematic.

The courts had great difficulty applying these rationales to feeding tube cases. Termination of sustenance evoked strong emotional responses, and judges were reluctant to sign their names to an order that many observers claimed was tantamount to a death sentence by starvation. Actually, death was usually caused by dehydration-induced electrolyte imbalance in seven to ten days. Unlike certain medical technology that could stave off death for only a short period of time, a feeding tube could keep a vegetative patient alive for years—in one noted case, a ghastly *eighteen years.* Some courts even adopted the argument that artificial provision of sustenance did not constitute medical treatment at all, and therefore could not be terminated under any circumstances.

For Mrs. Browning it was Florida law that mattered. This issue had twice reached the Florida appellate system. Appellate courts review the work of trial courts and the pronouncements of the former become the reported decisional law under which trial judges are bound. In the first case, the Supreme Court of Florida permitted the withdrawal of a feeding tube from a competent patient agonized by the final stages of amyotrophic lateral sclerosis—Lou Gehrig's disease. There, artificial feeding would only prolong life a few more months, and the patient clearly and consistently expressed his desire to terminate a life he described as unbearable suffering. The court concluded that the state had no right to interfere in what appeared to be a reasonable choice unquestionably made by a patient facing imminent death.

While a bit helpful, this case didn't apply to Mrs. Browning. She was neither competent to express a choice nor was her death, with artificial feeding in place, imminent. The status of the patient's competence was important to the Florida court. Its comfort zone in terminating artificial provision of nutrition was much greater when the patient could speak for himself or herself.

State authorities gave little or no comfort to the families of incompetent patients. Prosecutors argued that a surrogate could not choose death for the patient, even if the person had expressed such a desire while previously capable. They reasoned there was always a chance the once competent but now uncommunicative person had later changed her mind. How could one possibly prove this negative—that the patient *hadn't* changed her mind? Of course the State's logic nullifies all previous expressions of the person's intent, invalidates any living will the patient had executed, and takes from her the right to plan for such situations while she has an ability to do so. The result? Tube feeding is mandatory for all incompetent patients lacking the natural ability to eat.

The other Florida appellate decision was factually closer to Mrs. Browning's situation. There, a lower appellate court ruled that a feeding tube could be removed from a patient in an irreversible coma or permanent vegetative state. The court did not mention or discuss the issue of patient intent, but seemed to focus solely on the medical condition. In either a coma or vegetative state, the patient totally lacks the capacity for reasoning and other higher brain function, leaving only automatic brain stem activity extant. For judges in these cases, quality of life apparently was the determining factor. When illness or accident permanently reduces the person to nothing more than mindless flesh, this opinion suggested that artificial feeding, as well as any other treatment, may be terminated without inquiry into the subjective wishes of the patient.

Mrs. Browning clearly was not in a coma. And while a vegetative state is less precisely defined and more difficult to diagnose, Mrs. Browning was more than vegetative, as she appeared able at times to interact with her environment in a rudimentary way. The medical records and nursing home aides reported that she occasionally would smile when an employee's child visited. Although Mrs. Browning could not speak, the aides insisted she made infrequent utterances "in an attempt to communicate." The health care providers also claimed they could detect differing moods, and there seemed to be no question Mrs. Browning could experience pain. She often emitted low moans and grunts when handled.

This portrait of Mrs. Browning's consciousness directly contradicted the observation and experience of Mrs. Herbert, who was also her live-in companion and sole surviving relative. Doris Herbert, in her early eighties, visited her elder cousin at least twice per week at the nursing home. She had initially visited on a daily basis until it became clear to her Mrs. Browning was non-responsive and would remain as such. Mrs. Herbert scoffed at the reports and suggestions of her cousin's rudimentary mental abilities and sorrowfully proclaimed that Mrs. Browning had become nothing more than a cash cow for the nursing home.

Undoubtedly, feeding tubes had become big business. Regulations issued by the Florida Department of Health and Rehabilitative Services made it virtually impossible to remove feeding tubes from nursing home patients without obtaining a court order. If the patient were incompetent, as most were, the judge would insist on proof of a permanent coma or vegetative condition. And of those patients, few of their families, even if emotionally capable and financially able, chose to expend the time, money, and effort to hire a lawyer and go to court.

Why not bypass the nursing home and the court, bring your loved one home, and pull the tube yourself? How does prosecution for murder sound? With no appellate court or statute declaring artificial feeding terminable without court order, or terminable under any circumstance for a non-vegetative incompetent patient, your local prosecutor was just a phone call away from an officious nursing home administrator. Additionally, not many families were emotionally or physically equipped to administer this end-of-life care without assistance. As a result, Mrs. Browning was just one of the estimated hundreds or thousands of incompetent Florida nursing home patients kept barely alive through tube feeding. At approximately $2,000 per month per patient for the privilege of basic nursing home residence, feeding tubes indeed were a financial windfall in Florida to the probable tune of tens of millions of dollars per year.

Mrs. Herbert had reason to be suspicious of the nursing home's motives and its sanguine assessment of her cousin. Not only did feeding tubes perpetuate a clientele, they greatly reduced the cost of labor. Assisting an impaired nursing home resident to naturally intake food is very time intensive. Not only may a resident need help to get the spoon to his or her mouth, but the food must be cut or mashed and the resident may often require repeated encouragement to eat. How better to free up an aide's time, and the employer's money, than by commencing tube feeding? All the aide need do is change a bag once or twice a day, expending a few minutes rather than an hour or more in direct resident care.

Countless incompetent patients have been prematurely intubated for the sake of corporate convenience and profit. But why would the patient's doctor order such a thing you ask? The primary treating physician for many nursing home residents also happens to be the facility's staff doctor, who very often also happens to hold a financial interest in the institution. How's that for conflict of interest!

The sabre of conflict of interest was double-edged, and it didn't take long for Mrs. Herbert's opponents to raise it. As commonly would be expected, Mrs. Browning had chosen in her Last Will and Testament to leave, upon her death, her entire estate to her next of kin. Was $250,000 enough money in the till for Mrs. Herbert to "hasten" her cousin's death? The State Attorney thought so. Mrs. Herbert, as well as most other relatives in this position, see their prospective inheritance dwindle away through expensive and seemingly endless medical, hospital, and nursing home "services." According to the State, this potential conflict was serious enough to require families to obtain judicial consent to terminate tube feeding.

Let's have a little trial and invite the State Attorney, just to make sure persons like Mrs. Browning are protected from their loved ones! The State's position was decidedly anti-family and had the condescending and threatening odor of "big brother" seeking to intrude upon highly personal and private areas of citizenry life. Most people expect and believe that a spouse or child or other relative of an incompetent patient is primarily concerned with the loved one's welfare, and is not the sinister, money-grubbing operative portrayed by the State.

Despite Mrs. Herbert's apparent heartfelt plea that the feeding tube be removed because it was the expressed wish of her cousin, she was looked upon with suspicion and derision by the State, Mrs. Browning's doctor, and the nursing home staff. Various employees of the nursing home would sarcastically remark to her, "How can you think of killing your cousin like this?" or, "What kind of person are you who would starve someone to death?" This emotional blackmail and intimidation was commonly inflicted by health care providers upon family members trying to grapple with the heart-breaking decision whether or not to terminate tube feeding.

Obviously, many health care providers are compassionate and dedicated. But even this group sometimes clashed with the family, as each saw the patient quite differently. The contradictory patient assessments made by family and provider are due, in part, to relative perception. The doctor, nurse, social service worker, and aide never knew or observed the patient prior to the medical catastrophe. Their relationship with the patient is therefore limited in context to the reality of impairment, and the spectrum of patient behavior and response they experience is the narrow one with which they are very familiar.

Family and friends, however, have had a lifelong relationship with a vital individual, and now see an incapacitated patient who bears little resemblance to his or her former self. Fine gradations in patient behavior may be irrelevant to the family when their bench-mark for comparison is pre-impairment. No wonder viewers from such opposing perspectives may see something differently, or may form contrary beliefs as to what constitutes the best interests of the patient. While this dynamic may partially explain conflicting opinions about patient competence, it doesn't resolve gross discrepancies in observation, nor does it ever excuse the infliction of emotional cruelty.

Why not then just let an impartial judge sort out all these issues and make a fair decision solely based upon the patient's welfare? Aside from all the impediments previously mentioned, the process of obtaining judicial relief is exceedingly slow. Opinion after opinion sang the same refrain. After expounding at length upon the legal theories and social policies that entitle the patient to the relief requested, the court concludes by casually mentioning that the patient died months before the decision was entered! A year or two is nothing in the time frame of litigation. What good is a right to die with dignity, if the remedy for enforcing the right is useless? It became obvious that if the right-to-die were to have any practical effect, these medical treatment decisions had to be made by patient families, after consultation with health care providers, *without the requirement of judicial intervention.*

As I stood in front of Mrs. Browning reflecting upon these issues, I knew I had not answered for myself the question that brought me here: would I represent Mrs. Herbert and become the agent of Mrs. Browning's death? I had hoped for some help, some sign from Mrs. Browning. Although no closer to what I sought, I remained at her bedside, sensing that my question would somehow be answered before I departed.

# CHAPTER EIGHT

# *"Soul-Speak"*

As I continued to stay beside Mrs. Browning at her nursing home bed, I felt my mind relax and my weight sink into the ground. I began to feel light-headed as I became more reposed. Although feeling like I could drift into sleep, I also experienced a sense of heightened awareness. As Mrs. Browning lay motionless before my gaze, I suddenly heard a loud, deep moan and scream and wondered if the nursing home personnel heard it and would respond to the unfortunate resident. In the next moment, as this cry of pain and torment continued, I realized it was Mrs. Browning. I felt the mid-section of my body open and noticed a strange quality to the light in the room. I sensed her soul in agony. As she screamed I heard her say, in confusion, "Why am I still here . . . why am I here?" My soul touched hers and in some way I communicated that she was still locked to her body. I promised I would do everything in my power to gain the release her soul cried for. With that the screaming immediately stopped. I felt like I was back in my head again, the room resumed its normal appearance, and Mrs. Browning, as she had throughout this experience, lay silent.

My first thought shouted, *Did this happen . . . did I imagine it?* Quite typical for the rational mind, wouldn't you say? I knew without a doubt what had transpired was real and dispelled the thought as intellect's attempt to assert its own version of reality. It takes some practice and training to maintain in the conscious mind the memory of psychic or "paranormal" experience. The propensity of rational mind to immediately invalidate the psychic self often acts to suppress into the subconscious these experiences, which I am convinced we all have or are capable of having. The practice of developing psychic memory is actually the undoing of a strong cultural conditioning. The anecdotal evidence of children seeing spirits, having premonitions, and talking to loved ones who have just died is pervasive. This expression is not only ill-nourished, it is hastily and forcefully disapproved. No wonder that we, as adults, are not receptive to the inner voice and vision.

We go to great lengths to explain away what is not within our rational world. I remember a recent television program on P.B.S. devoted to scientifically explaining the miracles in the Bible. As I recall, the one I saw displayed highly trained and motivated scientists intent on proving that the Red Sea parted due to a unique combination of epochally low water levels, immense desert winds of rare but not unknown occurrence, historical magnetic shifts, and lunar tidal influences of an orbiting body that was slightly closer to the Earth three thousand years ago! I was amused and struck, not by the hypothesis or its probability of accuracy, whatever that may be, but by the fact that there was obviously such a compelling need to undertake this exercise in the first place. I don't intend to demean human curiosity or rational methodology; however, the Bible was given as inspiration for spiritual transcendence, not as a textbook for Earth Science 101.

I acknowledge that my experience with Mrs. Browning was highly subjective, and at the moment, not suited to independent verification. Further, I am sure a persuasive argument can be constructed to psychologically explain this incident as an expression of a willing imagination. I obviously already had great interest and motivation to take this case before I met Mrs. Browning. I also felt a compelling need to obtain some sort of approval or permission in order to relieve my burden of responsibility for the anticipated result of my efforts. What better way to justify a decision to take the case and validate the appropriateness of my actions than to conjure up Mrs. Browning's woeful plea? Isn't it more likely my internal psychological needs motivated a self-created experience, compared to the contrasting possibility that souls can converse? As you see, a lawyer and skillful advocate can do this very well.

My communication with Mrs. Browning was real, and of course you must choose for yourself whether or not to believe it—and it really doesn't matter to me if you do or don't. Nevertheless, I can offer some proof that "soul-speak," as I like to call it, is not always a purely subjective experience.

Before our son was conceived, my then wife and I went through a long and arduous process trying to decide if we should have a child. Given that our marriage was never very stable, the familiar arguments against creating progeny seemed at times hard to overcome. Adding to this my ex-wife's underlying fear of childbirth left us, after seven years of marriage and two years in the decision-making process, still unresolved. Having a baby is one of those few decisions which ultimately is nonrational. You can weigh the pros and cons *ad infinitum,* but eventually must leap off a cliff with a gut faith that what you are doing is right.

One morning, while still generally engaged in that process, I walked into my office, and about half way to my desk was hammer-struck. While almost seeing stars like a comic book character, I heard the soul of my yet-to-be-conceived child emphatically shout: "I'm ready to be born . . . will you stop this fooling around!" I barely made it to my chair, which helpfully supported my slightly wobbly weight. It took a second or two for me to say *wow* to myself and another few minutes to move on to the pile on my desk. The voice I heard was distinctly male, and I beamed with the idea I had a son—or was going to have a son—or sorta had a son out there—or something like that.

As I got into the day I didn't think much of the message, but felt a deep inner glow. I didn't mention the experience to my wife when I got home, not by design but by inattention. When we rested in bed that night in the dark, before falling asleep, I said to her, "You know, I had a very unusual experience today, I—" At that point her body straightened. She interrupted me and said, "Oh, my God. Our unborn child told me today he's ready to be born."

Stunned, I relayed to her what happened to me that morning, and we both lay awed in silence. A few moments later I asked her why she hadn't told me this before. She explained that like a dream one forgets upon waking and then later remembers during the day, my words "unusual experience" triggered her memory of what had earlier occurred but had been pushed into her subconscious. I asked her when she had received this message, and she told me it was about ten A.M., the same time I was touched by our son. I had no doubt we were the beneficiaries of the same soul transmission, the only difference being that just one of us consciously retained the message.

From that point there was no decision to be made about bringing a child into the world. We already had a son, and only the attending details of his physical incarnation remained. Upon our stopping birth control, Alexander was immediately conceived. During the pregnancy many friends and clients offered the prediction we were having a boy, and only one offered the alternate possibility. What a joy and relief to embark on the affairs of life with an absolute knowing that your course is true!

This degree of certainty, for me at least, is rarely provided. During the course of our marriage we had one other such independently identical psychic experience, involving another highly personal decision. I have learned to trust in myself and in my capacity to be conscious of the spiritual world. Not that I doubt much the objective reality of my experiences, but independent verification sure is nice to receive every once in a while.

As I drove from the nursing home, I carried with me resolute determination to sever the artificial cord that bound Estelle Browning to this earthly realm. Her agonized cry for release ran through my mind over and over again, and I felt our spiritual bond. I would express for her what she was no longer able to advocate for herself.

This was not quite the same bond created when Manny and Mary Fellouzis would later walk out my door with their signatures on the bottom line! Speaking of the bottom line, let's temporarily leave our union of spirits and return to our marriage of dollars.

# CHAPTER NINE

# Starting Discovery—
# The Big Case Progresses

ISCOVERY. Unfortunately for our story, not the latest in space exploration or an educational cable television channel, but the dreaded, interminable, controversial, contentious and most expensive part of litigation. Beloved by defense attorneys charging clients on an hourly basis. Despised by plaintiffs' counsel working for free—until the hoped-for percentage pot of gold at the end of the litigation rainbow. A murky playground to cleverly outwit your opponent, or for those who cross the line, an opportunity for skullduggery. A war of attrition in which you wear down your adversary with crushing loads of work. The constant subject of proposed judicial reform and the repeated focus of client outrage.

Let us put our subject in context. There are three stages to litigation: pleading, discovery, and trial. (Here comes a session of Basic Law 101.) In the first stage, the plaintiff's complaint and the defendant's answer and affirmative defenses frame the issues in the lawsuit. The complaint, the first document filed with the court, starts the contest. In it the plaintiff must state a "cause of action," the legal term for a remediable wrong. Although it seems so these days, not everything that happens to our dislike or injury can be remedied through the legal system.

Each cause of action consists of various elements. For instance, in a slander suit the plaintiff must prove that a statement about him was made by the defendant, its content was false, the statement was heard by someone other than the plaintiff, and as a result the plaintiff's reputation was damaged. What happens if Joe files a complaint claiming: Fred told numerous ladies that Joe has a sexually transmitted disease and the result of this blabbing is Joe's inability to get a date? The judge will heave this case out of court. Why? Joe failed to say in his complaint that Fred's statement was *false*. Remember, one of the elements of a cause of action for slander is the untruthfulness of the objectionable remarks.

Once the court determines that the complaint states a cause of action, the defendant files an "answer" admitting or denying each element of the plaintiff's claim. In addition, the defendant may raise "affirmative defenses," which in essence say, "If everything you allege in the complaint is true you lose anyway, because..." These defenses are varied. Some may be general to all cases such as: you filed your lawsuit too late (statute of limitations); you filed it with the wrong court (lack of jurisdiction); we settled this matter before (accord and satisfaction); the wrong isn't remediable (failure to state a cause of action). A specific affirmative defense may be, using the slander example: I was joking when I made the remarks; everyone knew I was joking, no one believed they were true, and therefore your reputation wasn't damaged.

Pleadings are important because they weed out faulty cases early in the litigation process and in other cases narrow the issues requiring resolution at trial. Again, using the slander example, unless Joe amends his complaint to say that Fred's remarks were a lie, his suit is dismissed. If Fred admits everything in Joe's amended complaint *except* the new claim of lying, the only issue needing court resolution is whether Joe indeed has a sexually transmitted disease, and if he isn't infected, how much money to award. Now that you are plea-masters and know more than you probably ever wanted to about this lively subject, let's blaze on to discovery.

The parties, now aware of the issues still in dispute, go about gathering information that they hope will prove their points in court. The primary ways to compel disclosure of information are:

submitting written questions to your opponent, which must be answered under oath (interrogatories); obtaining papers, documents, and other tangible materials from your adversary or other persons for inspection and copying (request for production); having your opponent admit or deny in writing certain facts or propositions of law you propound (request for admissions); and questioning the opposing party or witness under oath in the presence of a stenographic reporter (deposition).

The philosophy behind discovery is to promote settlement and prevent trial by ambush or surprise. If each side knows the strengths and weaknesses of the other's case, this vantage encourages pre-trial resolution. Despite the fact that the law governing discovery promotes disclosure, many attorneys will do everything possible to give up as little as they can. Unless the opposition specifically asks for something, they won't get it. A request for "all papers that help my case" is improper under the rules of procedure. In some cases an attorney never finds the smoking gun because he was lax in phrasing his discovery requests. Of course it doesn't help that the producing party is scrutinizing the request as narrowly as possible.

Another technique to avoid discovery is the dribble effect. You partially produce or answer a request and hope this satisfies your opponent. If it doesn't, the requesting party has to endure the tedious process of going to court to compel your compliance. And even if the court rules for your opponent, you again only partially comply, hoping your adversary will get too tired or discouraged to return to court. Of course, if you're hauled back to court again, you've made sure the dribbled response is minimally sufficient for you to argue to the judge you haven't deliberately disobeyed the court's prior order.

If you're not fond of dribbling, effective disclosure can be avoided by employing an opposite strategy, the avalanche. Bury the smoking gun in a mountain of information. Your opponent requests "all documents that may show that the product you manufactured is unsafe." You strategically place your client's incriminating internal memo among thousands upon thousands of pages of useless but similar-looking data. A less-than-diligent opposing counsel may not discover the needle in the haystack. And some nasty attorneys, usually at the client's prompting, lie and say the requested information doesn't exist, or turn a blind eye to the client's destruction of this damaging evidence. Some lawyers actually instruct the client to commit this nefarious deed.

I suppose this mindset figures the odds of getting caught are slim, and even if nabbed, the worst the court will do is fine you or rule that the other side automatically wins the case. If you're fined the client ultimately picks up the tab, and if the case is lost, well, you probably would have been defeated anyway if the destroyed or concealed evidence had been properly disclosed. As to losing your legal license, you've left no paper trail and deny knowledge of your client's slimy efforts. Ugh!

Now before I start receiving hate mail from my colleagues, let's proclaim that most lawyers are indeed honest and ethical. But counselors, how many of you can say you never play the discovery game, even a little? What is difficult for attorneys and makes the ethical line fuzzy at times, is that equally noble duties sometimes pull us in opposite directions. Yes, as officers of the court we must maintain the integrity of the legal process and deal honestly and fairly with all parties. Yet one of our most sacred duties is to zealously and vigorously represent and promote the interests of our client. In theory these duties are compatible, but in practice, lawyers are frequently faced with decisions that don't easily fall on either side of the fence.

Your opponent requests in discovery an important document. You know what document she really seeks, but the request is arguably imprecise enough for you to contend it doesn't describe the document you know your adversary wants. Do you produce it or respond that no documents exist fitting that description? Yes, the spirit of the rules promotes disclosure, and yes, justice depends upon the truth being revealed. Yet our system of justice is *formulated* to be adversarial. Therefore, if your opponent does not skillfully frame her request, how can you produce this damaging evidence without breaching your duty to zealously represent your client? A prerequisite to ethical conduct is the recognition that ethical issues exist. However these issues may be unraveled, we hope most attorneys at least spot the knot.

One of the first tangles I needed to unloose for Manny and Mary was the court's discovery and trial schedule. Here it was, September 1992, and discovery had to be concluded by early November with trial set for January. With nothing much done since the filing of the complaint and answer a year before, there was no way this case could be prepared for trial in a couple of months. We needed to delay. The technical word is "continuance," often the savior of busy or unprepared attorneys. Although courts, cognizant of public dismay over protractive litigation, scrutinize requests for continuance, this plea was a slam-dunk. Obviously the court, if possible, will not penalize blameless clients for the unpardonable sins of their lawyer.

But make no mistake, even if the result may be a foregone conclusion, obtaining the result almost always involves considerable effort. A request to the court, for anything, is called a "motion." Under the rules of procedure, all motions must be in writing. No, clients, your attorney can't just call up the judge when you need something to happen in your case. Before a motion is filed, the maker must confer with opposing counsel and then certify in the motion whether or not the other attorney contests the request. In state courts, motions are usually resolved by obtaining a hearing where the lawyers argue their respective positions before the judge. Federal court requires much more work. There, the rules demand every motion be accompanied by a written brief or legal memorandum detailing and analyzing the issues and legal authorities raised by the motion.

Legal writing is extremely time-intensive, and good legal writing more so. The rules of procedure limit the length of legal briefs and memorandums. That's why they call them "briefs." Contrary to popular assumption, voluminous writing takes less time and effort than terse expression. Skill and labor are required to concisely convey factual and legal issues that often are very complex. For this reason, among others, many attorneys dislike and avoid federal practice.

My motion for continuance, legal memorandum, and attached client affidavit consumed a day and a half of legal research, writing, and re-writing, and ended up as fifteen pages filed with the court. And this effort was for a foregone conclusion. All right, I do fess up to being chronically overprepared; however, I believe this has won me a few cases I otherwise would have lost over the years. It also significantly reduces my anxiety level in court. But even a modicum of the effort required in federal practice results in huge workloads. This is why large law firms, with their legions of clerks, paralegals, and junior attorneys assisting the lead counsel, usually handle cases like the one I bit off. Our slam-dunk resulted in a revised schedule pushing completion of discovery back to April 1993, and marking trial for July, buying us a little time to breathe.

Discovery started congenially, which means each side was willing to cooperate as long as something was gotten in return. The government had submitted to previous counsel a request for production of documents that was ignored and long overdue. In exchange for an extension of time to respond, I agreed to segregate from my clients' numerous boxes of business records the specific invoices that were sought. As further consideration for sparing my opponent the lengthy process of hunting through records, the government agreed to produce its documents before the date due under my request.

The mantle of the United States of America was worn in this case by David N. Geier, which he prominently would display whenever he thought it advantageous to his client. By stentoriously referring to his client as the "United States of America" rather than the "defendant," I believe he intended to project a moral superiority to his cause in contrast to the inferior claims asserted by the rest of us lesser litigants. I must admit to the effectiveness of his flag-waving, even in that era of anti-government feeling.

We had an opportunity to size-up each other during our initial meetings in November and December to produce and inspect documents. David first came to my office in Dunedin to review my clients' records and shortly thereafter I took my turn at the United States Attorney's office in Tampa. My antagonist looked a few years younger, perhaps in his mid-thirties, and a few inches taller, maybe six-foot-one or so. His thin and wiry build reminded me of Ichabod Crane. He definitely exuded career government. He was a lead trial attorney with the tax division of the United States

Department of Justice and carried that air of superiority or self-confidence that often seems grafted onto people holding positions of power for extended periods of time.

We cautiously exchanged some pleasantries and personal tidbits. His permanent office and home were in Washington D.C. He was married with a stepchild and frequently traveled to Florida to litigate in the federal courts there. When David mentioned his recent appreciation of cigars, I somewhat nervously retorted with my disdain of all forms of tobacco use. (As far as pop trends go, my part of Florida lags behind the northeast by a few years, so I hadn't heard about yuppies and their newfound love for cigars.) After discerning that my opponent indeed was not joking about his stogies, I realized how well I had unfortunately managed to insult him.

In the role of combatant, I have found it difficult to personalize my adversary and have admired the few attorneys who do this well. As a young attorney I utilized aggressiveness to compensate for the insecurity of often having to learn my craft by the seat of my pants. As with most novice attorneys I craved the respect of my peers, and although no one ever accused me of being collegial, I did acquire the reputation of a hard and skilled opponent. Only in the last few years, with more maturity and confidence, have I relaxed more around what I do and with whom I do it. No stranger to personal issues associated with professional competence and standing, I gained some insight into the less obvious motivations of my younger opponent.

Our professional strengths and weaknesses were not too difficult to assess. Federal tax law was David's only job, which gave him an enormous advantage. I had only started to scale the learning curve in this area of law. He practiced almost exclusively in federal court, which conferred upon him another sizable advantage. While I had handled a few miscellaneous matters in federal court over the years, I had never taken a case to trial there and lacked intimacy with the federal rules of procedure, a paramour well worth attending to should you wish to pay a visit. He also possessed the benefit of resources. If money buys justice, or at least access to justice, he represented the client with the deepest pocket in the world.

Of course I held a few advantages of my own. Being a little older I had been around the block a few more times than David, and although it wasn't the same block as his, I was a more seasoned competitor. Most important, I had upward of ten jury trials, while my opponent had never tried a case before a jury. Unless you're a lawyer it may be difficult to understand why the prospect of a jury showdown strikes fear deep into the bowels of practitioners. Many attorneys, probably the majority, never go to court at all. Just the thought of entering this arena keeps them at their desks drafting contracts, forming corporations, preparing deeds and trusts, and otherwise transacting your business.

For the rest of us who venture into court, jury trials infrequently transpire. First, most matters which could result in trial never reach that conclusion. The bulk are settled, many are dismissed, and some are abandoned by weary or discouraged protagonists. Second, the clear majority of civil cases that make it to trial are decided by a judge without a jury. The constitutional right to trial by jury does not extend to many types of cases, such as divorce, custody, probate, guardianship, mortgage foreclosure, etc.—the actions classified by courts as "equitable" in nature. Also, litigants entitled to jury trial often waive that right and choose to have their case heard by a judge. Jury trials are more expensive and time-consuming than those tried non-jury. Additionally, in many cases the parties conclude that the issues involved, which may be complicated or technical, would be better understood by a judge who has previously decided similar cases.

Lack of familiarity with jury work is not the only factor that daunts so many attorneys. Yes, jury practice is aggressive and combative. Yes, it requires you to think quickly on your feet. Unexpected circumstances, like a witness testifying differently than expected or the judge erroneously excluding a piece of evidence, force immediate changes in strategy. Yes, it demands intense levels of concentration. You can't space out and then dumbly look at the judge when he asks for your response to his question that just slipped by. Yes, there are countless events and details commanding your constant awareness, as inattention to one can result in disaster at any moment. And yes, this is incredibly stress-producing, which can destroy you physically, mentally, and emotionally if you haven't learned the art of transmuting this stimulus into a higher energy. While these elements are present in non-jury trials, they are ratcheted up in jury work.

With a jury, you perform in a fishbowl and they're the audience peering in. Unlike a judge who is more geared to just getting the facts, the jury is in the process of judging you. How you express yourself, how you hold yourself, how you sit, how you walk, how you relate to the judge and witnesses and opposing counsel—who you really are—all tell jurors whether or not you are a person they can believe and trust. You are in court to ask and convince this group of women and men to follow your direction, to accept the truth as *you* see it rather than as presented by your opponent.

It's not that the facts and law don't count. But in many trials the evidence provides each side with equally persuasive support for their position. If the evidence were one-sided, the case would have been settled long before. Therefore, juries rely on the attorneys to help them arrive at a resolution they feel is fair and just. Jurors want to do right, are exceedingly perceptive, and intelligently exercise their common sense. They almost always see through a facade and can determine if you really believe what you are saying.

This scrutiny of a jury can open areas of vulnerability many attorneys find uncomfortable. No matter how skilled a technician a trial lawyer becomes, no matter how proficiently he delivers the lines, no matter how well the advocate can make it appear she believes in what she is doing, this competence will only make you a good trial lawyer. No doubt this competence, especially in high degree, will bring considerable success. But greatness in a trial attorney takes heart. It takes, in addition to competence, the ability to reach down and speak from your inner truth, to express who you really are and what you really think and feel. This does not mean you always must approve of what your client has done, or suggest to the jury that the actions of your client were appropriate. But even in my hardest cases, I have always found an issue or argument I could truly espouse.

I once represented a very unappealing middle-aged man who clumsily and stupidly tried to pick up a young sales clerk at Sears.

He gave her a card depicting a copulating twosome spouting the words, "For a good time call [his phone #]." The young woman turned out to be fifteen, and my client was arrested for endeavoring to contribute to the delinquency of a minor. The law required that aiding delinquency be done "knowingly" in order to constitute a crime. Since the fifteen-year-old could well have passed for eighteen, the defense in the case was lack of criminal intent, as (arguably) the defendant didn't *know* he was propositioning a minor.

My client came across as reprehensibly as his conduct. At trial I denounced his actions almost as strongly as did the state attorney, to the state's considerable surprise. Whether the sales clerk was fifteen or eighteen did not excuse this inappropriate behavior. No matter how morally or socially objectionable his conduct, however, the only question for the jury was whether these actions were made criminal by statute.

My argument to the jury focused on the distinction between moral and criminal wrongs. I stressed it was not the function of the jury to become social police, nor was it within the power of the prosecutor to criminalize obectionable behavior not made unlawful by statute. I also emphasized that as we engage ourselves in the world, many things may occur that we find unpleasant and objectionable, but not necessarily criminal or legally remediable. Toleration is one of the prices we pay to live in a free society. I believed what I said to this jury and spoke from my head as well as my heart. I never once defended my client's actions. The jury's verdict was "not guilty." In an unusual postscript, the jury foreman immediately announced after the verdict that their decision was *required* by the criminal statute and legal instructions given by the court, and should not be taken as approval of the defendant's conduct, which they found despicable.

Coming from your heart does not necessarily mean being emotional—it is expressing from your essence, from the truth of who you are, without holding back or protecting. The vulnerability we feel, the risk we mistakenly think we are taking by being open-hearted, is of rejection that strikes deep. So we guard the best part of ourselves. We create personas to take our emotional hits, thinking this somehow insulates our inner self from experiencing hurt.

In talking one day to an attorney friend, who I didn't know professionally, I mentioned I acted basically the same way at work as I did with her socially. With astonishment she proclaimed she was a completely different person as a lawyer and could not function in that capacity if she were her "real" self. Inability to express who you are in what you do creates self-conflict which, if perpetuated, can prove destructive. We seek to protect ourselves by not risking. How many of us never fully commit in our intimate relationships? We never fully open, perversely thinking that if we are rejected we will be consoled by the self-rationalization, *My lover never got to see the best part of me.* A wise man once said it is hard to be open-hearted but harder to be closed-hearted. We are malnourished by our misguided and futile efforts to protect ourselves from life, which is our staff and source.

For me, being in jury trial and on trial is allowing myself to be vulnerable. It is an exercise in letting go, dropping into myself, and trusting that, even though there is a lot riding on the outcome, I can joyfully express at my highest potential irrespective of the tangible result. Without the awareness that our inner journey sustains us, external outcomes can take on monstrous importance. I soon learned what importance *Fellouzis vs. United States* held for my opponent as we started to play hardball.

If discovery is cheesy, the government's response to my request for documents was definitely of the Swiss variety—full of big holes:

> The defendant has redacted all information which is not factual and are merely opinions or conclusions . . . as such items are protected by the governmental privilege.

A sentence gone here;

3 PAGES HAVE BEEN REDACTED

A paragraph erased there;

NINE (9) PAGES HAVE BEEN REDACTED

> This request is objected to on the basis that tax documents involving third parties are privileged. Documents will be produced as requested to the extent they are non-privileged.

My vocabulary is not exactly minuscule, but "redact" was new enough to send me to the dictionary. Technically meaning "to edit for publication," I found the use of the word here slightly less benign. Numerous portions and entire pages of documents I sought were being withheld. But based on what privilege?

A "privilege," established by courts or by statute, recognizes a societal value in keeping certain types of communications or matters confidential, and thus non-discoverable. We weren't exactly asking for nuclear missile codes or the President's personal diaries. It didn't seem to me that a messy tax case involved the national security or issues of executive privilege, but I had never litigated a tax refund case, so what did I know? And what about the claim of third-party privilege and the unspecified assertion of privilege? We hadn't requested the tax papers of any other persons. Was this a red herring or was the government hiding something?

More disturbing was my opponent's claim of full disclosure. He represented that, absent privileged materials, the entire "administrative file" of the I.R.S. had been produced to me, and that this constituted all the documents I had requested. In comparing the I.R.S.'s "administrative file" to my clients' case file, however, I found the latter contained numerous government letters and notices absent in the former. I began to think the government was playing the discovery game, and my relations with the sovereign started to become less congenial.

In early January I sent David a firm and slightly testy letter trying to pin down his claims of privilege and clarify what the heck he meant by "administrative file." I also demanded a firm date for the production of the I.R.S.'s "Certificate of Assessments and Payments," which the government had promised to produce but had not yet delivered. With statute of limitations issues dependent upon the dates taxes were assessed and paid, this was an important document. David sang a constant refrain. He asked the Service to prepare it, and there was nothing much else he could do but wait to receive it. The government wasn't exempt from discovery rules requiring documents to be produced within a certain time, but its attitude certainly belayed that fact. My letter drew no response, and I still didn't have what I had requested, thought I was entitled to, and needed.

This was getting more difficult than I had expected, and we weren't even past first base. At least our next line of skirmish would bring some fringe benefits. We were headed for Hong Kong!

CHAPTER TEN

# Awakening in Hong Kong

"How can it be morning when it's dark here?" my six-year-old queried as we sat electronically tethered on opposite sides of the globe. I relayed some first grade celestial mechanics while gazing from my bed across the water that separated the Holiday Inn Kowloon from Hong Kong Island. Hong Kong Territory arose slightly earlier than I this day as my body still complained of the thirty-hour door-to-door trek—nineteen hours aloft—which had mercifully ended the previous Asian afternoon. Alexander did not quite grasp why it wasn't dark now everywhere, and in some way neither could I fully accept that my morning sun was obstructed from the view of Earth's other half. As Hong Kong was already in gear for another day of blazing commerce, the home part of my world was winding down after the dinner meal. Despite my obvious knowledge of rudimentary physical laws and the now-commonplace NASA images of our planetary sphere ever rotating between light and dark, I shared with my son the wonderment of this expanded perspective.

There is relative truth and absolute truth—a proposition today's moralists hotly decry. No doubt the sun rises in the east and sets in the west. It happens every day of our lives and has occurred every single day in the history of humanity. The probability it will happen tomorrow is great enough to propel any of us to wager the family farm, should there be anyone foolish enough to bet the contrary. Yet the sun neither rises nor sets. The illusion of an orbiting sun is provided courtesy of a revolving Earth. This illusion is so compelling it took the Western mind—after forgetting what the ancient Greeks realized—over a thousand years to re-dispel.

Moving from the relative truth of the wandering sun to the absolute truth of the spinning Earth is a leap into enlargement. As the breadth of our perspective grows, as we view life from a new and greater vantage, as we see how fixed beliefs suddenly can become fluid, vast parts of our world fall from the absolute to the relative. But as our expanding consciousness reveals ever-increasing aspects of our life to be the construct of transitory beliefs, do we reach an unchangeable core or, like peeling every layer of an onion, find nothing at the end? Is anything left for us as immutably true?

The sages answer this question by proclaiming all is God, and everything we perceive to be other than God is unreal. Accepting this as our axiom generates the following corollaries some find troublesome. If Universal Consciousness is the sole immutable truth, and this truth is perfection, love, peace, and bliss, then is our experience of life other than as perfection, love, peace, and bliss an illusion? If evil and suffering are not part of God, is our pain and suffering unreal, and are good and evil just arbitrary distinctions? Is our lack and limitation, our pain, our confusion, our lust and greed, our enmity, our rage, and all the aspects of our lives we deem negative, as compelling an illusion as the sun rising and setting? I submit that the ending lyrics of "Row, Row, Row Your Boat" betray musical mysticism rather than nursery nonsense—"Life is but a dream."

You have to keep your sense of humor when mentally investigating profound issues of Spirit. This is because pondering, while enjoyable and sometimes helpful, almost never results in God-realization. If intellect were the means to commune with the Divine, we would find those with exalted I.Q.s palling around with God in numbers disproportionately greater than the rest of us. I've never found spiritual enlightenment to be a pronounced trait of our mental giants, have you?

We have to laugh as well to remind ourselves that intellectual efforts to know God not only bear minimal fruit, but often are themselves the impediments to what we seek. The great nineteenth century Indian saint, Sri Ramakrishna, analogized the experience of God to drinking wine. Upon taking a few sips of the Divine drink, we are God intoxicated beyond measure. So when he goes to the metaphorical tavern he asks the barkeep for a cup, takes a swig, and revels in God's bliss. But when we go to the tavern, we interrogate the dispenser of the elixir. We demand the barkeep tell us how many bottles of wine are in the tavern, the proportion between white and red, how many different varieties he keeps, the vintages, the method of chilling the wine, the temperature he maintains the Chardonnay, and so on. Although one swallow of the house beverage is all we ever will require, we never imbibe, being constantly engaged in our endless inquiries.

We often miss the experience of Spirit in our effort to understand its nature. No wonder Jesus said it takes the mind of a child to enter the gates of heaven. To be more blunt about it, our need to understand God, with our resulting conceptual beliefs in and about God, is probably one of the largest obstacles we face in our quest for Divine communion. Even the idea that Spirit lies beyond comprehension, which is another mental construct we can cling to, can become an impediment.

With these caveats, let's return to our pondering. Is pain and suffering an illusion, as the sages say? This proposition at first blush is difficult to accept, especially since each of us has probably experienced the "reality" of some physical trauma or excruciating emotional torment at some time in our lives. Nevertheless, pain is a relative belief, a judgment we have made, which then shapes our experience. The root of the experience of pain is "sensation," defined here as awareness of energy in the body. Like anything else that comes into our field of awareness, our mind tends to react in one of three ways, positively, negatively or neutrally. We habitually attract the positive, repel the negative and ignore the neutral. If we judge the sensation to be positive, we experience it as pleasure and want more of it; if we deem it negative we tend to view it as pain and want to get rid of it as soon as possible.

The desire to eradicate unwanted sensation, the drive to avoid experiencing it, and the fear it will indefinitely remain or get worse, is the attitude and posture of *resistance* we assume around this body energy. In trying to resist sensation, a somatic tension and psychological wall is constructed around the affected area in an attempt to insulate us from the negatively judged energy. This effort actually protects and immobilizes the sensation preventing its natural release. Fearing the sensation amplifies its intensity, which generates greater avoidance efforts. These weapons we use in our seeming fight against pain create the overlay that, to a large degree, *becomes* the very thing we are desperately seeking to escape. Therefore, much of what we experience as "pain" is actually this resistance, which is not innate but is learned.

The etiology of the word "pain" comes from the Latin *poena*, which means penalty or punishment. At the root of our linguistic psyche, pain is retribution for our untold and innumerable transgressions. No wonder pain has gotten such a bad rap, and no wonder in our culture we will go any length to avoid its imposition. It is time for a major change in attitude.

Physical pain is the organism's method of communicating a fault or weakness in, or danger to, the system—a warning to attend to the organism to prevent damage or injury. Not only a wonderful messenger, bodily pain is one of nature's fundamental diagnostic tools. Pain creates the pathway to locate and remedy an underlying disorder. How many of us, in response to pain, thank our body for the wonderful service it provides? When the display light in your auto goes on and warns that your oil is low or your brake linings are getting thin, do you curse the light, tape it over, and ignore it? Although I might complain a little that some work may now be needed, I'm generally appreciative of this advance notice and even a bit amazed at the vehicle's ability to provide this valuable service—betraying me, I suppose, as a simpleton in mechanics. Does your own body's intricately more sophisticated warning and diagnostic system deserve any less appreciation?

The attitude of gratitude fundamentally alters our experience. It promotes joy and happiness through embracing, rather than rejecting, what comes to us. Changing the way we encounter pain, and deprogramming ourselves from the pervasive conditioning that pain is bad, decreases our resistance. As a result, by assuming this posture of acceptance rather than conflict, our experience of the sensation is less "painful."

The arbitrary judgment we make about a bodily energy phenomenon can create pain. Is pain then really just in the eye of the beholder? If I have an incredibly intense burning sensation in my foot I may find it unpleasant or agonizing, but that same sensation felt by a quadriplegic might generate a response of ecstatic joy. We have the power to alter our judgments, and if pain indeed is a judgment about a sensation, we can change that mental conclusion.

Okay, you say, attitude may make a difference, and perhaps there is a relative aspect to our relationship with pain but—it's *real* because sometimes "it just hurts!" I say, in piercing the heart of pain we find bliss. The means of this discovery is one-pointed attention. If we can focus on the sensation generating our experience of pain, that pain can be transcended. By making sensation the object of attention without distraction, you start to experience the sensation without overlay.

What seemed monolithic now takes on varied forms. You notice a place where the sensation exists and a place where it is absent. The "boundary" between the two appears to be fluid and moves in different directions. The sensation has diverse textures and feels: sharp here, dull there, more intense or concentrated there, thin or amorphous here. As you sharpen your focus, you start to see in ever-greater detail, like looking through a microscope, and can move from the edges towards the center of the sensation. What were waves of pain now look like vortices of closely banded energies, and what once seemed solid is now constantly reconfiguring. Moving deeper you see small spaces between the bands, and by entering such an area where sensation is absent, you fall through that space into the heart of sensation. And in this heart there is a stillness, like the eye of a hurricane or the center of a spinning wheel—a place of perfect repose and silence amidst the deafening tumult. And in this stillness is unspeakable joy.

What I have described is meditation. I have performed this meditation many times in my life and on a few occasions have, as a result, transcended rather significant pain. I don't mean I was able to *bear* the pain. I mean I found that place of inner peace that was infinitely larger than the pain. Meditation is a way to transcend the rational mind. This mind works by comparison. Whenever we experience "this," there is always the "that" of our previous experience to place beside it. Dropping the rational mind means to become one-pointed. When we leave the duality of comparison and judgment, we fall into the single, infinite, and Divine present.

In my meditative experience the pain didn't disappear, but became a small bubble floating on an infinite ocean of consciousness. And when I would oscillate back to my rational mind, that small bubble could become my entire excruciating reality. Interestingly, I have found that intense pain can sometimes be more readily transcended than lesser pain. Because I can more easily "bear" routine discomfort, there is less impetus to move through it. As for unbearable pain, we move towards God, as we are often apt to do, because we've run out of other options.

As the duality of mind creates pain, so we could make the same argument for right and wrong. As Hamlet proclaimed, "There is nothing either good or bad, but thinking makes it so." Of course we don't fully live in the reality that all is God. For this we have compassion, for each other and for ourself, because the inevitable result of living outside that reality is suffering. There is a story of a renowned Zen master whose young son died. One of the master's many disciples, while walking through the fields, saw his master sitting by a tree, sobbing. The disciple, aware of the death, said, "Master, why are you crying? You have taught us that all is God and everything else an illusion." To this the master replied, "That is true. Yet the death of a child is the greatest illusion of all." Although we live in the relative world and suffer its slings and arrows, we are always connected to the immutable truth. Like the prince in beggar's robes who has forgotten his lineage, our job is to remember and reclaim our birthright.

Upon wishing my corporeal lineage a good night, I luxuriated awhile in bed, slowly infusing the morning light and, after endless hours confined in a plane, playfully stretching to my heart's content. In my nascent emergence from jet lag, I was beginning to appreciate the first-class accommodations provided by my client and travel companion, Manny. The dark burnished mahogany furniture and the forest green and burgundy fabrics, leathers, and room colors combined to ooze comfort and elegance. With the curtains now open and the balcony windows ajar, the March morning air began to waken me.

# CHAPTER ELEVEN

# The First Major Assault— Being Falsely Accused

H ONG KONG AND FLORIDA'S WEST COAST share similar climates—meaning mid-March perfection. The crystal blue skies added to the sparkle of Hong Kong Island's impressive skyline. I beheld the view from my ninth-floor perch across the mile-or-two-wide channel now busy with container traffic and the commuter Star Ferry. The island ascended steeply from the sea to Victoria's Peak, terracing by nature's design the skyscrapers rising from its slope. The composite effect was very pleasing, due in great part, I later learned, to the application of *feng shui* in building placement and design.

After a slow shower and shave I curtained some outside light, put a fresh towel on the floor, and began yoga and meditation. Each place has a different feel, and this practice is an excellent way to get in touch with the local energies. Inner work can also be very grounding and is an effective way to unwind jet lag.

The physical feat of getting to Hong Kong capped an exhausting whirlwind of two months of legal activity. Drifting into meditation, the pictures of those preceding events ran over and over again through my mind. As the images replayed they generated feelings of nervousness and insecurity. Had I made a misstep? Was there some procedural sin I committed, waiting to toss this case back into the abyss from whence it came? After dragging people half way across the world, would my Hong Kong witnesses even show up for their depositions? Adding to this unease was my opponent, with knives sharpened, waiting eagerly to pounce and fillet should I stumble in the least. I wasn't merrily singing "Life is but a dream" at the moment!

In January, after serving the government with extensive Interrogatories and Requests for Admissions, I sat with my clients to plot which witnesses we would depose. There are two primary purposes for a deposition. First and most obvious, you get to hear what a person has to say about the case before he enters the witness box. This provides an opportunity to investigate his account through independent means and prepare an attack or rebuttal if his testimony is damaging to your case.

Second, it locks in the story of the witness. If the trial testimony later varies, you can impeach the credibility of the witness by serving up her prior words. "Mrs. Jones, you have testified in court today that the sky was blue on the day in question. Do you remember six months ago I took your deposition at which time you swore under oath, on page 22, line 7, that the sky was gray on that day. Does your memory get better as time passes . . . were you telling the truth then . . . are you telling the truth now . . . what *are* we to believe?" The witness loses a lot of wiggle room once pre-trial testimony is taken and transcribed by the stenographic reporter.

As you can surmise, depositions are most helpful when witnesses are adverse. If witnesses are favorable, you almost never initiate their deposition, because that will confer an advantage on your opponent. Why provide your adversary an opportunity to learn more about your case? And since favorable witnesses are likely to be sympathetic to your cause, they will usually talk to you voluntarily before trial, thus obviating the need to compel their pre-trial testimony by subpoenaing them for deposition.

We journeyed to Hong Kong to depose its residents Eric Lee and Dominic Ng. The latter's testimony was critical to our case. As the general manager of the Nathan Ivory Factory, I hoped he would corroborate Manny's story that a supposed $350,000 U.S. retail ivory boat was sold for $17,000 in Hong Kong as an act of oriental gratitude. Also, with his worldwide experience in the ivory trade, we hoped Mr. Ng would appraise the boat's fair market value at the time of Manny and Mary's museum donation. Eric Lee, as purchaser of my clients' wholesale import business, was to confirm that the items later donated by Manny and Mary were clearly identified as part of their personal collection and specifically excluded from the salable business inventory.

Why take their pre-trial statements, since these were favorable witnesses? A less common purpose of depositions is to preserve or garner testimony for use at trial should the witness later be unavailable to appear in person. For instance, if a sickly deponent later dies or becomes too frail to appear in court, his pre-trial deposition can be read in lieu of live testimony. Also, depositions may be read at trial when the witness is beyond the tribunal's jurisdiction. The federal district court can issue a subpoena compelling a person to appear, but only if that person resides within a hundred miles of the tribunal. Hong Kong was well beyond the long arm of the court. The testimony of our witnesses was for reading at trial as neither, understandably, agreed to personally appear in Florida.

Although United States courts have no jurisdiction or authority in Hong Kong, there is a way to secure a grip over a foreign witness. By treaty or perhaps by custom, the court of one country can request the court of a foreign sovereign to issue legal process to compel the latter's citizen to submit to deposition where the witness resides. This formal request from one court to another is called a "letter rogatory." The foreign court is not bound to grant the request, but usually assents as a matter of judicial comity— you scratch my back, and we'll return the favor when you ask. Of course, I hadn't the slightest idea how to go about arranging a deposition in another country and had never heard of a letter rogatory prior to my numerous hours of legal research necessitated by the circumstances of this case.

Despite my clients' assurance that Eric and Dominic would appear voluntarily, I knew better and suggested we go the official route to secure their presence. Not too many people jump at the prospect of involvement in the legal system. And no matter how cooperative witnesses may seem, voluntary efforts often evaporate due to inconvenience, delay in being examined, and worries over the anticipated unpleasantness of being cross-examined. My judgment was soon displaced by the price tag. After finding a reputable Hong Kong law firm, we discovered it would cost thousands of dollars to have a barrister present the letter rogatory to the Hong Kong court and obtain its order requiring the witnesses' appearance. (Don't you love a lawyer being "shocked" over the fees charged by another?) I won't tell you what it cost just to use the offices of the firm to take the depositions and have them fetch the stenographic reporter.

The clients' decision to keep their fingers crossed and forego compulsory attendance did not end my procedural headaches. A duly authorized person must administer to the witness the oath to tell the truth before testimony begins. In the United States, all stenographic reporters are notaries and authorized to swear in witnesses without court approval. Luckily I discovered that public notaries as we know them don't exist in Hong Kong, and court reporters there have no authority to administer oaths. This brought me back to the law books, which revealed that a non-notary foreign reporter must be "commissioned" by the court to give the oath. I could easily have missed the reporter/oath issue and, upon asking the reporter to swear in the witness, suffered the ignominy and disaster of scrapping the depositions due to this oversight. Try explaining to your client why he's paid over $10,000 to come to Hong Kong for no purpose and why, upon his return home, he would have to pay the government a greater sum for its costs and fees!

You would think the momentous decision to approve a reporter was sufficiently noncontroversial to generate a stipulation between counsel. But despite calls and letters to my opponent in an effort to amicably and simply work out the technical details for the depositions, no response was forthcoming. The result?—my time, energy, and effort to produce an Emergency Motion to Commission Reporter with accompanying Memorandum of Law.

We couldn't even agree on a deposition date. As soon as Manny was able to get a commitment from Eric and Dominic to a certain day, I informed David of the proposed date six weeks hence. The time to complete discovery was winding down. Our witnesses had the hectic travel schedules expected of wealthy and powerful businessmen, and March seemed to be the only available time to take this trek. Air transport and hotels had to be booked, we needed to retain the reporter, and various other arrangements required immediate attention. After a week of David's silence and after another futile fax, I filed notice of depositions for the March 10th proposed date and filed my emergency motion to commission the reporter. A few days later I received the government's response— notice that David was taking *my* clients' depositions on March 4, the day before we were booked to depart for Hong Kong!

Battle room strategy was going on here. The time to hit your adversary with a massive workload is when he's already maxed out. In addition to all the work in this case above and beyond arranging and preparing for the Hong Kong depositions, there still remained other clients I represented and a ton of work to clear my calendar— and when do I get some time to pack my socks?

The deposition of your client is a major and critical litigation event. Because deposition locks in trial testimony, you have to prepare your client as if this were the court appearance. Cases have been lost or severely compromised because the client was not fully prepared for deposition. I knew I would need about two full days I didn't have to ready Manny and Mary, and felt the screws tighten.

Often a keen sense of timing is needed to maximize the advantage gained from deposing the other party. The government's strategy was not without risk. Absent unusual circumstances, you get only one shot to depose the opposing party. My adversary obviously wanted my clients' story before he encountered Eric and Dominic on the record. The downside was, as additional information developed in the case through the course of discovery, the government was foreclosed from further pre-trial direct questioning of Manny and Mary.

Closely following the government's deposition notice was its next missive: scheduling the deposition of Dominic Ng on March 10, 1996, "will work a hardship against the United States." Apparently, the government had now decided to send its own expert witness to Hong Kong to attend our depositions along with counsel. Unfortunately, the scheduled date was inconvenient for its hired gun. *Well, why the heck didn't you tell me this when I first called you to arrange these depositions, or at least tell me before I set them?* This latest notice was particularly rankling, as I had just agreed to give David an extension of time to respond to my Interrogatories and Request For Admissions, thus relieving him from a pre-trip burdensome due date.

Since experts charge beaucoup bucks by the hour, I was astounded the government would pay a small fortune just to have James Godfrey by David's side in the unlikely event the latter needed technical assistance while our witnesses were being questioned. How easy for me as opposing counsel to be indignant over the hemorrhage of our tax dollars!

We eventually worked out dates. Dominic's deposition was pushed back a couple of days and Manny and Mary's were moved up a bit, as there was no way I was going to permit them to be deposed the day before our departure.

My clients both got "A's" for their depositions. Part of that we can attribute to their diligent homework—getting the facts straight—which was no simple task when the events requiring recall began over seventeen years before. No small part was due to their intelligence, strong verbal abilities, and good common sense. And let's not neglect David's mediocre performance. He failed to explore many areas where a little digging would have exposed valuable caches of facts helpful to his cause. I can only speculate that his time pressures inhibited more extensive preparation. Finally, my coaching contributed some.

Yes, attorneys coach clients and no, that doesn't mean lawyers tell their clients to lie. The first thing I advise any client or witness regarding testimony is to tell the truth. Not only is veracity required by law and personal ethic, it provides the best of all practical strategies. Most people don't lie well, and even those who do, get tangled in the additional lying it takes to conceal the initial falsehood. Once a witness lies, even in small part, a massive opening is created to destroy not only the witness's credibility but the case of the attorney who called that witness.

What is "coaching," then? First it is reviewing the facts over and over again with your client until you are sure you both understand them. Second it is educating the client about the legal issues in the case so he understands which particular facts are legally significant. Next is teaching your client how to answer questions. This is critical. Many clients respond to inquiries they don't fully understand or start replying even before the examiner finishes the question. Listening is a learned art that often must be imparted to many clients. And yes, how an answer is expressed makes a big difference.

"Mr. Fellouzis, why did you donate these items to the museum?" "Well, I thought more people could see them that way, and why not take advantage of the tax loopholes?" "Loopholes" obviously is a pejorative expression and "take advantage" doesn't help much either. After reminding the client that tax deductions are authorized by Congress for beneficial social purposes, such as supporting charitable and educational institutions, the answer now becomes: "Mary and I wanted many more people to have the opportunity to appreciate these works of art, and we were encouraged to do so by the legal provisions of the tax code."

Last and most effective in coaching, and more fun from my seat, is a highly rigorous cross-examination of your client as if you were the opposing attorney. Most of my clients find my practice cross much more onerous than the actual examination of opposing counsel, which they later report as tame by comparison. A movie producer was told his lead actress was holding up the set because she was afraid to momentarily grasp a live snake as required in the scene. About an hour later the producer burst on to the set brandishing a seven-foot constrictor, held it under the terrified actress's nose while shouting she was going to do the scene, and just as promptly exited with the serpent. Within a few minutes the actress reportedly did the scene in one take with an eighteen-inch snake provided by the director. But maybe this isn't the best analogy to use when talking about lawyers!

Even if we cast aside as humor the likening of attorneys to reptiles, I must confess that my clients' depositions were not a high point for the profession. A week or two before, the government served another request for documents, asking for all the import and customs records regarding the donated items. David wanted the documents at the deposition despite the discovery rule allowing me thirty days to produce. He also wanted at deposition the documents we had previously produced which he had already examined and had the opportunity to copy. Although not bound by his request, I initially and reluctantly agreed to bring them.

Upon reflection, we changed course a bit. Given the government's porous response to my document requests and the jerking around I got in the scheduling of the Hong Kong depositions, my clients and I decided to show up for questioning with a few large boxes of records containing the documents requested. We had plenty to do ourselves and refused to spend valuable time searching through records we weren't legally bound to bring just to make the government's job easier.

My opponent, clearly unhappy at this turn of events, became more frustrated as the depositions progressed. Manny and Mary were proving to be tough witnesses, and he never could get his hands on the particular documents he anticipated using. The examinations lasted more than a few hours.

Upon us wearily concluding and gathering our materials to leave, David, in the presence of my clients and the stenographic reporter, jutted in my face without warning and accused me of stealing my clients' money! The government had furnished me copies of its documents without charging for reproduction costs, and neither had I charged the government for making copies of our documents. David blurted out that I had billed my clients for reimbursement of nonexistent government copy charges in a scheme to bilk Manny and Mary.

I felt as if the blood had exited my head and cemented my feet to the floor. How could a member of the bar and representative of the Justice Department engage in such outrageous, careless and scandalous behavior? Obviously he had no information whatsoever about my billing relationship with my clients and wouldn't have the slightest idea in the world if I were stealing cost money, which of course I wasn't. The reporter looked up with an expression like "boy is that guy out of control," and Manny and Mary were as frozen as I in disbelief. After a few seconds I stammered something about how ridiculous and untrue his statement was, and my clients and I hastened our exit. In our car ride back to my office, my shock began to wear off and I started to boil. My clients calmed me down a bit, reminding me that David's conduct adversely affected only one person's reputation, his own.

A few days later and now half a world away, my meditation revealed a lot of juice still left from the deposition tete-a-tete. As my mind served up images from the incident, I could feel the reactive emotional tug of my anger and contempt. I could really steam myself up if I chose to stay on that locomotive, especially since it felt so good to keep on blaming David for my distress. After some time, by continuing to watch these images with the intention not to invest energy in their emotional offspring, the succession of mental pictures started to slow and dispassion started to arise.

No matter how compelling or engaging a motion picture, if you diminish the speed of the projector, the illusion of the drama begins to dispel. Eventually, as the projector slows down, you will start to see that the movie is really a series of individual frames whose rapid succession gives the appearance of solidity. And between each individual frame is a small space. Our minds work in the same way. Internal moving stories are created from the rapid succession of our thoughts. And because our stories are personally compelling and trigger emotional reactions, we become identified with these dramas, which become our reality.

Most of the movie-going public will remember *Alien,* the sci-fi picture with Sigourney Weaver that came out in the late 1970s. In one incredibly intense scene, an astronaut, John Hurt, is lying unconscious on a table in the spaceship's mess. While surrounded by the crew, his chest starts moving up and down accompanied by a loud thumping. With more heart-pounding suspense—we think he may be recovering—suddenly the grossest and slimiest looking alien with lots of teeth bursts from his chest and bolts away, to the absolute horror of his shipmates. This was the first scene of its kind in movie history and obviously has been oft repeated.

I saw *Alien* in Tampa on its opening day without knowing what to expect. When an afternoon real estate closing finished early, I went to a three P.M. show at one of those massive screen, one-picture movie houses. I was the only person in the dark, cavernous theater, and as you might expect, was scared completely out of my wits. Why was that? The story was so compelling, the sets so authentic, the acting so expert, the illusion so masterful—projected celluloid became real for me. But no matter how compelling the illusion and no matter how much I identified with this story, if I sidled up to the screen to give Sigourney Weaver a squeeze, all I'd get is sandy grit on my cheek.

What we are is the eternal light of consciousness. This light projects the contents of our mind onto the screen of our lives. Like the beacon of the movie projector, whatever is put before it is displayed. The reel we are playing could be a tragedy, comedy, or perhaps an adventure. Spiritual growth is the process of becoming less identified with what is appearing on the screen and more identified with the light of the projector. No matter how cata-strophic, exciting, painful, or ecstatic the projected dramas of life, they are as illusory as my gritty hug with Sigourney. Irrespective of the tonnage of explosives erupting on the screen or the number of worlds colliding, notwithstanding that the child on the screen was starved, exploited, beaten, and abused, and despite the endless misfortunes befalling the characters, the light of the projector can never be harmed.

By starting to realize we are this light and not what it projects, we discover we can change the script of our lives by altering the contents of our mind and choosing to focus more on some images and not others. Some of us then start to become rather proficient at creating our lives, so by the end of the reel, it's a pretty sweet story. And what happens when the reel runs out? As the infinite light of consciousness continues to illumine, perhaps we will rest a while before the reel of our next lifetime premieres.

For me, meditation has been indispensable in loosening the grip of my illusory dramas. While meditation may be practiced any-where at anytime, initially it is easier when seated in a quiet place without external distraction. This facilitates the mental relaxation that enables us to begin to see the spaces between our succession of thoughts and sensations. By focusing on the spaces between these "mind moments," insight often occurs.

Suddenly I noticed a space between the image of David accusing me of larceny and my feeling of anger. What once appeared inextricably linked, I now recognized as two distinct phenomena. With this realization the anger immediately waned. Unease arose. Focusing on this sensation brought up mental images of my meeting with Manny and Mary to sign our fee agreement. These images generated feelings akin to guilt or self-negativity. I again focused on the spaces between the images and feelings, and a light flashed. I realized in some way I have held the belief I was being unfair or avaricious in my fee negotiation with my clients, hence the feelings generated by those mental pictures.

Simultaneously I saw what had hooked me in the experience with David. Part of me believed that in some way perhaps I was "stealing" from Manny and Mary in garnering the fee agreement, hence my reactive angry stance to David's comments. (As we discussed before, anger usually is an avoidance mechanism covering feelings we find difficult to experience.) With this flash of insight my meditation instantaneously dropped to a deeper level. I felt no need to delve into my beliefs surrounding the fees—no impulse to figure out if the belief was justified. My breath became more expansive, there was much less mental activity, and a light and pleasant feeling of "all-rightness" welled up through me.

After a while I emerged from meditation and slowly started to dress. I enjoyed the sensation of fabric newly touching my skin and appreciated the dancing colors outside the window. As I dressed, I saw the incident with David as if it were a painting or photograph I was observing from a distance. From this vantage spontaneously arose a passionless understanding. Had there been nothing in me to disturb or awaken, David's aggressive and negative barrage would have passed through me without generating upset. I could just as well have responded by ignoring him, or chuckling, or having compassion for *him* being lost in his own unconsciousness.

But I had a lesson to learn. I saw how my latent belief about "stealing" was related to my self-worth. If our fee agreement were fair, did I mistakenly believe I was overreaching because I doubted the value of my time and talent? If the agreement were unfair, was I motivated by greed, which is just another manifestation of the belief of self-lack? Either way, my self-concept here was grounded in deficiency consciousness. Any belief other than that we are whole, complete, full-filled and perfectly cared for is ultimately illusion-based. Had I not been asleep to my illusory belief, perhaps I wouldn't have received David's prodding. But the universe provides what we need to resolve our own stuff. As for David, I played as much a part in his self-created drama as he did in mine, so our encounter was synergistically perfect. We don't notice this synergy, because we usually remain unaware of the role we play in the fulfillment of the needs of others.

One day when I was living at the Kripalu Center, the facility was closed to visitors and the residents were happily out and about the summer countryside. I had a very strong desire to find a resident who had a book I wanted to borrow and read that day. The halls were deserted, so I concluded there wasn't much chance of obtaining my reading material that afternoon. For some reason I felt an urge to go to the main chapel, so I decided to gather my music and play the Steinway grand there. Upon entering this huge space, which holds more than half a thousand, I saw only one person, lying on his back in the middle of the floor. He just happened to be the person I had been seeking. As it turned out, he had lent the book to someone else, so it was unavailable to me that day. But please notice, my strong desire had been to find the *person* who owned the book, not the book itself! Be precise in what you ask for.

I started playing the piano in the chapel and after a few minutes noticed the book owner had left. I continued in reverie for about an hour. The cathedral ceiling approached forty feet in height, and the chapel had wonderful acoustics. As I started to walk out another resident appeared from behind the large mosaic screen in the front of the chapel and said, "I was just sitting there and had such a strong desire for someone to come and play some classical piano. Thank you."

My path to the chapel fulfilled not only my desire, but the desire of someone unknown to me. Nevertheless, though we all act as each other's agents, as principal to our own karma, we bear the sole responsibility for working it out.

So I left it to David to deal with his own business. I slowly selected my pocket contents and then, moving towards the hotel room door, paused by my image reflected in the wall mirror. Convinced I was sufficiently self-pampered this morning, I took a step forward, twisted the handle of the door and with tingles in my chest, opened into an Oriental world of newness and excitement.

# CHAPTER TWELVE

# *City of Colors*

FIERY REDS, BRIGHT YELLOWS AND BLAZING GOLDS, blacks, greens, and other colors kaleidoscopically filled the sky as I looked up from the Hong Kong street. Banners, streamers, ribbons, placards, and signs of all sorts densely hung between the three-and four-story buildings on each side of the byway. This artificial sky, labeled with exotic-looking pictographs, appeared all the more remarkable since the road and walkways beneath it were not particularly narrow. Multitudes streamed by while I momentarily gazed above, as "pause" did not seem to be in the vocabulary of this great city. I allowed the rapid pulse to move me along until the next delight grabbed me in this feast for the senses. Every available space was filled over capacity. Storefronts, building facades, and windows were plastered with display and advertisement, and sidewalks brimmed with stalls and carts of food and ware. Motion and sound combined to relegate "bustle" to the description of quaint cities of the economic past. The older English architecture felt a bit out of place—the seeming remains of a colonial impress now utilized by vibrant Chinese inhabitants. What a joy to be here!

And what a joy to be here with Manny. With over twenty trips to Hong Kong and numerous local friends and contacts, he showed me the city he loves from the inside out, his pleasure barely exceeded by my own. As we traversed the boulevards and alleyways and entered the businesses of friends and associates, I was treated to Manny the raconteur. Each person and locale seemed to spur a

110

story that wove bright human textures and patterns on the panorama before me. We had a few days before depositions, providing my guide ample time to enchant me with the object of his affection.

Amidst this love affair I was repeatedly struck and amazed by the entrepreneurial spirit driving this metropolis. There was no doubt whatsoever commerce was king, subsuming what appeared to be every thought, activity, and relationship. I half expected a young street vendor to whip out a satellite-linked portable computer, check the latest commodity prices, and correspondingly adjust his price for a cup of rice noodles. But while I continued to admire this mercantile drive, I later came to sense an imbalance in this energy that focused on business to the exclusion of all else.

Manny, although retired, kept up his commercial contacts for the benefit of his son, who operated an import/wholesale business. This resulted in a succession of lunches and dinners at fine restaurants, courtesy of the prospective exporters. Each meal presented at least one sampling of highly expensive exotic fare, proclaimed without fail by our proud hosts to enhance male potency. I didn't exactly feel a surge from the shark fin soup, but then again, I didn't get to try the snake gallbladder!

I was soon completely spoiled by the "regular" Chinese cuisine, which defies comparison to its lesser cousin masquerading in the States. Each restaurant sported huge aquariums, and I naively commented that the natives must find this aquatic decor aesthetically pleasing. My companion chuckled, explaining that the Chinese here wouldn't think of eating seafood not killed immediately before preparation—quite a contrast to our "fresh" fish that is iced for days or weeks. No wonder the Chinese consider us barbarians.

Manny no doubt enjoyed playing the gracious host and savvy guide, but he hadn't brought me ten thousand miles at his expense strictly for entertainment. While business may not reign supreme in the States, we nevertheless soon began to tend to ours. The civilized Chinese way was to start at the dining table, where it was our turn to treat.

Our first meeting with Eric Lee and wife commenced with their immediate display of genuine affection and respect for Manny. Eric and his extended family had come to Hong Kong from China

twenty years before to escape poverty. For years they acted as
Manny's agents in Hong Kong, a timely opportunity that contributed to the struggling family's success. After years of hard work and
the eventual purchase of my clients' business on favorable terms,
Eric's wealth now exceeded Manny's, probably by multiples. As an
expression of Eric's gratitude and regard, Manny became the
godparent to the Lee's daughter—a salient fact my opponent never
ferreted out in the course of the proceedings.

Our primary guest was a few years younger than I, short and
stocky but not fat, and sported a full head of straight black hair. I
immediately liked Eric and wife, both of whom I found to be
congenial, good humored, and down-to-earth. I soon learned of one
of Eric's most formidable talents, his renowned ability to consume
great quantities of noodles, which had apparently earned him
victory in numerous sanctioned as well as impromptu competi-
tions. I mentioned my own ability to ingest pasta in significant
quantities, but any impulse to compete immediately withered
under Eric's gaze, sparkling as it was with keen delight over the
mere possibility of burying yet another opponent.

Next, to my wonder, our server wheeled to our table a massive
earthenware mound resting on top of a transport almost large
enough to fit a patient. There was no competition over who was
going to have the honor of smashing the Shanghai chicken. With
the waiter presenting a ceremonial yet fully functional hammer,
everyone insisted *my* muscle was required to crack open our dinner,
since this was my first trip to Hong Kong. I was told this four-by-
two-foot hive of dried mud contained a specialty dinner Manny
had arranged a day in advance.

As the story playfully went, early one morning a hungry thief on
the outskirts of Shanghai stole a chicken and while under hot
pursuit, buried the loot in the mud for the twofold purpose of
escaping apprehension and preserving his prospective meal. Upon
returning to his quarry at the end of the day, our hero found the
mud hardened by the hot summer sun. After grabbing a large rock
and breaking open the hiding place, the thief to his delight discovered a succulent dinner, the unintended result of nature's slow-
bake oven.

My first couple of tries with the hammer didn't even crack the surface of the mound. Throwing caution to the winds, I wound up and gave it a big whack, creating a fissure and spatter of small mud chips sufficient to generate the applause and delight of the waiter and much of the restaurant. I left the excavation to our server, who eventually retrieved a large well-tied brown bag from beneath the slabs of baked earth. Our emerging dinner was now brought to another station, where it was carefully removed from its sack onto a large platter—soft and tender meat dripping and falling from the bones amidst exotically fragrant wafts of steam. Numerous vegetables followed the chicken out of the bag and on to our table, providing me, a vegetarian, at least some sampling of this remarkable dish. A gentle anise flavor permeated the fare, either from a liqueur or perhaps the plant itself. The combination was subtle yet striking and the taste of the dish almost rivaled its presentation. With the risk of being repetitive—what a joy!

The next day we taxied into the New Territories to meet Eric at his place of business. This frontier-sounding name designates the bulk of the Colony's four hundred or so square miles and lies north of the city centers of Hong Kong Island and Kowloon. As we moved over the large brown rolling hills, massive high-rise apartment complexes took over the landscape. While the terrain was still relatively open, compared to the urban hubs, these habitations for Hong Kong's working class seemed, along with sprouting factories, bent on consuming the countryside. Half a hill gone here, the side of a small mountain obliterated there—all in the process of being digested into submission by ubiquitous excavation equipment. Growth management is a concept likely foreign to or rejected by this ultimate arena of laissez-faire. By the time we reached Eric's we saw more of the countryside left to enjoy. But even with more space about, real property was still a highly valuable commodity, and the size of his enterprise indicated a significant wealth in land.

The fenced complex held numerous buildings, all newly constructed. The main structure combined a large purchasing gallery, offices, and workshops. Enclosed warehouses stood at various places, but most impressive to the eye were long open-air covered storage areas with rows of massive, brightly colored ceramic pots. Each close to my size, the hundreds of vessels took up quite a bit of real estate. These I learned were reproductions of Chinese antiques, many manufactured in Canton Province and a substantial number fabricated in Eric's own factory located elsewhere. Much of our host's business was in reproductions, including beautifully crafted furniture of classic oriental design.

Despite the dazzle and interest of the new stuff, my attention quickly focused on the old. In the main building a large workshop was devoted to the processing, cleaning, and restoration of incoming antiques. Ceramic figures of all shapes and sizes painstakingly proceeded through various stages of work. Horses, camels, demons, deities, court figures, overlords, and solemn attendants emerged from the past, some with exquisitely preserved glazes of green, brown, and yellow. Many were still covered with mud and dirt, evidencing recent unearthing. An area with various antiques ready for sale or shipment adjoined the workshop.

What an opportunity! I needed a crash course in Chinese antiquities if I were to successfully refute the appraisal and expected testimony of the government's hired gun, and here was a classroom. If I didn't have time to become an expert myself, I hoped I could learn enough to at least sound like one—and is that what makes someone an "expert" anyway? Sometimes it takes a thief to catch a thief.

Larceny, I discovered, was now fueling the market in Chinese antiques. That mud and dirt I saw clinging to the figures betrayed the illegal excavation of Chinese earthen tombs. While grave-robbing is a time-honored tradition, it was held in check for a generation by the communist regime's imposition of brutal penalties for any such offense. With commerce now replacing ideology as the driving force in mainland China, smuggling the nation's past into Hong Kong for resale was becoming a very lucrative business. Whether by subterfuge or bribery—the latter now the means in China for accomplishing just about anything—the goods buried by predecessors for use in the afterlife streamed into Hong Kong as profit for their progeny. While receiving smuggled goods in the

Colony was most likely an offense, a third party's purchase from a fence apparently was perfectly legal. More laissez-faire.

We had previously had the pleasure and good fortune to meet one such entrepreneur, Mr. Wong. We were brought to Mr. Wong's small antique shop on the island by Manny's former agent who now procured goods for his son. Hong Kong's premiere and established galleries were located on a strip of Hollywood Road, but at Mr. Wong's we found ourselves on a side street. His store, crammed with porcelains, some smaller jades, and numerous items of great variety, lacked the organization, presentation, and "big" storefront pieces of the pricey Hollywood Road shops.

Mr. Wong was middle-aged, thin, with almost crew-cut hair that stuck straight up, and wore black pants and a short-sleeved white shirt. A cigarette constantly dangled from his lip as if it were permanently appended. He spoke no English and we spoke no Cantonese, so Manny's agent handled the introductions.

As we surveyed the merchandise and found something to our liking, Manny identified the item and then asked for a price. If not sure of the period, or if we wanted verification, we had our agent ask Mr. Wong to date the piece. After a while we could hold an item or point to it and say directly to Mr. Wong, "what's this?" and would promptly receive our answer by dynasty, and if Ch'ing Dynasty (1644-1911), by reigning emperor. Manny seemed to be impressed by this expertise and accepted our host's opinion even when contrary to his own.

Upon asking Manny why he trusted Mr. Wong's word, I was promptly given a lesson in Oriental customs and practicalities. Manny's agent would suffer dishonor by bringing her customer to a vendor who engaged in deceit. The agent's loss of face would have to be rectified by the agent compensating her customer in some way. The dishonor of the agent suffered at the hand of her long-standing vendor, however, would cause the latter a much greater loss of face, thus requiring a vastly more substantial remedy between vendor and agent. Apparently this was something more than just business reputation or ethics, and Manny felt secure under the canopy of moral custom provided by our agent's introduction and involvement.

As Manny started to buy in good portion, I couldn't refrain from joining the act. Given recent historical perspective, I learned that current prices were exceedingly low. In this arena for over twenty-five years as an importer, collector, and now advisor to his son, Manny was astounded at this new market trend, which he discovered soon after our arrival. Supply of goods, particularly *fine* goods, had significantly increased. On Hollywood Road we saw forty or fifty of one type of piece that Manny would declare numbered one or two on previous trips. The wave of smuggling was only one part of the equation.

Manny's theory, on good authority, posited that local dealers and collectors were flooding the market with their stockpiles of antiques in anticipation of China's impending takeover of Hong Kong. Supposedly, since the mainland outlawed the possession or sale of artifacts over one hundred years old, many in Hong Kong feared their goods and collections would become unsalable under Chinese rule, or worse, subject to confiscation. An orderly market was now disrupted by an unrestrained transitory supply, thus creating a price plummet and purchasing opportunity. A late Ch'ien-Lung (Emperor from 1736-1795) bowl with surreal-looking bats in blue and red underglaze struck my fancy, along with some later Ch'ing Dynasty covered vases. With Manny gushing about a possible market skyrocket once the mainland took over, I thus began my life as a collector of Chinese antiquities.

After completing our shopping fest we labeled our purchases, which were set aside at the store for later packing and shipping by our agent. Little did I know our spree was just the appetizer. We spied Mr. Wong and the agent whispering in a corner, and their furtive glances let us know our attention to their huddled interchange was not welcome. A short while later our agent came to Manny and asked if we were interested in seeing the proprietor's "special" collection of goods. Our palates purred at the prospect of more aesthetic delicacies, and we unhesitatingly accepted the invitation.

We all proceeded to Mr. Wong's auto and were chauffeured through an increasingly narrow maze of side streets. We dead-ended in a shadowy alley with small connected buildings on each side. One or two appeared to be storefronts with tiny covered windows and the balance presented padlocked metal garage-type doors. We edged up to a particular door, and Mr. Wong signaled this was the place.

As we exited the car and approached the entry, I was a bit unnerved by our host's continual rotation of the head, obviously performed to detect anyone who might be watching. He quickly turned to release the substantial lock and as quickly pivoted back as if someone might, in that brief lapse of observation, decide to spy on us. Looking outward to the alley he reached behind and lifted the roll-up metal door. The shadowed light of the alley exposed just the first few feet of the opened space, keeping its recesses well hidden. As Mr. Wong stepped back and beckoned us into the darkness, I felt as if I were in a Charlie Chan movie and half-expected some sinister figure or perhaps the police to pop out of nowhere. As soon as we were in, the door slammed down behind us, and for a moment there was nothing but blackness.

We heard movement in the dark, and after a few elongated seconds light appeared. A bare bulb, on a wire hung from the ceiling, dimly revealed a long narrow room with an earthen floor about eight or nine feet wide. Another bulb further down showed me that the room stretched at least fifty feet in length. Aladdin could not have been more astounded upon entering the secret cave of the forty thieves. From ground to ceiling on each side running the length of the room were yard-wide dirty wooden shelves laden with treasure. As we started to walk down the narrow path between the troves, I heard Manny gasp, "George, look at that Han Dynasty [202 B.C.-220 A.D.] fortress . . . that celadon is Song Dynasty [960-1279] . . . look at the size of those Ming [1368-1644] tomb figures!"

On and on it went as we proceeded down the aisle, and even I recognized that many of these antiques rivaled or surpassed the big-ticket storefront items displayed by the Hollywood Road galleries. Many pieces looked as if they had been there for ages, while others revealed the moist dirt of recent excavation. I admired the gorgeous "celadon" ceramic vessels about three feet high with relief figures of fantastic dragons and other mythological figures. Celadon, the light green color said to resemble the hue of sea water, is most associated with glazes used in Song Dynasty ware.

I was so mesmerized by the succession of beautiful and incredible pieces, I didn't bother to ponder the nature or scope of the proprietor's extracurricular activities. At least not until I approached the end of the room, where an entry led to an unshelved additional room containing an enormous, elaborate wooden and metal altar. Painted in gold and red, with a large Buddha intricately carved among various attendant figures, its well-aged splendor was trumpeted by its size. Almost as wide as the room and as high as the ceiling, it was about four feet in depth, and I imagined it used to adorn the wall of some far-off ancient monastery—hard to get this piece out of China stuffed under your coat!

Our astonishment with this storehouse was just about rivaled by our amazement over price. These same pieces were selling on Hollywood Road at three to four times Mr. Wong's amounts, and we realized he must be one of their suppliers. With most gallery antiques now fetching only one-third to one-quarter the prices of previous years due to the current glut, Mr. Wong's private market was irresistible. "That piece went at Sotheby's in eighty-five for twelve thousand," Manny said, "and Wong wants nine hundred. I couldn't find that pot in Hong Kong for less than two thousand my last trip, and he wants one-fifty."

Our previous question, "what's this?" was now replaced with our new inquiry, "how much?" Manny bought heavily and I, befitting my circumscribed financial condition, purchased modestly. Perhaps someday, if Manny augured correctly, I may make a happy and considerable profit from our meeting with Mr. Wong. But it doesn't really matter, because I followed the first rule of collecting: buy only what pleases you and will bring you joy. The tri-glazed pair of Ming tomb figures inscrutably staring from my office credenza and the nearby Tang Dynasty (616-906) celadon wine vessel do just that.

Of more mundane delight, at Eric's I was pleased with his quick grasp of the legal issues in our case and his cooperation with my extensive deposition prepping. After the proudly given tour of his facility, Eric and I had retreated into his office, where our work took upwards of three hours. Convinced my witness was as prepared as he would ever be, we expressed to Eric our appreciation for his efforts.

But before our legal showdown, I still had one witness to meet. I first spied Dominic Ng already seated as Manny and I were escorted into the dining room at Hugo's, an establishment so posh there are beautiful attendants to slipper your feet, should your toes jealously demand comfort during the lavish massage of your taste buds. He rose to greet Manny as we entered, and the quickly shrinking distance revealed a well-coiffured gentleman of impeccable dress. Our guest was small in stature by Western standards, yet broad faced and robust, and appeared to be in his early forties. After a genuine exchange of salutations we happily sat down for a luncheon of fond reminiscences, wild stories, and fascinating conversation—and yes, a meal of extraordinary imagination and quality.

Dominic had married into the ivory business, wedding the daughter of Mr. Au, the owner of the now-defunct Nathan Ivory Factory. The demise of the ivory trade apparently cast no misfortune on Dominic and family, now well-positioned in numerous other ventures. Manny told me our guest enjoyed great wealth, a fact highlighted when Manny and Dominic took to comparing their ruby-ringed fingers. I had often admired the beauty of Manny's stone, valued, he previously disclosed, in excess of fifty thousand dollars. Dominic's ruby was an eye-popper by comparison—two to three times larger and paling Manny's in brilliance, clarity, and color. My client, also a certified gemologist, later appraised Dominic's ring at no less than two-to three hundred thousand dollars.

While examining monster rubies was no doubt ruddy fun, I found our guest's stories of procuring ivory in Africa much more interesting. Trips to exotic locales, encounters with local purveyors, examination and grading of tusks, auctions of the commodity by willing governments—on and on we went until it was time to politely acknowledge the demands of our business. Dominic agreed to spend the following afternoon with me to prepare for his deposition.

We met at my hotel room and, as it went with Eric, the session proceeded well. Dominic's testimony was much more extensive and crucial to the case. Not only did I want to establish the reason for the drastically reduced purchase price of the ivory boat, I also wanted to garner as much evidence as I could to establish market value. Salient factors were: the prices at which Nathan Ivory previously sold similar boats; the cost of producing the boat, which involved the cost of ivory as a raw material; the fluctuations in the commodity market between the time the boat was made, sold to Manny and Mary, and donated to the museum; differences in wholesale and retail treatment of the item; and comparison of the Hong Kong market, where the piece was sold, with the United States market, where it was donated. In addition to giving "fact" evidence that would be useful and relevant in determining value, I hoped to have Dominic qualified as an expert witness. This would permit him to express an opinion on the ultimate issue here, the fair market value of the boat at time of donation.

We went through his story again and again until the witness could relay it with certainty and ease. We were riding well until stumbling on the issue of Nathan Ivory's previous sales. Each of the six large boats produced prior to Manny's was sold for more than $100,000. Great. But Dominic wouldn't tell me the names of the purchasers. Not so great.

My witness felt honor-bound not to disclose these identities, claiming that the privacy interests of his buyers would otherwise be infringed. I stressed he was required to provide this information if demanded by my opponent, but Dominic suggested that Hong Kong law protected trade secrets, thus relieving him from complying with this demand. Unfortunately, Dominic was not under the authority of the Hong Kong courts for purposes of this deposition, so even if such a legal protection existed, it wasn't available and wouldn't be recognized by the United States court. I reminded Dominic it was permissible to say he didn't remember the names, if in fact that were the case. Although he wouldn't come out and tell me one way or another, I got the message that a customer plunking down six figures for a seven-foot carved boat was not an event soon forgotten. All I could do was politely and firmly convey that our entire effort might be jeopardized if he willfully refused to answer this question.

As our session came to an end and my witness prepared to depart, I intended to repeat my admonition, but was cut short when Dominic asked to meet again that evening. His request felt a bit odd, since we had more than covered the material. But if a star witness needs more time, you dutifully agree—and of course I did, notwithstanding my desire to use the evening to complete my preparation for the morning contest.

After a light dinner I returned to my room to finish organizing my materials and when just about done, the knock on the door announced Dominic's arrival. As I slowly and reluctantly walked over, my body and mind signaled that they had worked enough today. I mustered up some energy, greeted Dominic, and ushered him to the chairs now positioned to enjoy the view of the night harbor. He tepidly asked a question or two about the deposition and then brought up the subject of meditation, which apparently intrigued him. Perhaps I had made an offhand comment at lunch or Manny may have passed a remark to him previously, but either way, Dominic knew I meditated and wanted to hear about my practice. Within a few more minutes it was evident this was not intended to be an evening of business, a fact neither one of us felt a need to explicitly acknowledge.

Few pleasures surpass fellowship in Spirit, and my body and mind happily relaxed into this unexpected treat. My guest soon revealed he regularly practiced tai chi as his spiritual discipline. We compared our respective practices and discovered the similar effects they had on our lives. Our conversation naturally modulated from subject to subject as we explored the nature of Spirit, our experience of transcendent states, and the application of spiritual principles in the daily world. We beheld with fascination a universal process that unfolded each of us through a different culture and spiritual tradition.

Without awareness of passage of time, we both sensed the evening's age and gradually shifted to more conventional time and subject. Dominic inquired a bit more about the deposition as if to confirm for social purposes our meeting indeed was a business affair. I offered an answer or two and repeated my afternoon admonition about disclosing customer names. We shook hands by the door, looked deeply into each other's eyes, and ended our evening without word.

CHAPTER THIRTEEN

# Back in the Trenches

WHILE SILENCE MAY BE GOLDEN, its polar opposite was the purpose for our assembly at Wilkinson & Grist the next morning. Manny and I were first to arrive at their offices on Charter Road, Hong Kong Island, and were politely ushered into the conference room reserved for our deposition. Moments after we declined the proffered coffee, our stenographic reporter ambled in and introduced herself. I strategically selected my seat and started arranging papers and exhibits when through the doorway my opponent burst onto the scene.

David's physical entry was none other than routine, but just the sight of him seemed to puncture my exotic ambiance of vacation and adventure and immediately transport me back to the trenches for more warfare. I felt the unexpected jarring of disparate worlds in collision and found decidedly unpleasant the familiar smell of the battlefield. What a wonderful example of mental and emotional bodies being out of synch. Despite my obvious intellectual awareness that we were here to resume litigation and that David would be walking through the door any moment, I was unaware of how I *felt* about it. Since we so often disconnect from our feelings, these wake-up calls, uncomfortable as they may seem, can justifiably be celebrated as clarions of consciousness. Sometimes we need to give ourselves a reason to celebrate, especially when our habitual reaction to discomfort is negative.

I readily confess I didn't pull out the party hats and noisemakers upon David's arrival. With this our first meeting since Manny and Mary's depositions, it shocked no one that our greetings were barely perfunctory. While waiting for Dominic to arrive, I was too preoccupied with the palpable unease in the room to become concerned with the possibility our witness might renege on his voluntary commitment to appear. There was no getting around it, my adversary intimidated me. His style, or tactics if we ascribe intentionality, appeared at the moment to be working. David could be pleasant and charming when he wanting something from you or when the tides were moving his way. But when the sands of fortune were shifting in the other direction, he was often abrasive and combative, and if he felt himself boxed into a corner he could become shockingly mean-spirited.

I have known other attorneys who acted so outrageously hostile, opponents eased off potential skirmishes rather than chance an encounter with such mercurial wrath. A seasoned attorney won't capitulate and fold her case under this type of attack, but she may ask herself whether the particular issue at hand is worth the onset of another aggressive, personal barrage. Practicing the scorched-earth variety of law doesn't win you many friends and, except perhaps when used against some lesser opponents, is ultimately ineffective. A litigator worth her salt will redouble her efforts in the face of adversity—which doesn't mean yelling louder than your opponent—because winning *your* case is a bully's ultimate comeuppance.

To help the government win its case was our latest entrant upon the scene, James B. Godfrey, appraiser and expert advisor to the United States. I was surprised at Godfrey's age. He couldn't have been a year or two either way from my forty, which put him in his late twenties at the time of his appraisal. Pretty young, I thought, to acquire enough training and experience to assume expert status. James was a handsome man of slightly rugged but cultured look, of medium height and build, and, as I recall, his robust brown hair suggested the copper red prominently displayed in his mustache. We looked rather alike—a fact certainly not influencing my estimation of his appearance. After our few amiable words, I recognized I sensed much about him. I liked James and felt we were similar in many ways.

Our witness arrived and we were off. Dominic's direct examination was long and complicated, and along the way I had to deflect numerous objections of my opponent. I accomplished what I needed and was generally pleased with the result, but for one error on my part. Two of the cardinal rules in examining a witness are to stop when you're ahead and to forego a question when you don't know what the answer will be. Abe Lincoln, no less, is the attributed source of the most famous account of an attorney who asked one too many questions.

A frontiersman was being prosecuted for biting the ear off his brawling opponent. The state attorney garnered incriminating testimony from the only witness to the scuffle and turned the witness over to defense counsel. "Sir, did you actually see with your own eyes my client bite off the ear of Mr. Jones?" "Well, no, I can't say that I did," stammered the witness. This is the time to firmly state, "No more questions," and promptly take your seat. Our blabber unfortunately followed with, "Then why do you say the defendant bit his ear off?" which prompted, "Well . . . uh . . . I saw him spit it out of his mouth!"

My excessive tongue-wagging didn't butcher my case, but it did provide David a wide opening. In order to use Dominic's deposition in court, I had to show that the witness did not reside within the court's jurisdiction and otherwise was unavailable to attend the trial. Routine enough. I asked Dominic where he resided and received the expected answer of his Hong Kong address. For some reason, I foolishly asked the witness if he maintained any other residences, a question I didn't know the answer to, and to my shock he stated he also lived in Los Angeles. I quickly glossed this over and established he had no plans to be anywhere near Tampa, Florida, while the case was scheduled to be tried.

When we eventually got to cross-examination, this was the first thing David honed in on. He wanted to know how much time Dominic spent in the United States, where he traveled, what he did, and so on. It turned out that the witness, unbeknownst to me, had a green card, spent more time in the U.S. each year than in Hong Kong, and even had been to Florida in the recent past. Although David could not shake the witness's claim of unavailability for trial, he insinuated that Dominic's deposition could easily have been taken domestically and claimed we had pulled the government to Hong Kong in a ruse to inconvenience them and drive up expenses. I didn't think my adversary could get very far with this pony should he choose to trot it before the court, but even so, I decidedly squirmed through this firestorm caused by my own ineptitude.

Dominic's soft-spoken demeanor proved an effective foil to David. My opponent tried to engage Dominic in a discussion about the politics of ivory:

"You went to a conference . . . on International Trade in Endangered Species?"

"Right."

"In fact, you went there to advocate the continuing slaughter of elephants to produce ivory, is that correct?" How else could the rapacious demands of Nathan Ivory and the other merchants of death be satiated!

That merited my intrusion.

"I object to the form of the question, it is inflammatory."

David toned it down a bit.

"Did you advocate the continuing killing of African elephants to continue the ivory trade, was that your position at the conference?"

"No."

"Did you argue against the continuing killing of African elephants?"

"Yes," replied the ever-polite witness.

"So you wanted to stop the killing?" David asked with increasing bewilderment.

"Yes."

"And that is the position that you represented to the conference on behalf of the ivory traders?"

"Yes."

"To stop the killing of African elephants?"

"Yes. . . ." continued Dominic as I restrained a smile.

"But you wanted to continue the right to kill the elephants for their tusks . . . to utilize their tusks?"

"No, we don't need to kill elephants to utilize their tusks," the witness answered in a reassuring tone.

"I am sorry—" David stammered.

"We don't need to kill the elephants to utilize their tusks. That is why I went there to explain to the people—"

"That you don't need to kill the elephants?" interrupted David.

"Not necessary."

I finally asked Dominic to relieve the befuddlement of the nonplused questioner:

"Mr. Ng, by the way, how can you obtain ivory for carving without killing the elephant?"

"I would put it like this . . . the natural death of elephants. . . !"

This was the tenor of their exchanges, at least until David got to the previous sales of ivory boats. I heard it as if I thought it couldn't happen, but here it was:

"Who else has boats . . . are any of the boats in the hands of any major collectors in the international ivory market?"

My stomach felt as if it had just crested the top of the roller coaster and was about to plummet. I pleadingly looked at Dominic and, after a pause, there came the plunge:

"Well as a matter of business secret, I can't answer you."

My opponent's posture straightened and his voice also rose. After it became clear the witness possessed the ability to answer but was refusing to respond, David chiseled it into the record:

"Is it correct that you will not tell me the names of any other individuals or organizations that currently have one of your boats or that you sold one of [your] boats to?"

"No."

"You will not tell me, will you?"

"I will not."

With that, David abruptly ended his cross-examination.

The silence jolted me. I knew, based on the length and scope of my direct examination, there remained at least an hour or two of material left to be explored on cross. *Oh God, no!* David wouldn't scrap the rest of his cross-examination unless he knew for sure the entire deposition was now useless. On re-direct, my pleading voice couldn't move the witness to answer the question. There was nothing I could do to force a response, as Dominic was not bound by subpoena. Hoping for a lapse in memory, I specifically asked if he remembered the names, but was rebuffed as expected. I did manage to elicit that all the buyers resided outside of the United States. This might be worth something. Learning the identities of the purchasers would only provide the government a means to verify Dominic's account of the sales. Now, at least I could argue that the undisclosed evidence was immaterial. Even if a buyer contradicting Dominic's story could be found, the dwindling time for discovery precluded another foreign deposition.

I couldn't talk until we stumbled onto the street. Without knowing quite why, Manny realized from my grim expression it was bad. I burned inside, as if my flesh were being worn away by a corrosive agent I ingested. My mind spun. *The trip a waste, maybe the entire case down the tubes. . . . I should have insisted our witnesses be under legal process.* I told Manny I wasn't sure, but thought the entire deposition was rendered inadmissible by Dominic's refusal to answer. Manny didn't understand why a problem with only one question should make such a difference. As we walked I sullenly tried to explain the great importance placed upon the right to confront adverse witnesses in our system of jurisprudence. Manny was shocked to hear that courts, to preserve and enforce that right, not only may strike the testimony of a recalcitrant witness, but in rare cases have dismissed a claim or even thrown out an entire case.

After a brief lunch, circumstantially marked by lack of appetite, we reconfigured around the deposition table with the addition of Eric. He clearly testified on direct examination that Manny and Mary had physically removed the ivory boat, jade incense burner and jade table screen from their business inventory and placed these items in their personal collection. I relinquished my witness to my opponent and was pleased as Eric, under tough examination, stuck to his story. As cross continued I surmised this testimony, along with that of my clients, should be enough to establish Manny and Mary's entitlement to a tax deduction for the fair market value rather than the purchase cost of these donated items.

Realizing he wasn't going to crack Eric's account, David took another tack. His tone became condescending and somewhat harsh, and the content of his questions became more personal. The interrogator does have some leeway on cross-examination to probe into personal matters of the witness. While these questions are not directly pertinent to the issues of the case, they can be relevant if they touch upon the honesty or bias of the witness. It is sometimes a fine line between probing credibility and purposefully trying to embarrass or humiliate a witness, the latter obviously not permitted.

When, "I don't think you have the right to ask me to disclose that," is shouted to the opposing attorney, it's a sure sign your witness is getting rattled. With this outburst I could see David smack his lips in anticipation of a knock-out, now that he had Eric on the ropes. Not only do hotheads blurt, but in a deposition setting there's no judge and bailiff to prevent an irate witness from bolting out the door. The added danger here was lack of subpoena, which allowed Eric, without legal impediment, to terminate his deposition anytime he wished. By contrast, when under legal process a recalcitrant deponent can be jailed for contempt of court to compel his testimony. If Eric refused to complete cross-examination, his entire deposition would be inadmissible. *Oh, no, not this one too!*

Here came David's flooring punch:

Sir, this case involves a large amount of money . . . and I am entitled to find out and continue to ask you questions concerning matters which I deem important. . . . You are being purposely vague with me and very flippant and I resent that, but I will continue to ask questions and if you want to refuse to answer those questions, you can go ahead and refuse to answer them, but I am entitled to ask them to you. Are you—

With Eric itching for the exit, I interrupted:

I object on the basis that you are harassing the witness, you are characterizing him in a testimony that is totally subjective, the questions you are asking are wholly irrelevant, they have nothing to do with his direct examination.

Objecting is an effective approach when your witness is becoming upset. It doesn't really matter what you're objecting to; the important thing is your interruption of the flow of questioning. By breaking the exchange between witness and examiner, you diffuse the thrust of your opponent and give your witness time to regain his bearings. That's the easy part. Your adversary, however, is usually smart enough to know what you're doing, and without the presence of a judge ordering him to desist is not going to stop just because you object.

David continued to press, and I continued to object while politely but firmly reminding the witness he was required to answer. I didn't want to be boxed into a position where I was forced to instruct Eric not to answer a question, which I would only do if it appeared he would otherwise leave. David would then surely challenge the use of the deposition, and unless the judge agreed my objection to the unanswered question was valid, the entire deposition would probably be thrown out. My gosh, what were the odds of trashing two depositions taken in the same case on the same day? I don't know whether my persistent objections wore David down, deflected his attention, or worked to calm Eric, but luckily we seemed to get by that flash point and complete the examination with the witness and his deposition testimony intact. Not until we were back on the street did Manny and I exhale a sigh of relief.

That brief release did little to lift the weight of the discomfort and depression I suffered over the morning debacle. Knowing how miserable I felt, Manny kindly offered the solacing thought that through our efforts here, we at least secured Eric's deposition for trial—a magnanimous gesture on Manny's part, considering this was his money, case, and future.

My intensity of feeling clearly displayed to me the degree to which I was attached to the outcome of this lawsuit. The depth of this burning emotion vastly eclipsed any reactive feeling I may have had about my performance or competence. No matter how many times I told myself that I had tried my best and there was nothing I could do about it at the moment, I still felt the same. Obviously I believed winning this case was vital to me. On some level I also believed I held deficiencies—lack of fame and fortune—that would be filled by my external triumph, which was now in jeopardy. How frustrating to be intellectually aware of why you're caught in reactive emotion yet still be unable to release it. Now, with this overlay, I had two emotions I didn't want to be with. When you start running in that endless loop of not experiencing how you feel, sometimes the only thing you can do is remind yourself to breathe and chant, "Lord, this too shall pass."

A late afternoon yoga session seemed to put some space around my distress, and the feeling became more accessible. Sometimes things turn out much better than the aroused speculations made in the midst of disaster. I started to percolate a bit. Maybe there was a better shot at salvaging parts of Dominic's testimony than I had initially thought. I wanted to burrow into the law books to unearth court rulings on this issue, though that would have to wait until after the long journey home. But, as you might readily guess, returning to Florida was the least of my desires. We had more time to our advantage to continue our Hong Kong saga!

# CHAPTER FOURTEEN

# The Joy of Creative Discovery

Y OU KNOW YOU'RE IN THE GROOVE when the imaginary line between work and play disappears. And so it was as we scoured shops, galleries, wholesalers, and dealers in our quest to find anything that resembled our big-ticket items: the ceremonial jade incense burner (koro), jade table screen, and ivory boat. We showed pictures of the pieces to those in the trade, hoping to pick up any leads. Though comparable sales are the best evidence of fair market value, even a listed price for a like item could substantially help our case, if, of course, that price was right.

Assuming a comparable could be found, the passage of time would have to be factored in. We had to prove fair market value as of donation date, which now was thirteen years in the past. Any evidence of current prices would require foundation testimony to explain how today's values have been affected, if at all, by the intervening period. This didn't concern me. The disparity between the parties' appraisals was so huge, a hypothetical table screen today selling at $90,000, the amount my clients claimed at time of donation, would still blow away the government's $1,200 estima-tion. Common sense told me thirteen years could not explain away that chasm.

My ruminations went for naught since, try as we did, pieces comparable to our own couldn't be found. The ivory market was dead. A worldwide ban on the export of raw and finished ivory had been enacted in the late 1980s, effectively killing the carving trade.

Most shops did offer a few small items for their limited domestic market. When shown the picture of our seven-foot carved boat and asked what it would cost to now produce such a piece, most proprietors laughed, exclaiming, "Where would I get the money and ivory to make it? . . . and even if I had one, we're not allowed to sell it!"

While ivory lay moribund, the market for jade was flourishing. Shop after shop prominently displayed new decorative carvings of urns, animals, deities, and various other traditional subjects. Stores paraded jades of brilliant "Emperor" green as well as numerous other colors. Lavender seemed to be popular along with a rusty brown shade. Often the piece was mottled, with splashy color combinations accentuating an already ornate design. Jadeite was easy to spot, as its surface was shinier and therefore bolder than the waxy-looking surface of nephrite.

Jade is reputed to be the most valuable commodity to the Chinese, followed by gold and ivory, and the prices for these newly produced decorative arts bore that out. Items of comparable size to our koro were selling for $30,000 and up. Price tags in the hundreds of thousands of U.S. dollars routinely hung from the larger and more elaborate pieces.

The steady procession of jade, along with some of Manny's tutoring, enhanced my aesthetic sensibilities and added discrimination to my eye. With this developing vision, I began to easily distinguish the newer pieces from the much-less-common antique jades. The advent of electric tools for carving, finishing, and buffing made for smoother and more polished surfaces; yet, I found the current elaborate designs more a display of mechanical prowess than expressions of artistic sensitivity. I preferred the balance of form and technique exhibited in earlier works. We did find one or two antique table screens and a like number of antique koros. Even I could recognize that these mid-to late-nineteenth century pieces were markedly inferior in craftsmanship and design to our eighteenth century jewels.

The first part of the eighteenth century and throughout most of the reign of Emperor Ch'ien-Lung (1736-1795) is renowned for carvings of the most exquisite craftsmanship produced from the highest quality jades. This era of artistic creativity was marked by political stability and great Imperial wealth. With the late eighteenth century and nineteenth century political and economic decline of the Ch'ing rulers, the Chinese arts diminished in quality. Later Ch'ing works were often copies of eighteenth century pieces and were produced from inferior materials with less skill—many nevertheless still outstanding works of art.

Godfrey, the expert, claimed our table screen was a cheap nineteenth century reproduction of a Ch'ien-Lung piece, yet the nineteenth century screens we found were at prices exceeding Godfrey's $1,200, and they didn't come close to the size or quality of our piece. Neither could the antique koros rival Manny's. Ours, reputed to be produced during the reign of Ch'ien-Lung's father, Yung-Chen (1712-1732), had its surface carved in three distinct layers, a feature I had yet to see in any contemporary or antique ceremonial jade incense burner. One or two dealers, upon seeing pictures of our jades, told us the only place we were going to find anything like that was in a museum. So eventually that's where we headed.

The newly constructed Hong Kong Museum of Fine Arts and Antiquities gleamed on the Kowloon side of the harbor. A long escalator took us to the second level, where the antique jades were exhibited. The beauty of these works was splendidly evident, even without my newfound discrimination. Fortunately though, my rapid immersion into the world of jade had made enough of an impression to enable me to more fully appreciate these elevated expressions of nephrite carving. I later usefully learned that jadeite was not found in China until its import at the end of the eighteenth century, thus explaining its absence in the museum's collection.

I quickly found the eighteenth century pieces by their appearance, and was much pleased with my ability to discern style, newly baptized as I was in this art form. The one or two incense burners of this period on display were the closest we had seen to our koro, but as best I could tell from the detailed pictures, Manny's piece was better carved and still stylistically distinguishable. We saw nothing resembling the table screen and decided to consult with the museum curator for a professional estimation of our pieces. On the way to the administrative offices, we veered off upon spotting the antique porcelains, a diversionary delight befitting my new status as collector.

With some luck we tracked down the curator for the jades, a thin, longhaired man in his early to mid-thirties, and showed him our photos. The pictures apparently interested him enough to pause his hectic pace for a minute or two of examination. Asked to identify and date the jades, he offered an opinion that the pieces appeared to be eighteenth century. After politely deflecting our questions about value, we asked whether he was aware of any similar carvings elsewhere on display. Finding a near match exhibited in a museum could prove very helpful. This would rebut the government's claim that the donated items lacked museum quality, a proposition placing the Carnegie Museum, the recipient of my clients' largess, in questionable light. The curator claimed no offhand knowledge of like items on display, but offered us the resources of the muscum's research center, which he suggested might aid our quest.

We gratefully accepted his offer and were led to a large room, brightly lit by the wall-to-wall windows showcasing the harbor. Now transferred into the custody of a studious-looking young female attendant, we spent hours exuberantly pouring through books, catalogues, and magazines that portrayed museum and private collections of jade from around the world. "Hey, Manny, look at this one, it's pretty close. What do think about that one? Wow, this piece is incredible." The fact that our efforts didn't yield much in the way of results was no bother to us at all. We both just experienced an adventure that was as joyful as it was exciting.

So much joy and excitement springs from the freshness of discovery. An entirely new world had opened for me. Antique Chinese jade and porcelain, a subject that couldn't generate more than a few general sentences from me before, was now rich in image, focused, and abundantly alive.

This process of learning and discovery often involves the exercise of discrimination, which is the power to distinguish and thus recognize and perceive with clarity. Discrimination is enhanced by the concentration of our attention, and whatever we focus our attention upon grows magically before us in scope, texture, subtlety, and degree.

I remember my experience with doors when redecorating our office a few years ago. We decided to replace the painted flat-doors to our individual offices with custom wood-paneled ones. I had never really given much attention to doorways before, and now was reviewing catalogues of numerous makes and styles. Two-paneled, three-paneled, boxed, framed, squares within frames, rectangles within boxes, beveled—you get the picture. I encountered endless choices and varieties. I noticed during the two-or three-week selection process that doors seemed to be the first thing I saw wherever I went and whatever I was doing. While watching movies or TV, I found myself studying doors as characters walked in and out of rooms, missing much of the dialogue. At someone's home or office, I lingered in portals engrossed in detail that hadn't existed for me before, and just about everywhere, doors seemed to be popping out all over. You know the popping out phenomenon—if you or your spouse is having a baby, all of a sudden the pregnant population proliferates!

This faculty of attention not only expands and enriches our experience of life, it also creates it. Life willingly and automatically complies with our attention by providing us the subject of our focus. When I have doors on the mind—doors are what I'll get. And because this God-given power is unlimited, there is no end to the variety, splendor, beauty, diversity, intricacy, and grandeur we can derive from our co-creative partnership with life.

The mystics describe the experience of God as ever-new bliss. Our joy in the creative discovery of life is a small sample of the bliss that *is* the Universal Creative Principle, and that joy reminds us that the process of our individual lives is this Principle at work.

Since our faculty of attention co-creates our reality, it becomes extremely important to decide where to direct that concentrated awareness. What do I want to focus upon and expand in my life? I can attend to TV reruns and watch my torpidity grow, or I can focus upon my tennis game and watch my fitness gel. I can concentrate on my belief that life is hard and cruel and have unending examples of suffering pass by my window, or I can suffuse my mind with the belief that life is joyous and watch a steady stream of delight.

In the right exercise of free will, we intend to place our attention where it will truly serve us, which is also where it best serves others. Since, however, we often are not fully aware of what is best for us, many times we are not sure where to focus our energetic attention. This is when discrimination helps us. This ability to differentiate, this power to perceive with clarity, enables us to better choose *where* to place that attention. Because our creative consciousness will get for us what we want, whether boon or bane, it sure helps to know that what we want is what we really need. (See Appendix "B" for an exposition of how society debases the value of discrimination.)

One thing *I* could discern was that the table screen and koro were worth much more than government-appraised value. Mind you, I wasn't sure exactly what they were worth, or how I was going to prove it, but I had seen enough to know that the I.R.S.'s estimation bore little resemblance to the marketplace. This did two things. First, it increased my confidence in my clients and their case, and second, it hardened my resolve against the government— as if my experience thus far in litigating this controversy had not been enough to forge my determination.

While Manny and Mary may have been less than lily white, I could identify more readily with their feelings of being mistreated at the hand of the sovereign. I conjectured that the I.R.S.'s initial attitude toward my clients was: we'll lowball the valuations, tack on huge penalties and interest, and if the taxpayers live long enough and have enough money to fight us indefinitely, maybe they'll get lucky and get some of it back.

And what about Godfrey? Did he purposely lowball his appraisal? Was he asked to, or did he just figure that this was what the I.R.S. wanted? What better way to get more lucrative expert witness work than by giving your employer what it desires? Or perhaps the government just innocently relied upon his appraisal, which simply proved to be unskilled? I toyed with these thoughts and decided, in the name of objectivity, to see how more facts played out before indulging in further speculation.

Unfortunately, it took no speculation to realize that our time for playing was near its end. Manny and I savored our final dinner and later cruised the streets for some last-minute shopping at the outdoor markets. Exotic sounds and the smell of kerosene lanterns led us through the night alleys to an area of open-air makeshift theaters where classic Chinese opera was being performed. In each stall four or five older men were playing homemade musical instruments that seemed to be concocted from tin cans and junkyard parts. Makeshift bows vibrated twangs from the stringed instruments, which in combination with the unusual percussive sounds and the high-pitched winds, yielded an unexpectedly well-formed and pleasing composition.

The musicians were accompanists for the costumed actors who periodically emerged from curtains that were no more than rugs or blankets hanging from a rope tied across the top of the stall. The heroine, or villainess, I suppose, depending upon the drama, wore so much makeup it appeared her face was painted on. For greater effect, our masked madam was accented by long fingernails lacquered a piercing red. As I listened more intently, I realized the performers neither sang nor spoke, but created a high nasal cadence somewhere in between.

As we moved from stall to stall sampling the different theater, I became more impressed with the performing artistry and wondered whether these were amateur or professional productions. Manny claimed this night theater was mostly the avocation of the working class, an endeavor not totally without recompense, given the sums in the baskets strategically placed in front of the stalls. After a while my partner wanted to move on, but I felt transfixed by the sounds and smells and feeling of this place. I dropped out of my thought and received a strong sensation that I had known all about this before, having been a musician in such a street theater. I bounced back as Manny again reminded me that the next day's scheduled departure left no more time for night lingering. As we made our return to the hotel, I silently wondered whether I had lived a former existence in China—given the numbers, highly probable if you believe in reincarnation.

The morning brought my sojourn in China to an end. At our last breakfast before leaving for the airport, I saw on the front page of an English-language Hong Kong paper a story about a late-winter storm hitting the U.S. east coast. Must be quite a doozy, I thought, to make a headline ten thousand miles away. After describing the unprecedented blizzard paralyzing much of the northeast, the article went on to report huge floods in the southeast, specifically mentioning deaths caused from rising waters in Pinellas and surrounding counties in Florida. When you're sitting halfway around the world, reading in a foreign newspaper about massive flooding in the county where you reside, it definitely engenders a sinking feeling. Manny and I both called home and got the same busy signal. Well, here was something else we couldn't do anything about until our return.

Soaring back over the Pacific, I surveyed the legal landscape formed by our Asian efforts and noticed my emotional reaction had moved down a number of notches. Pain had changed into a disappointment that held some seeds of promise. Maybe Dominic's crime was not so heinous. Perhaps the court might only strike the evidence of previous sales and accept the rest of his story. These sanguine assessments along with the deep vibratory hum of jet engines seemed to ease my mind, and I started to relax into the long journey.

As I drifted off, I more and more appreciated the extraordinary experience provided me in Hong Kong. As I closed my eyes, the movie *Casablanca* appeared in my mind and I heard the sweet sound of Ingrid Bergman humming "As Time Goes By"—"*La, lie lie, la la lie . . . la, **lie lie**, la la lie. . . .*" And on the airfield with the lovers parting at the end, instead of Bogart saying, "We'll always have Paris," it was me in a trench coat with a Bogie accent telling Ingrid, "Schweethart, we'll always have Hong Kong!"

Even if the case turned out to be a complete bust, so what? I just had an adventure of a lifetime that never could be taken from me. As I descended into an airplane half-sleep, the last thought I heard was, *I wonder what the next adventure will be?*

## CHAPTER FIFTEEN

# *The Bowels of Litigation*

S LUDGE, MUD, AND MUCK. Having pushed open my front door, I stood transfixed as I beheld the incongruous mixture of my living room and the sea floor. My daze was eventually broken by the intrusive pungent odor of low tide emanating from the interior. Apparently the briny deep had taken well to my sealed home, creating a rich soup of microorganisms well fed and multiplying on the organic parts of my furnishings and other contents. A dark brown and gray gook covered the floor and about two feet of wall and everything else taking vertical space. As I surveyed the disaster from the doorway, I noticed bits of shell and seaweed on the drapes. Oh no, my record collection, unfortunately on the bottom of the bookshelf, was history—the sleeper sofa, all the guts will rust out—oh, my God, the piano! My mahogany McPhail upright, purchased in law school and painstakingly refinished a few years ago, was a beautifully crafted and carved antique as well as a fine instrument. I didn't want to ponder at that moment the ramifications of combining salt water with iron and brass.

So far I felt remarkably calm. Maybe I was just stunned, or perhaps numb from jet lag and fatigue from the return trip ending yesterday. My father had broken the news at the airport the previous evening by telling me we weren't heading back to my house. I was told my neighborhood had been in the bay, with the now-receding waters probably permitting us vehicle access the next day. As we pulled up that next afternoon, the piles of mud-soaked carpets, furnishings, and debris on front lawns revealed that most homeowners were already hard at work. I had noticed the high water line about five feet up the exterior walls of my house, but could barely imagine what the tempest must have been like here during the night it hit.

The "No Name" storm, a moniker betraying its unexpected onset, apparently took everyone by surprise. The weather prognosticators accurately predicted a heavy squall line coming through around midnight. They didn't forecast the hurricane winds and rising seas that followed a few hours later. Most residents, after weathering the midnight thunderstorms, went to bed thinking it was all over, only to be aroused at four that morning by the sound of waves crashing into their homes. The sea rose so swiftly exit proved impossible, and everyone was forced to ride out the fury in darkness—a frightening situation, especially since you don't know how high the water will get before it stops rising. Our battering of six to eight feet above high tide was destructive. The ten-to twelve-foot surge just a few miles up the coast proved fatal.

Summoning up the nerve to step through my doorway, I entered my home with a big squish and splash, surprised that carpet could retain so much water. Proceeding through the mire, I discovered each room looked dismally the same. Luckily my business suits and other good clothing hung sufficiently above the water line. I lost some sweaters and jeans in the bottom of my dresser and the shoes now littered on the closet floor. Fortune seemed to smile a bit as I opened the door to the garage.

My beloved auto, a Mercedes 240D with an almost-perfect beige body and hard-to-find standard transmission, appeared to be in good condition. I approached the car, hoping the water hadn't made it up to the engine, and started to consider the extent of the repairs probably needed. My speculation was abruptly ended by the horrible surprise waiting for me as I opened the door. To my amazement, the inside of the car was melted! The dashboard, seat covers, roof lining, steering wheel, and everything else made of plastic were now a soot-covered ooze congealed in surreal shapes rivaling those in a Dali painting. The salt water must have shorted out the electrical system, causing a high-heat, low-flame fire. To be without house was bad enough, but to be without wheels—this truly was a catastrophe.

Unfortunately, I had no time to concern myself with the effects of a once-in-a-hundred-year flood or any other such trifling personal inconvenience. Mid-March was upon us, and discovery had to be completed by April 16, making the crushing demands of *Fellouzis vs. United States of America* the immediate focus of my existence. I found temporary sleeping quarters, rented a heap, and spent most of the next two months living at the law library and my office. During this time we descended into the bowels of litigation, a dark and slimy domain making my alluvial homesite pleasant by comparison. Put on your hip boots—we're about to wade in!

I first had to dive into the law books to quench my burning need to know the legal consequence of Dominic's refusal to answer the deposition question. As I suspected, the majority of such cases required the striking of the witness's entire testimony. I did find some courts that gave the witness an extra chance, throwing out the testimony only if the person refused to answer after a judicial command to do so. I thought this minority line of cases might be enough to convince our judge to issue a letter rogatory requesting the Hong Kong courts to compel Dominic to answer the question. I was convinced the government would move to strike his deposition, so I was modestly pleased to find a countermeasure, weak though it was, to that anticipated attack. The law, in a way, is like statistics: if you look hard and wide enough, you can almost always conjure up something to support your position.

Case law, which is the precedential decisions of appellate courts, is also a wonderfully intriguing historical and sociological record. The controversies detailed in the judicial decisions resolving those dusty disputes yield rich and highly personal accounts of the issues of the day. A case I found while researching Dominic's deposition spat involved the espionage prosecution of a German soldier held in a P.O.W. camp here in the States during the Second World War. Another P.O.W. testified for the government, but refused to answer defense questions that would have revealed the operations of a counterintelligence collaboration between German prisoners and U.S. authorities. The case was replete with facts about the housing and treatment of German P.O.W.s, U.S. efforts to enroll prisoners in its spy network, and various other details of the war I had never heard of before. More interesting were the contemporaneous beliefs and attitudes shaped by the war, which seemed to come alive through the court's opinion.

You never know when one of these social histories will turn up. Once while researching some procedural point, I came across a libel case between Marjorie Kinnan Rawlings, renowned Florida author of *The Yearling,* and her former friend who was aggrieved by some explicit prose. I was fascinated by the court's unintended exposition of the mores and values of rural Floridians in the 1920s.

Some such decisions are shockingly riveting. In law school I remember reviewing a case where two creditors asserted contrary lien rights on the same tangible goods of a bankrupt. Said another way, lenders were fighting over the remains of their debtor. In this 1850s Virginia opinion, the chattels in dispute were slaves. I was aghast at the court's matter-of-fact description of the "goods," as if human beings were two legged livestock, and only slightly less disturbed by its morally oblivious legal analysis of the competing liens.

Unfortunately, this was not the time to indulge my interest in historical study through the eyes of the law. I loaded a musket and fired a perfunctory salvo across the government's bow. This heralded my immediate intent to file motions to compel production of the Certificate of Assessments, compel production of redacted materials, request issuance of a Letter Rogatory, and permit the deposition of James Godfrey. For you procedure buffs, unlike state rules, the federal rules of procedure require court approval before you can take the deposition of your opponent's expert. And before requesting such permission, you must obtain from your adversary, by interrogatory, the names of its trial experts along with summaries of their opinions.

My one-paragraph shot prompted a three-page mortar in return: the government does not agree to Godfrey's deposition because I haven't "indicated the need" to take it; the Certificate of Assessments will be produced when the I.R.S. gets around to providing it (maybe sometime after trial will suffice); the redacted materials contain the "mental process" of Service employees and are protected as a matter of "public policy" (however, if you wish to waste more of your time by telling us why you really need this information, we'll reconsider your request before denying it again); and finally, because the deposition of Dominic Ng was taken in a manner "seemingly calculated to avoid cross-examination," bring him to the United States if you want to ask him more questions. As if all this weren't unpleasant enough, I was informed the government would be scheduling another deposition of my clients, because plaintiffs had not produced, prior to the first deposition, requested documents showing the purchase price for the donated items.

The last was a bald-faced attempt for an extra bite at the apple. David had twice inspected our documents and was provided separate folders for each item containing photographs and any purchase receipt. Re-depose my clients? Over my dead body! I put down my musket and brought out a piece of artillery. Up to now I had written directly to David, although the letters I received from the Justice Department, obviously composed by David, had contained the imperial subscript, "James A. Bruton, Acting Assistant Attorney General, Tax Division, By: Steven Shapiro, Chief, Civil Trial Section, Southern Region." In my first correspondence to Mr. Shapiro, I informed him plaintiffs would proceed to file their motions and suggested that the cessation of Dominic's cross-examination "was seemingly calculated to enhance a motion to strike the witness's testimony."

On the issue of re-deposing Manny and Mary, I meticulously recited our extensive efforts to provide David with all the information and materials he had requested. Perhaps the government's erroneous excuse for another deposition lay in a miscommunication between Shapiro and his trial counsel? I further intimated that the failure to inquire about purchase price at the previous depositions was an omission of his subordinate having nothing to do with plaintiffs. (Oh yes, if provoked I really can get nasty—in an artful way of course.) The consequence, should the government file a notice to re-depose Manny and Mary, was not intimated. We cocked the hammer with our declaration that plaintiffs would consider such a notice "frivolous and filed with intent to harass them," and left no doubt we would strike accordingly should they be foolish enough to pursue this line of attack. That's the last we heard of another deposition for Manny and Mary.

For me, it was time to move the court. A sixteen-page "Emergency Motion to Issue Letter Rogatory," a six-page "Emergency Motion of Plaintiffs to Permit Deposition of Defendant's Expert Trial Witness," and eleven pages of "Plaintiffs' Motion to Compel Production of Documents" compressed forty hours of labor into less than three days. This is when the senior partner summons his juniors at five P.M. and tells them he wants various motions on his desk the next day. He saunters home, and his subordinates stay up all night. How wonderful life would be if I had underlings of my own.

I must confess, as taxing as it was, I enjoyed parts of that legal research and writing. Aside from raw learning, which always holds an interest, an issue sometimes pops up that truly deserves emphasis. The dispute over redacted materials brought to focus the competition between the governmental cloak and the individual's right to an open trial. The cases were mixed. I thought the better-reasoned decisions properly recognized that documents such as those disputed in our case, although possibly a source of embarrassment, were not so important to the operation or security of the government to justify its claim of secrecy. I even found, in a decision requiring disclosure, a Patrick-Henry-quoting judge analogizing to the Boston Tea Party the litigant's effort to pry loose I.R.S. files. Truly impressed by the role of the judiciary in our political system of checks and balances, I cited this opinion in my motion and raised my own cry against the dangers of an unaccountable sovereign.

In the meantime, additional requests from David for production of documents were consuming more time and energy. We finally hunted down and produced all the import records for the donated items acquired overseas. I had requested copies of the witness interview transcripts compiled by the I.R.S. during its fraud investigation, and now had more materials to review. The bloodhounds had taken statements from my clients, their accountant, his secretary, Matthew Weissman who appraised the 1979 and 1980 items prior to donation, his son Neal Weissman who assisted in the appraisal, and Eric Lee who appraised the 1981 donated items, just to mention a few. Many of these witness declarations came close to incriminating Manny and Mary in overt wrongdoing, and at a minimum, cast them in a highly unfavorable light. Curiously, none of these transcripts contained the witness's signature, nor did the I.R.S. produce any interview recordings.

The government requested all my clients' records showing when and how they insured the items prior to donation. If these "art objects" were *really* worth so much, they would have been covered—right? This proved to be yet another tale. A year or so before the donations, my clients got a binder adding the major items to their homeowner's policy, specifically insuring each for a substantial amount. Like just about everything else in this case, what initially seemed helpful came with a problem at the tail end.

Manny and Mary never paid the premium on the binder, so the policy wasn't issued and the goods remained uninsured. It sure looked as if my clients never intended to cover the goods, but were creating a paper trail to display values and confirm that these were personal items. According to Manny, he and Mary intended to insure the objects but changed their minds when they got the bill for a disagreeably high premium. Instead, they put their money into a security system. But why were they surprised at the cost, since they already were insuring other items in their collection and knew the premium rate? The rationale felt weak to me, and no doubt to David, who served notice he was taking the insurance agent's deposition. Also rolling in was David's call to set a date for the Weissmans' depositions in Philadelphia. Well, why not? I had a lot of time on my hands!

My interactions of late with David bore marks of a borderline civility eroding at more than the edges. I avoided phone contact as much as possible, as the disdain and animosity transmitted from the other end was becoming less contained. If I wistfully thought our relationship had now reached its low ebb, this dream was shattered by my opponent's last-minute response to my emergency motions.

According to David, my motions for the letter rogatory and Godfrey's deposition were "hidden" in the back of the packet I sent him that contained other documents. He claimed he was "understandably not aware" of the motions and further proclaimed his ignorance asserting that I "did not advise the defendant that such 'emergency motions' had in fact been filed or served." In a limited argument opposing the substance of the motions, David also blamed me for "manipulation of the discovery rules" and asked the court for an extension of time to file a more complete response.

Dem's fightin' words! Sparring with an opponent is one thing; accusing the other of misconduct *before the court* is quite another. The gloves were off, and I was not one to run from a fight. After all, I had my reputation to protect! David's allegations were so fantastic it was hard for me to believe they weren't contrived. Every time a motion or any other paper is filed with the court, a copy of what you file must contemporaneously be "served" on the opposing attorney. "Service" can be accomplished by hand delivery, but is permitted and almost always done by mail.

The packet I mailed David with the two emergency motions did contain documents he had previously requested. However, that document response consisted of only twenty-six pages that were stapled together. There was no possible way the sixteen page rogatory motion and the six-page deposition motion, each separately stapled, were "hidden." Also, the same day I sent copies of the motions, I faxed a separate letter to the government advising them I would proceed with the court filing, and I even sent David a copy of my letter to the court clerk that specifically listed each motion transmitted for filing.

All of this I of course recited to the court in my opposition to the government's motion for extension of time. I suggested that "Defendant's counsel did not bother to examine what was served upon him and now presents a purported excuse" for an extension. I soundly lambasted David for his "ludicrous and scandalous" assertion the motions were "hidden." Rather restrained, wouldn't you say? I followed sagacious advice I had long before heard and incorporated into my practice: if you're really angry with your adversary or the court, compose your motion or other paper, but wait a day or two to cool down; reread it and then file it if you still think it's suitable.

The broadsides continued unabated. Without bothering to get court permission to supplement his initial response, David soon filed an additional opposition to the rogatory motion. First we were grilled over Dominic's residence. Plaintiffs "'neglect' to advise the United States that their 'expert witness' maintains a residence in the United States." We have "misled the defendant during the discovery process into believing" Dominic could not be deposed domestically. This entitles the government to recoup the expenses it incurred resulting from plaintiffs' "blatant misrepresentation."

That's the nice part. On Dominic's refusal to answer the question, it was "a mere sham to prevent the United States from conducting an in person cross-examination." We are not just guilty of "manipulation of the pretrial discovery process," but have "connived to place the United States at an extreme disadvantage. . . ." Our motion was "not submitted in good faith" and "should not be condoned" by the court. Finally, plaintiffs should be sanctioned by the court to "prevent similar occurrences in future matters."

We also sell children into slavery and skewer babies. Obviously David didn't subscribe to the "wait two days before you file it" rule. I was not in a comical mood after this bombardment, now accused, among other things, of intentionally tampering with a witness. All the matters *really* requiring my immediate attention—which had displaced all the other things needing my immediate attention—were instantly moved aside. This was blasphemy that could not be left unanswered.

I first branded the government's allegations as "totally baseless and apparently filed by Defendant in an act of desperation." I addressed Dominic's residence issue by attaching the letter first sent to him, offering to pay his way to the U.S. should he agree to come here for deposition, a proposition he declined. The government's claims of a "connivance" to restrict its cross-examination were dismissed as ranting and trickery. I suggested that the defendant stopped cross-examining Dominic after his refusal to answer, in order to enhance a motion to strike the entire deposition. Now, with the possibility the question would be answered, making the deposition usable, "the Defendant is resorting to any means whatsoever, including the use of frivolous and scandalous allegations, to try to prevent this result." I referred back to my opponent's "hidden" papers farce and noted that "whenever the Defendant makes an error or blunder, it resorts to using baseless allegations against the Plaintiffs to divert this court's attention."

Statements filed with the court are absolutely privileged, which means that the laws of libel don't apply. Therefore I mentioned it was incumbent upon parties to exercise restraint by making sure any assertions made to the court are fact-based. Then I added that the court system should be respected by not using it in "the unseemly and embarrassing manner in which it is being used by the Defendant." I concluded by expressing shock that the good ol' red, white and blue "has such seeming disregard for standards of fair conduct and rules of fair play," and I urged the court to stick to the *merits* of the matter in making its decision.

Had enough yet? We were slinging so much muck—though I thought mine more skillfully tossed—we became the gossip at the federal court. My secretary, upon calling the clerk's office for some information on the case, received an off-hand comment and a few chuckles from a deputy clerk about the ballooning tirades. I could imagine the clerks, judicial assistants, law clerks, and other court personnel having a popping good giggle with each incoming scandal sheet.

Want a little more? David's response to our motion to compel production of documents labeled my recitation to the court "misleading and questionable." He also claimed the motion was "simply part of a continuing pattern to drive up the expense of preparing this case for trial without producing any identifiable benefits..."

Okay, I hear you. The stench down here can get pretty nauseating, especially for the unaccustomed, so we'll ascend from the bowels, move on to some drier and open terrain, and take these hip boots off!

# CHAPTER SIXTEEN

# Taking the High Road

ATTORNEYS ARE SUPPOSED TO DISSUADE CLIENTS from engaging in personal attack and mudslinging. When counsel sorrowfully devolve into this bashing, it drives everyone up a wall. Aside from the toll it takes on the lawyers, it frustrates the judiciary, absolutely infuriates or further inflames clients, and undermines public confidence in the dispute resolution capacity of our legal system. Unfortunately, the problem here lies not just with the attorneys. We are society's creation and in many ways your alter egos.

Why does Japan, at half our population, get along with fifteen thousand lawyers while we congest on an ever-burgeoning legal clan of seven hundred thousand? The reasons are well-documented, the primary being Japan's strong cultural emphasis upon each person's duty to the social order—quite different, but not necessarily better, than our free spirited American individualism.

When a Japanese airplane crashes because of pilot error or improper maintenance, the families of the victims don't file suit. They dutifully accept from Nippon Air the hundred or so thousand dollars in yen equivalent—*but* the C.E.O. of the airline goes to each family's home, takes off his shoes, gets on his knees, and bows to the family in contrition. When we consider ourselves aggrieved, it is amazing how much of our need for redress is satisfied by the wrongdoer's expression of remorse and plea for forgiveness. Upon recognizing that those whom we believe have harmed us also suffer from their own wrongdoing, our compassion is often awakened and healing promoted.

By contrast, on the American business and political landscape, penitence is a scarce feature, and we have to roundly search to even find a genuine "I'm sorry." As for the occasional corporate or institutional public remorse, it more often sounds like part of "damage control's" plan to minimize liability than a heartfelt response. Wouldn't it be so refreshing to hear the president or his press secretary get up one day during some brouhaha and instead of spouting the political spin say: "We goofed. Our actions there were ill-motivated and inappropriate. We were reacting to criticism and unfortunately got caught up in defensive posturing. Our goal is to take the high moral road, but sometimes in the heat of battle we lose sight of that goal. We'll try harder next time."

Of course, these leaders are also our creation, and their need to be "right" at all costs is reflective of our individual postures. When we misspeak or act less thoughtfully than we would like, how often do we own up to the consequences of our unconsciousness? By the way, if the other person isn't available, or further interaction is inappropriate in that situation, "owning up" means acknowledging to ourselves our temporary shortcoming and in our heart sending the other our apology and love. In our intimate relationships, do we provide a loving space for the other to remain in judgment we consider misplaced? How readily are we able to let go and let our loved one be "right?"

Even though David wasn't exactly my beloved, the swelling acrimony and unpleasantness of the relationship prompted for me these same questions. Relationships provide the grist for growth, and having one that is particularly distressing surely signals there is a lesson to be learned. I examined my actions and motivations to determine what role I played in provoking this personal contentiousness. I became very careful in my interchanges with David and consciously applied techniques to prevent blind protective reactions on my part to his continuing animosity.

Being the object of another's anger, frustration, and negativity is particularly difficult—especially when the external situation restricts your ability to remove yourself from the encounter, such as when dealing with a superior at work. Energetically, you usually perceive the negativity blasted your way as a threat and will compress your own energy into a defensive posture. And as we have discussed before, closing yourself down restricts your own energetic flow and is ultimately enervating. How then to remain open in the face of such attack? Know that you cannot be harmed by the negativity of another, no matter how intensely it may be focused at you.

That sounds all good and dandy, but in practice often proves extremely difficult. The hotter the situation, the less likely we are to consciously manage our own energy and thus we fall prey to the energetic demands of another. These energetic "hooks" sent our way invite us to transfer control of our energy to our antagonist. If someone directs anger at you and you fight back, you're hooked.

Fighting back doesn't only mean becoming overtly angry in return. If you remain impassive knowing this will further infuriate your opponent, you are simply employing a different combative strategy, and you're just as hooked. In either case, your energy has been utilized to fulfill the demands of another. And that demand and need of the other is for you to *interact* with his negativity. Someone who is angry desperately wants to enroll you in his or her venom. Once you climb in the ring you have already lost the battle. Even if you exit as the situational victor, you are always the energetic loser. The need of your combatant to use you for negative energetic intercourse has been met. If you wrestle with someone smeared with pitch, irrespective of the outcome, you will always end up tarred.

The techniques I used to help avoid getting hooked to David's negativity involved visualizations designed to reinforce the belief I could not be harmed by our interchange. In one, I became a transparent permeable field of energy through which anything could pass without harm or disturbance. David's barbs were visualized as energetic arrows. When one was fired, I watched it approach, easily pass through me without becoming intermingled with my own energy field, and then fall away harmlessly behind me. This visualization worked well when I was feeling more centered and less threatened.

Other images embodied a more protective structure. Sometimes I imagined a transparent golden-white energetic force field a few inches wide encapsulating my body at arm's length. Any salvos, again visualized as energetic entities, were diffused by the force field into neutral energy components and then absorbed by it. And when I really felt vulnerable, I covered myself in a suit of impenetrable white armor off of which even the most intensive rake shot would harmlessly fall.

As with any visualization, mine were more effective when vividly created and highly detailed. I often closed my eyes while speaking on the phone with David, which enhanced my ability to construct these images. Of course daydreamers well know that shut eyes are not a prerequisite to internal vision. Practice also helps develop this skill, as I discovered through the much-repeated application of protective visualizations during the course of my separation and divorce.

Obviously, this technique is not particularly effective if you don't remember to use it. Sometimes when caught off guard— answering the office phone in the absence of my secretary, for instance—I got hooked into David before I could recall this resource. Only after hanging up the phone and rocking back in my chair feeling energetically wasted might I realize I had completely forgotten to employ a visualization. Remembering that a particular event calls for visualization also reminds us that the situation requires our higher consciousness. Perhaps even more than use of mental imagery, it is our intent to remain conscious that makes visualization so successful in these situations.

The ability to be under attack without responding in kind is one of the benchmarks of spiritual progress. As aptly described by an early Christian abbot, when a beginner on the spiritual path suffers an attack, he cries out in pain but overcomes his strong desire to strike back at his assailant. A more developed aspirant has learned control of the self, holds no desire to harm his attacker, and will neither cry out nor return a blow. The monk advanced in spirit cries out under assault, not out of concern for himself, but in compassion for the harm his attacker self-inflicts by the act of aggression. The biblical turn of the other cheek does not necessitate passivity. It means not allowing yourself to be captured and lost in the unconsciousness of another. There may be numerous courses of right action to follow when faced with such aggression or negativity.

Many years ago I had a criminal felony jury trial in which my client and friend was accused of battery on law enforcement officers. The alleged offense involved quite a melee, and in addition to serious bumps and bruises all around, one of the officers suffered what was claimed to be minor but permanent eye damage. My client claimed self-defense, and tensions were still running high by the time of trial. The two Assistant State Attorneys were loud, determined and brash, and tried their best to rankle me throughout the proceedings. Whenever I would examine a witness they shuffled their papers around, opened boxes, dropped books on their table, played with paper clips, twanged rubber bands—all in a manner obviously calculated to distract my attention. Maybe they learned this in prosecutor school. I, of course, took the high road and remained quiet and courteous during their turns.

As the trial wore on with the hour getting late, I heard a large thump at their table behind me during a critical part of my examination of an important witness. This one momentarily got to me. Before doing anything I paused, took a deep breath, let my upset pass, and felt free of their energy. Without thinking, I slowly turned around and looked at my snickering opponents, then turned to face the jury. I looked in the jurors' eyes for a moment without saying a word, then swiveled to resume my examination of the witness. My point was made and received without rancor or animosity and without any desire for retribution. My intuitive action was the appropriate and perfect response to this situation.

At other times when facing belligerent counsel, I have forcefully spoken out or objected to misdeeds when it felt the right thing to do. The power of action depends not so much on what you do, but how you are when you do it. Had I stared down my opponents and gazed at the jury as a ploy of counterattack, I would have surrendered my energy by engaging my adversaries in *their* fight, and my action would not have been as effective.

Effective action sure was something I was searching for in my relationship with David. Trying this case was the most difficult legal challenge I had ever faced, and this rancor, in addition to generating personal distress, was proving to be a significant hardship and impediment to my efforts. At the moment I certainly wasn't the advanced monk wailing over the karmic misfortune David was causing himself by flailing me. I barely maintained enough control to prevent volatiles from exploding. So I came up with a revolutionary idea—I would talk to him about it! This seemed an endeavor best done in person, and the upcoming Weissman Philadelphia depositions would provide opportunity and venue.

The cold, wet, and gray Philadelphia April presented a perfect advertisement for Florida living. The landscape looked bleak from the air, and our taxi ride to some Federal building in the city heart did nothing to dispel the dreary urban visage. (No letters please; I'm sure the city is wonderful when sunbathed and verdant.) Manny and I found a deli around the corner from our destination, parked our paraphernalia, and enjoyed a brief respite. While partaking the excellent downtown fare, we speculated about the Weissmans' upcoming testimony.

I had never talked with the elder Weissman, recovering now from a recent stroke, and had spoken to Neal Weissman on only one occasion. After considerable effort to arrange that conversation, all I got was the younger Weissman's bitter assertion that both he and his father were systematically harassed by the I.R.S. as retribution for appraising Manny's pieces. He even claimed the I.R.S. investigators demanded false evidence, threatening criminal charges of complicity in Manny's "fraud" should they refuse to change their story to the government's liking. As to *my* client's professed belief the government was "out to get him," I found my initial reaction of implausibility steadily eroding.

Discussing government conspiracy theories had its fascination, but I was much more interested in the I.R.S.'s written "record" of the statements supposedly given by the Weissmans to investigators. Did these witnesses *really* tell the government their appraisals were mostly Manny's handiwork? Weissman wouldn't talk of it. Still deeply suspicious—perhaps he thought I was an undercover

I.R.S. agent—he declined to say more about the case, but did instruct me to contact his lawyer should I want to press my inquiry. Counsel dealt as parsimoniously with the facts as did his clients and told me neither father nor son would talk off the record. As we exited the deli and moved around the corner, it looked as if my client was thinking as I was. Would Matthew and Neal Weissman now repudiate under oath the unsigned statements attributed to them by the ever-vigilant government sleuths?

We arrived somewhat early at the appointed place and found David unloading his files, looking more comfortable and confident in this bosom of federal bureaucracy than he did in the wilds of Hong Kong. The witnesses hadn't appeared yet, so here was my chance. I asked David if we could talk in private, and after a bit of skeptical hesitation—his face seemed to say, "I wonder what he has up his sleeve?"—he agreed. I found it difficult to move out of battle gear and speak from the heart, but I did the best I could.

I carefully avoided recounting any particular incident or ascribing blame to anyone. I told him how our current state of affairs distressed me on a personal level and suggested it was possible and much more desirable to do our respective jobs without engaging in personal attack or acrimony. I also expressed my belief that he as well would prefer to litigate in more personally amicable surroundings. Finally, I shared with David my desire to rehabilitate at least a working relationship and told him I hoped he too would consider this a worthwhile objective.

My opponent had probably heard just about everything in the course of litigation, but apparently not this! I won't go so far as to say David was stunned, but the combination of his hanging chin and blank gaze could have passed for a momentary catalepsy. After an awkward pause he managed to stumble out a few words to the effect that he was a nice guy and of course preferred to get along with everyone. Upon regaining his composure a bit, he started into a "if you didn't do what you did I wouldn't have had to do what I did" type argument, which I promptly defused by reminding him it was unproductive to now start apportioning blame for past flare-ups. We ended with David cautiously agreeing to approach our relationship anew.

Some victory always accompanies even our most dismal fail-
ures. The depositions quickly degenerated into the nasties, and by
the time we concluded, David and I were more at odds than ever
before. My adversary got first shot at the witnesses, and it soon
became evident their testimony held no resemblance to the
government's written "statements" from the fraud investigation.
David appeared more frustrated the further along he went. At one
point in the proceedings, he was thumbing through his files looking
for a particular document. I spotted the object of his search stapled
to the back of another document and reached over to his file to
point it out to him.

*"Don't touch my file,"* he exploded. We lawyers are very sensitive about maintaining the integrity of our files; however, given
my Good Samaritan explanation, I found David's threat of prosecution for attempting to interfere with government property a
bit extreme. I obviously knew by then my pre-deposition attempt
at reconciliation was doomed. Nevertheless, I found great value in
my earlier conversation with David. I expressed who I was and
took a risk in doing so. And what better way to transform a
profession deemed heartless than by acting with humanity? We
are always victorious when we align our outward expression with
our inner truth.

Also true was my surprise that David didn't question either
deponent about their reputed statements. When the buck was
passed to me, I had to make a quick call. Do I ask about the prior
declarations? The Weissmans would not personally be attending
the trial, but their deposition testimony would be read in court. I
certainly wanted the Weissmans to disavow these prior statements,
but only if they were otherwise mentioned by the government at
trial. As I recalled my basic evidence, a prior conflicting statement
of a witness is not admissible in court *unless* the witness is first
presented with the statement and given an opportunity to explain
it. Since David hadn't brought up the statements here at deposition, I concluded he was barred from discussing them at trial. Either
my opponent knew something I didn't, or he just made a costly
error. I hoped I remembered my evidence well and opted not to
raise the issue.

The depositions were turning into a gold mine. I couldn't have asked for more favorable testimony. Neal Weissman, who did the research legwork for his father's appraisals, gave great valuation testimony. The ivory boat contained forty-two finely carved ivory figures *(netsukes),* each about five inches in height. The witness gave a good account of the market for like figures at the time of appraisal and testified to sales fetching up to $4,000 per netsuke. At that price just the figures on the boat were valued at $168,000. How in heck could the boat *and* figures be worth only $35,000 as claimed by the government? I sure looked forward to making that argument.

Although we hadn't engendered much brotherly love in the city so highly named, Manny and I rested a little farther into the seatback during our taxi return to the airport. Both depositions were a big plus for the case, and we especially savored this victory since we wouldn't have deposed the Weissmans had the government declined to do so. Winning a skirmish does not necessarily mean prevailing in the war, but we were looking for success wherever we could find it, and this provided a small but ample opportunity for some good cheer. Funny how the landscape didn't look as bleak leaving town. Little did I know that the government was activating its strategic arsenal for a launch designed not just to win a battle, but to obliterate the entire landscape of this case.

# CHAPTER SEVENTEEN

# The Crushing Difference of a Day—Is All Lost?

"THE DEFENDANT ASSERTS that no 'claim for refund' was 'filed' on January 31, 1991, in accordance with the express provisions of the Internal Revenue Code and applicable Treasury Regulations." Although the envelope bearing the claim for refund was postmarked January 31, 1991, and claims timely mailed are deemed to be timely filed, "Plaintiffs *improperly addressed* their claim for refund;" thus, "Due to the incorrect designation on the envelope, the presumption that the claim was filed when mailed does not apply." Good Lord, please tell me this can't be true. This entire case, all the time and effort and sweat and blood, can't be flushed down the toilet just because an envelope was misaddressed!

This response by the government to our Request For Admission, if determined by the court to be true, effectively would send our case to the showers. Of the two substantial payments by my clients to the I.R.S., the one made in 1988 for $300,000 had significant statute of limitations problems and recovery was a long shot. The other of $422,033 made February 1, 1989, thought to be secure from the evil statute's grip, now was in jeopardy. If your memory is outstanding, you will recall that a taxpayer must claim a refund from the I.R.S. within two years of the date of any payment sought to be recovered. If you're a day late you're out of luck and your claim is barred. Therefore, January 31, 1991 was the last day for filing a claim to refund the $422,033 paid February 1, 1989. All agreed the claim was mailed on January 31, 1991 and received by the Internal Revenue Service Center in Atlanta on February 2, 1991.

A claim is "filed" upon receipt *except* when mailed before a deadline but received after the due date; then it is considered filed as of the mailing date. We were in the ball game with our mailing date, but six feet under with the date of receipt. Before I had agreed to take the case, I exercised my caution and checked the "timely mailing, timely filing" law. While I found the statute did require the claim be properly addressed to get the benefit of filing upon mailing, I had no reason to suspect the address, especially since the government had generally admitted to a January 31st filing date in its Answer to the plaintiffs' Complaint.

Apparently my cautiousness lacked sufficient muscle. Though I had reviewed the law, I failed to research its related Treasury Regulations. Provisions of the Internal Revenue Code, which are federal law, are supplemented by regulations issued by the Department of the Treasury. While a Code section may only be a paragraph long, the regulations detailing the procedures for implementing the Code provision are sometimes very lengthy. My belated foray into the regulations now revealed that refund claims were required to be sent to the Internal Revenue Service Center covering the geographic area in which the taxpayer resides. For Manny and Mary that was the Atlanta center, and that's where the claim was received.

However, the envelope containing their refund claims was addressed to the "Internal Revenue Service, *District Director,* Atlanta, Georgia 39901." I soon discovered that the "Center" and "District Director" were not identical entities. Damn that Davis! Not only did my clients' former attorney wait until the last day to mail the claim for refund, he couldn't even get the address straight. But even though the envelope may have been technically misaddressed, it was delivered by the postal service directly to the Service Center and not to the District Director. Did this direct and prompt delivery somehow make the address "correct?" Surely if the claim for refund arrives at the proper place without delay we still get the benefit of the timely mailing/timely filing law—right?

Not according to the cases interpreting the Code section and regulations. These judicial decisions were Draconian. The requirement that a claim for refund be properly addressed to be deemed filed upon pre-deadline mailing, admittedly was intended to prevent delay in the receipt and processing of claims. However, almost all the courts visiting this issue found little relevance in the intent or spirit of the law. Since the Sovereign can only be sued by bestowing upon its subjects the grace of its consent, that permission must be severely and strictly construed. Ah, the King as State— another wonderful anachronism carried over from our English jurisprudential roots.

So, in the eyes of the courts, "correct" meant exactly that. Cases were lost even if the only error in the address was a Zip Code one numeral off. Interestingly, an otherwise proper address lacking a Zip Code was deemed "correct" because these codes, as routing aids devised by the post office, were distinguishable from the address itself. Thus, even though a refund claim without a Zip Code took much longer to be delivered than one with a botched code, the former was "filed upon mailing" while the latter was filed upon receipt, and therefore filed late.

Such absurd results didn't faze the courts: "If you want to sue the government follow the letter of the law. And by the way taxpayer, if you bothered to mail your refund claim before waiting until the last day, your misaddressed envelope would have been received before the deadline and would have been timely filed. So don't blame *us* for your screw-up." Okay, so the judiciary didn't exactly phrase it that way. But evidently, at least in this area of the law, the mercy used to temper justice was in scarce supply. Was this my legal karma exacting retribution? Had I excessively enjoyed maneuvering the occasional dismissal of my opponents' cases on technical and sometimes obscure grounds?

"For want of a nail the shoe was lost; for want of a shoe the horse was lost; for want of a horse the rider was lost; for want of a rider the message was lost; and, for want of a message the battle was lost." (Benjamin Franklin, with extrapolations.) I just *could not* believe it. My clients' $422k, now swelled with interest past $700k, was being nailed into a coffin and buried by a marginally improper address on an envelope properly delivered and received. Could I really be the recipient of this cruel joke of such cosmic dimensions? But what about the pleadings, you say?

The Complaint, Answer, and Affirmative Defenses are supposed to narrow down the issues, so only those in dispute need be presented at trial. If a defendant in its Answer admits an allegation made in the Plaintiff's Complaint, that fact or issue is resolved and settled for the purposes of the litigation. (If you remembered all this, you were born into the law—see your nearest recruiter.) Since the government generally admitted in its Answer that the claim for refund was *filed* on January 31, 1991, wasn't this issue conclusively put to rest? And if so, why did I bother asking the government in discovery to agree to this fact?

When a day's difference separates success from doom, pleading the date of such event demands thought and precision. These were qualities both Davis and David lacked in their respective preparations of the Complaint and Answer. Davis failed to precisely plead a January 31st filing date, alleging that each tax years' claim for refund was filed "on *or about* January 31, 1991." Is anyone surprised? David's Answer admitted the refund claims for 1979 and 1980 were filed "on or about" January 31, 1991, but also curiously admitted the 1981, 1982, and 1983 claims were "filed *on* January 31, 1991." Both Davis and David were loose with their language, as probably neither believed at the time there existed a limitations issue regarding the $422,033 payment.

Lawyers routinely use the phrase "on or about" when imprecision is desired. If Mr. Jones fell at the market, his suit for injuries might allege he stumbled "on or about" March 10th. If at trial he testifies he fell on March 9th, or the store report indicates the date was March 12th, his Complaint can't be used to trip up his story because March 9th or March 12th is "about" March 10th. Imprecision gives this wiggle room. However, with limitations issues, you need to cement your position. You either want your client enduringly wed to the light of a living cause of action, or your adversary perpetually consigned to the black death of untimeliness.

The shades of gray in these pleadings were of no great concern to me when I, along with my adversary, thought the timely mailing/ timely filing rule applied. I had requested the discovery admission as to filing date just to sew up the minor ambiguity in David's Answer. Now with the government disavowing timely mailing/ timely filing, the exact wording and effect of the pleadings took on crucial importance. How often our careless words assume unintended significance.

I was sure neither Davis nor David imagined when drafting their pleadings that anyone, a couple of years later, would be burrowing in the law library looking for cases defining the phrase "on or about." I actually found a case or two offering some exposition. Unfortunately they declared the phrase to mean what I thought it meant. How could my uncompensated months of labor and mountains of work possibly hang upon some court's elucidation of such minutia? Envelopes, addresses, grammatical conjunctions—I was still too seared and in shock from the government's nuclear event to appreciate the absurdities.

If the pleadings stood up, the 1981-1983 claims were in; but how could I possibly prove, without timely mailing/timely filing, that the 1979 and 1980 claims were actually filed on January 31st? The government only admitted filing "on or about" that date, and in fact the claims were received on February 2, 1991. My devious and slightly feverish mind finally came up with a strategy utilizing the villainous envelope causing this mess in the first place. A separate form was required and prepared to claim the refund for each of the tax years in question. Each form was put into the one and only misaddressed nefarious envelope mailed to the Service. Each then, by the laws of physical nature, had to be received by the Service at the same time. If three of the forms were admitted by the government as filed *on* January 31st, can we not irrefutably presume that the other two forms in the same envelope had to have been filed on the same date?

My concoction wasn't much, but at least it was something that I could argue in an effort to save two of our largest refund claims— if, of course, the pleadings held up. An Answer can be changed with the approval of the court, and under many circumstances permission to amend is freely given. If it were me running the government's case, I would be on the horn to the judge with every reason in the world justifying a change in my Answer to: "The United

States denies the claims for refund were filed on January 31, 1991 and asserts they were filed on February 2, 1991 when received."

David took longer than I would have, but his pleas to the court to amend the government's Answer eventually were forthcoming. He presented strong arguments, not the least of which touted the government's immunity from suit. Since the Sovereign can only be sued by strictly complying with the laws permitting suit, "the statute of limitations is a jurisdictional requirement which *cannot* be waived." Thus in our case, because plaintiffs failed to comply with the statute, "sovereign immunity remains intact and mandates that the refund action be dismissed." Pleadings be damned!

I suffered through the throes of anger, frustration, and despair. Here we were in May, with the trial scheduled in just two months. Not content to obliterate the landscape, the government was intent on bombing us back to the Stone Age. Motion upon motion exploded around me, and unsuspected issues detonated like un-warily hit mines. The government was now disputing the dates the donations were made to the museum. Although the items were received by the Carnegie at the close of each respective calendar year, donations were not formally "accepted" by the museum until approved by its Board, an event that occurred the following year. What in hell did that do to the case?

The government now wanted to depose our expert witnesses and at the same time asserted to the court our experts should be prevented from testifying at trial. There were more motions to defend, trial exhibits to mark and organize, pretrial statements to draft, trial briefs to research and submit, witnesses to interview, testimony to prepare, questions to submit for jury selection, pro-posed jury instructions, verdict forms, mountains of materials, reams of paper, tons of research—and for what? Just to have the case thrown out at the end because of an address on an envelope?

This work was so challenging to begin with, it now seemed impossible to continue under this shroud of futility. Even the victories weren't much help. We had basically prevailed on the motions considered to date by the court. Although we didn't get a letter rogatory, the court ordered the government to produce the Certificate of Assessments and the redacted materials, and also gave us permission to take Godfrey's deposition. Despite David's attempt to have the court change its mind about the deposition, and after enduring bitter and interminable interchanges to reach an agreement on Godfrey's compensation and other such details, we were scheduled to fly up to Charlottesville, Virginia to square off against the expert.

I was spending just about every waking hour on this case and had to turn away *paying* clients for lack of time. Now I could expend endless additional hours preparing for and attending an expert's out-of-state deposition. Why sacrifice my time and energy arranging the deck chairs on a sinking ship? Why in God's name did I ever take this case on a contingency fee, let alone settle for a one-third cut?

*Fellouzis vs. United States* was not the only vessel in my life on the shoals. I had moved back into my house, now stripped to the floor and walls, only to learn that the owners would start major renovations in October with their flood insurance proceeds. I had to be out for good by then and despaired at my inability to fulfill my deep desire to remain. I wanted desperately to live on the Gulf and had neither the down payment nor current income level to qualify for a sufficient loan to purchase a waterfront home in the area. The flood money stoked an already hot market and created a measurable boom in new construction and renovation. Not too many old shacks were left on the water selling for just the price of the land, which itself was rather sizable. Nonetheless, I made creative offers on the few properties I at least could fantasize snaring. My proposals were rejected, more often than not with the addition of seller disdain. As my numbered days dwindled, I would sit in my yard and longingly look across the channel at the homes well-perched for viewing the sun disappear into the glistening sea.

Nowhere close to disappearing were my marital problems, even though I was now legally divorced. We had not yet worked out a settlement agreement, and our property and support issues seemed unresolvable. We both had attorneys. Somehow the agreements we painfully negotiated, once formally prepared, were no longer acceptable to my ex-wife's lawyer, who authored most of the now-contested provisions in the first place. As for my attorney, I uncomfortably wondered whether sympathies developed in her practice devoted to wives occasionally intruded into judgments and advice offered in my case. On her behalf I freely admit to not being the easiest client in the world.

Dividing our property took some doing, but was not the worst of it. Calculating the amount of child support proved tougher, as I was suffering from post-separation diminution of earnings. From my point of view, I should pay based on my current income. From the other side, prior earnings provided a fairer benchmark for calculation of support. Don't all self-employed divorced men purposely earn less just to spite their ex-wives? Despite my indignation over the accusation I wasn't working much these days, we ended up somewhere in between our differing points of view. This pleased no one—the hallmark of a fair settlement—but it was something we could both live with.

Alimony was another issue. My ex-wife, a tenured junior college professor, was making more money than I earned at the moment. I boiled at the prospect of having to continue to support her, especially when I was now living on near-rations. If placed in indentured servitude, how could I ever hope to get on my financial feet or even think of buying a house? Damn it—I carried her for most of our marriage, and it just was not fair. She could take care of herself now!

I was aghast to see how the judicial attitude towards alimony had changed in the ten years since I handled divorce cases. Back then an educated, well-employed woman in a fourteen-year marriage would have close to no chance of obtaining alimony. Now I was reading cases of *permanent* alimony being awarded to college-educated women in marriages of as little as seven years. I felt increasingly beleaguered as I saw my future slipping away and was harder pushed by the vitriolic intensity with which my ex-wife pressed her claims.

The object *I* was pressing with increasing intensity these days was the duffel-sized punching bag that somehow had found its way from my flooded home to the office file room. By nine or ten at night, the frustration, anger, and stress led me to some heavy duty pummeling and screaming. On some nights I kept pounding that bag until my screaming turned to shrieking and then to crying.

Occasionally I became self-critical about these outbursts. We still maintain significant attitudes of condescension and even snobbery towards those who can't "contain" their emotions. It wasn't too long ago a presidential candidate was booted from the race over a tear shed while defending his wife from scurrilous attack.

Despite our knowledge of the harmful, even fatal, effects of suppressed emotion, we haven't managed to learn how to effectively integrate emotion—no surprise, since many of us don't even have a clue most of the time what it is we really are feeling. The ability to control emotions is one of our primary yardsticks in measuring childhood development, and as a society fixated on "advancement," we persistently and excessively conscript our children into emotional confinements that are unsuitable as well as premature. No wonder then we are a society of emotive immatures.

Suppression is not the only form of emotional avoidance. Acting out or expressing an uncomfortable or "negative" emotion is just a different modality used to avoid underlying beliefs or issues we on some level choose not to face. By contrast, emotional integration results from experiencing emotion on an energetic level, apart from the story, drama, explanation or justification we may graft upon our feeling. This experience of emotion may be silent or may manifest in sound or movement.

The line between integrative experience and avoidance can be extremely subtle. As we become more sensitized to our feelings, we start to view our emotions and emotive life as if we were looking out of a door someone has opened. Although we can become very adept at identifying our feelings and even analyzing our emotional selves, we hardly ever step out the door. We mistake our *recognition* of feeling for emotional experience. This results in a stoicism of sorts and the belief we are "in touch" with our feelings. What we really are experiencing is a refined form of emotional suppression. Likewise, emotional expression can bring you close to the door whose threshold you mistakenly think you have crossed. Have I really dealt with my feelings, or am I just acting out my emotional dramas?

Were my punching bag sprees emotionally integrating or simply an avoidance mechanism? Of course it didn't matter. Either way, the exercise was worthwhile. Given our heritage of emotional repression, there is a value in choosing the expressive modality of avoidance—like a painfully shy or withdrawn child having a tantrum. Such a child achingly needs to step into and express its power, and its proclamation "I am here" delights us, even if it does come in the form of obstinacy.

As we are stepping into emotional health, it's all right to allow ourselves to emotionally express as a means of avoidance. The outward forms of expression often resemble the body's natural release when emotion is integrated. Like it or not, being able to yell and shout and cry, and yes, even shriek and shudder, helps us in learning the art of emotional integration. How many of us are afraid of "what might happen" if we truly experience intense emotion? Gaining comfort with these forms of expression reduces our fear of becoming "out of control" and therefore encourages us to let go into the safe and innate process of energetic release.

While my late evening poundings did blow off some steam and keep me somewhat together, each new day's escalating pressures made me wonder whether the release I really needed was withdrawal from the case. Although the prospects were darkening, we hadn't lost yet, and could I really write off this effort without seeing it through to the end? And what about my duty to my clients?

Manny and Mary came in for a powwow, and given the recent turn of events, presented a downtrodden demeanor rivaling my own. Reviewing with them the "misaddressed envelope" cases did nothing to cheer us up. I teetered around the suggestion we call it quits, but just the mere hint brought Manny's robust proclamation that, having gone this far, we would fight to the bitter end. Whatever thoughts I may have had about withdrawing were cast aside. Although legally I probably was able to jump ship, I just couldn't do it. I was not going to abandon my clients. With my feet then firmly planted on the deck of this submerging vessel, I did request, in all fairness I thought, some better accommodations.

Not in my wildest imagination had I anticipated the crushing load of work this case presented. Instead of just having to prove what some antiques were worth, it seemed I had to legally establish every issue under the sun before I could even get inside the court room to talk about valuation. While I knew from the start the first payment was shaky, no one had any idea the biggest payment had a statute of limitations problem. I explained all this to Manny and Mary and also told them how the rest of my practice was suffering under the time demands of their cause. I readily and truthfully confessed that I never would have taken the case had I known at the beginning what hindsight now revealed.

They didn't appear too impressed by my problems, nor did they seem to recognize what was obvious—I was hurting. I asked if they would consider paying for a law student or research assistant to help free up some of my time. They said it was out of the question. I told them this case needed a team to get it ready for trial and I didn't know how one person could get it all done. Their response? "Work less; just do what you can do." After seventeen years of practicing law, I could no more do a half-assed job than I could change my skin. Thanks a lot!

I then suggested it was equitable under the circumstances to adjust our contingency fee agreement. We all realized that, had we known then what we knew now, this case could not have been handed away at any contingency fee. I modestly proposed we increase the fee percentage from one-third to forty percent. A higher percentage wouldn't ease my workload, but at least I'd feel better knowing there was more to win, and would also get an uplift knowing I was really appreciated by my clients. My suggestion was met with outright displeasure. "A contract is a contract. That's the deal."—and I was stuck with it. Not only was I standing on a descending deck, it felt as if my feet were nailed to the planks!

Not coincidentally, the other major areas of my life also were provoking in me identical feelings of despair, futility and loss. Moving beneath the different surface circumstances and issues brought me to the same place: I was afraid of being harmed. In some way I believed if certain events occurred—loss of the case, a bad divorce settlement, moving from my home—I would be grievously hurt; not conditionally, but fundamentally and irremediably. Where was abundance consciousness? Where was "Thou art whole?" Where was the knowing that my innate and immutable nature was complete, perfect, and inexhaustible? Where was the safety and respite in the Infinite? And what good is this consciousness if it deserts you when you need it the most? After all, the winning lottery ticket in the pocket of a beggar won't deliver him from poverty to wealth unless he knows it is there.

CHAPTER EIGHTEEN

# Rescued on Dream Wings

N O MATTER HOW STORMY THE SEAS, our ship is *always* anchored to its source. How do you remember and experience that connection when you feel aimlessly tossed about? Give up the struggle. Recollection of consciousness is not a fight, it is a shift—like the ocean fog moving in and off shore. When the wind moves one way you are densely cloaked, and when it blows the other way the sky is blue and the sun is shining. When the winds are variable your clarity and scope of view changes quickly and often. When the fog is in, it is futile to try to blow it away, move it, hit it, or fight it into leaving. The effortless breath of wind is all that is needed. There is nothing to do. The breath of wind dispelling *our* darkness is the recollection of who we really are.

Trying to fix ourselves, adjust our circumstances or "work" ourselves out of our forgetfulness just perpetuates our struggle—as if we existed in a two-dimensional plane, oblivious of a third dimension. On a flat surface where length and breadth are the only realities, innumerable combinations of lines and points and pictures can be created. When our quest for happiness and insight involves struggle, we are endlessly moving and working within this two-dimensional world. We may become extremely proficient at arranging and manipulating the pictures and events on this plane, and it may even appear to us that we have made progress toward our goal of transcendence. Yet no matter how long or how deftly we operate on this plane, existing in this two-dimensional space will never bring us the realization of our true nature.

Spiritual transcendence occurs when we ascend from the surface. Vertical movement adds the perspective of height and allows us to see our prior world in a way that could never be realized without this added dimension. In the esoteric *chakra* system, spiritual realization correspondingly is described as the awakening of spiritual energy beneath the base of the spine and its movement up the spine to the crown of the head.

Paradoxically, then, because part of us is always spiritually transcendent, and because we never can lose this ascendant attitude of our being, all we need do when we are forgetful is allow ourselves to remember this truth. All we need do is wake up from our sleep. Unfortunately, this is just too simple for us. We find it difficult to realize there is no learning to be done and no work to accomplish. You can never "learn" how to play the piano; you can only *play* the piano. Obviously some perform more proficiently than others, but the only way to discover your adeptness is by playing. In the same way, the more often we live in spiritual transcendence—the more often we "play"—the more skillful we become at remembering during those times of forgetfulness. All we ever need know is our true identity—just put our hand in our pocket and pull out the winning ticket we have had all along.

Many years ago I had a difficult business and social relationship in which I felt controlled and enfeebled. I was convinced this person, large in physical stature, was intentionally trying to defeat and harm my interests, and I felt powerless to prevent it. One night I dreamt we were having an interchange, and I was wheelchair-bound, paralyzed from the waist down. He seemed all the more tall and imposing from my reduced height, and I felt that much more helpless to stand up to him. I then looked at myself and the wheelchair, and the thought crossed my mind, *Wait, I'm really not paralyzed, I don't have to stay in this chair.* I started to dismiss this thought by convincing myself that of course I was crippled. *Why else would I be sitting in this chair?* But something inside me told me, *No, I do have the capacity to stand. All I need do is arise!* I asked myself, "Could this *really* be true?" I think I woke up before testing my hypothesis. But I realized from the dream that my relationship "paralysis" was a self-created lie. This recognition improved my ability to interact with the person, although, as in the dream, I never did fully stand up.

Dreams can often be wonderful reminders of who we really are. A day or two after my debilitating conference with Manny and Mary, I dreamt I was packed into a New York subway car. I felt the pressure of being pushed against the car wall and the other passengers. There seemed nothing I could do to relieve my distress. We arrived at the subway station, but exiting onto the platform offered little relief. Masses of people still jarred and pushed against me as I tried to move towards the stairwell. I became more frustrated as my elbowing for space was met with gruff indifference. I then saw a piece of wood on the ground, like the top of a skateboard, and stepped on it. Instantaneously the board elevated a few inches off the ground and I moved effortlessly through space, propelled only by my will. I swiftly weaved and bobbed through the crowds up and out of the station. Amidst my exhilaration I asked myself how it was possible I could do this. I promptly and emphatically answered, saying to myself, "Of course I can do this. I've *always* known how to fly. I just forgot for a while I knew how!"

Shortly after waking that morning I remembered the dream. The recollection immediately brought the same feeling of exhilaration and transcendence I experienced in my reverie. My body tingled and pulsated. I felt rested, highly energized, and deeply connected to the part of me that knows everything is perfect and as it should be. For the next couple of days I glided above the morass and consciously tapped into this place of centeredness whenever I began to feel beleaguered. With the case demands relentlessly pressing, my ability to remain centered started to wane. Again, the dream world seemed to guide me to freedom. Oppressive or limiting situations would miraculously transform into spontaneous joy upon the self-suggestion that ecstasy indeed was my true nature.

One of my favorite dreamscapes was the ice-skating rink or pond. Not much of a skater during waking hours, I found myself stumbling on the ice, becoming increasingly frustrated with my inability as the other skaters whizzed by. The thought, *I can do that, can't I,* released my Olympic figure-skating potential. I blissfully glided and turned and pirouetted on my skates to the delight of the onlookers making space for me on the ice. Waking and recalling these dreams the following mornings again imbued me with a transcendent peace and energy—at least for a while.

Many spiritual masters find the contrast between the dream and waking states analogous to the difference between our normal waking state and spiritual enlightenment. Because mind, usually the subconscious, creates the dream world, dream realities are the product of thought. Since when we dream we usually are unaware we are dreaming, we experience that self-created reality as if we were actually awake—amply demonstrated by our measurable physiological responses to imagined stimuli.

The binding reality of the dream world disintegrates when we awake from our sleep or when we realize *while* dreaming that we indeed are dreaming. In the latter case, we become free to alter our dreamscape according to our will, as we are at liberty to create whatever our mind desires. Correspondingly, when we truly realize we are spiritual beings, it is like waking up and finding our "normal" life to be nothing but an illusion. We awaken to the reality that the physical world is an expression of consciousness and that this world is as much a creation of mind as is the world of dreams.

This is why working with the dream state can be so beneficial for us. In some way, by exposing the illusion of the dream world, we also enable ourselves to prick the delusion of our waking state. At times I have practiced "lucid dreaming," which is being fully conscious while you are dreaming, that you are indeed in bed, dreaming, and asleep. You need two skills to enjoy lucid dreaming. The first, common to all dream work, is the ability to remember your dreams once you awake. Like my transcendent dreams of gliding and skating, the benefit of lucid dreams is not maximized if the dream-memories reside in the unconscious after awakening from sleep. The techniques for recalling your dreams are well-known and need not be repeated here. The second skill is being able to know that your dream is a dream.

But how do you realize you're dreaming while you are dreaming? I use a simple system of "reality checks" described in a book I read on the subject. This system utilizes the fact that whatever we are habituated to in our waking state will routinely appear in our dreams. Pick a commonplace function you perform five-to-ten times every day, such as turning on a light switch, putting your car key in the ignition, or flushing a toilet. Each time before you do this task, ask yourself the question, "Am I awake or am I dreaming?" Your initial impulse will be to answer, "Of course I'm awake," but don't jump to conclusions. I've had many a dream where I paused to ask this question, only to give myself an erroneous answer. Take a moment or two to investigate your surroundings to verify if indeed you are awake or dreaming. Here are a couple of helpful tests.

Dreams contain only frontal reality. In that world there is no necessity to create a landscape outside your field of view. Thus in a dream, if you pause to use your peripheral vision, you notice that reality starts to break down on the fringes. At the far edge of your vision, your dream setting, whether it be a room interior or grand view of nature, dissolves into black nothingness. Like a miner with a headlamp, only what's in front of you is illuminated; everything else falls into darkness. The other test betrays left brain limitations in the dream state. While dreaming, if you look at anything written and then turn away, when you turn back the writing is all jumbled. Both tests I have found to be true without fail.

After just a few days of applying your "reality checks," you will find yourself performing in a dream the routine task you have chosen and asking yourself in the dream, "Am I awake or am I dreaming?" In my first consciously induced lucid dream I asked that question, summarily dismissed the possibility I might be dreaming, but taking on my new habit, decided to investigate. I stopped a moment what I was doing, gazed peripherally, fully expecting to see the walls of the room I stood in, and was shocked to find that the room narrowed at its sides and lost its detail as it disappeared into a black void! It reminded me of being on a lit stage looking out, but noticing at stage side a few props in the shadows and then just darkness. I checked again, then gleefully shouted, "I'm not awake, I *am* dreaming." With that my dream instantly changed. I felt as if an electric current were pulsating through my body. Everything in the dream became fantastically clearer, sharper, and brilliantly colored, and the entire dreamscape vibrated with a luminescing hum.

I decided to test the physics of this reality and said to myself, "I wish to be outdoors," and with that expression of intent I instantly found myself in an incredibly beautiful natural setting. My new world was filled with verdant forests and meadows, crystal blue lakes, streams, rolling hills where I stood, and mountains in the distance. I could hear the gentle, sweet sounds of birds singing and water flowing. The sky was mostly sunny and blue, displaying wonderfully puffy clouds—the ones just calling for someone's playful creation of some exotic animals or pictures from their shapes. But most prominent in my world was a breathtaking rainbow painted across the sky in colors almost too beautiful and vivid to behold. In my bliss I thought, *I'd love to walk on a rainbow,* and immediately I stood at one end of this ribbon of spectrum as it met the ground. The rainbow almost looked solid and three-dimensional with steps across its spectrum, each one a different color. I walked on, chose a color and started to ascend into the sky.

Many people report similar experiences in lucid dreaming and also find that working with this tool can be empowering and life transforming. Seemingly intractable life issues are shifted by de-signing different dream scenarios and outcomes. Scientists and others use it for problem-solving by creating and then resolving the blocked situation in the dream. Sometimes the dream solution actually works; other times it is the imprinting of the feeling of resolution in the dream that spurs the solution in the waking state. I'm not here to be an advocate of lucid dreaming. What I am suggesting is that we utilize our given capacities to wake up. Lucid dreaming, as a playground to practice manipulation of reality through mind, helps me remember I have the same capacity in the waking state and entrains me to utilize that God-given gift.

Our waking reality is what we believe and expect it to be. I experienced a simple demonstration when looking at an unbe-knownst broken clock. On walking into the courthouse one day, I quickly looked up to check the large clock in the lobby, as I thought I might be running late for a hearing. I distinctly saw the second hand moving as I caught the time. A step or two later I paused as I realized the time seemed to be off. I looked up again and noticed the displayed time was about an hour earlier than I estimated it to be. This time as well the second hand moved. I again looked and now focused on the second hand. It traveled the distance of five seconds, stopped, and then snapped back to where it had started.

I then realized the clock was broken and had not moved a bit since I first saw it. I closed my eyes, opened them, and the second hand still moved three seconds and snapped back. Finally, with some exercise of will, I saw the second hand rest in place. My expectation the second hand would be in motion created for me that illusory reality. The expectation was so habitually set, I had to consciously dispel the illusion even after it had been unmasked.

We all fill in the spaces of life with our acquired beliefs and expectations. Why not then construct life upon the belief we are God's children possessing the creative attributes of the Universal Mind? Outlandish you say—the mind of God may alter substance, but our physical reality doesn't change just because we want it to. But it does. What we create on the physical plane emanates from mind. If I want a new house, I form an idea of what it will look like, where it will be located, and most often create a plan to manifest my idea. My plan might be to learn how to build it myself or perhaps earn and save enough money to have someone else build it. When the hammers and nails and boards of wood eventually start to take the shape of my home, can't we say the seed material creating this structure was my thought, and not the building products now appearing as a result of my idea?

Of course we can. But even conceding that point, isn't implementation of ideas through exertion on the physical plane a far cry from thinking something and having it effortlessly and instantaneously happen? Not really—all of us have had our thoughts "miraculously" manifest, probably more often than we allow ourselves to admit.

How many times have you had a strong and sudden urge to talk with someone and a minute or two later they just "happen" to call you? Have you ever out of the blue thought of a distant friend you lost touch with a couple of years before, and then receive a letter from your old buddy the next morning? How many of you mentally see that open spot and then get a parking slot right in front of your crowded destination? Haven't you ever had a hankering for a particular dish and then find it's the special of the day at the new restaurant you've chosen for lunch?

What we mightily try to chalk up to coincidence has nothing to do with chance; it is the cosmic law of cause and effect at work. And our "miraculous" manifestations are really no different from the building of our home. With *co-incidences,* since cause and effect dramatically and effortlessly occur so close together in time, the connection is easier to see. In the house example, because the path between cause and effect is more circumspect, the relationship is less obvious. Nevertheless, both illustrate the same principle at work.

If we indeed are endowed with the God-given ability to create the physical world by the use of mind, why doesn't the Cadillac you want pop out of thin air when you sit down, concentrate on your imagined auto, and express your wish? Have you ever tried—really? My facetiousness is only partial here. While we all have unfocused wants and desires floating around, not many of us consciously and deliberately harness our mental energy for the purpose of manifesting a specific result. Most of us don't know how. Techniques for applying "spiritual thought" are designed to increase effectiveness of mind. One popular method divides the process into four components: expressing the absolute truth; connecting this truth to ourselves; declaring as unreal any belief blocking the intended result; and knowing with gratitude that what we have proclaimed is already done.

Let us say you believe you are of insufficient wealth to obtain your dream car. Your declaration might be: "Spirit is always complete, whole, sufficient unto itself, and ever abundant. God knows no lack. As a child of God, as a vehicle for Spirit to express itself in this world, I inherently and always possess wealth beyond measure. I am ever abundant and now easily and effortless obtain a Cadillac automobile. Any thought or belief I may have in lack or insufficiency is unreal, has no power over me whatsoever, and is now dispelled. Thank you, God, for the knowledge of this truth. I fully and completely know that what my word has spoken is done."

Had the obstacle to your Caddy been a belief you didn't deserve it, the spiritual thought would have emphasized self-worth.

So, if you never consciously have used your mind to create your world, perhaps you can suspend a bit your judgment about the efficacy of this practice. I concede, of course, that even with the right application of this mental principle, for almost all of us the car won't instantaneously appear out of the ether. (Please notice the word "almost.") Our mental condition is one primary reason it does not.

Our minds are largely undisciplined, agitated, unfocused, and therefore resistant to the concentration needed to harness mental energy. And the degree to which our thought manifests depends upon the energy with which we endow that thought. Given our fractionalized mental state, it's a wonder we manifest at all—our limited success a demonstration of Infinite Mind's power to shine through our dross. When Jesus proclaimed "Rise, Lazarus," he wasn't wondering at the time what the disciples would be cooking for dinner that evening. His cousin awakening from death was the one and only thing occupying his mind.

Throughout the ages in all spiritual traditions, the importance of mental discipline has been recognized and, in one way or another, has been taught. Yet even the untrained mind is not the greatest impediment to effective spiritual thought. That culprit is doubt. Our disbelief is what most inhibits the manifestation of our mind's projections. This doubt is so pervasive that, even if we could eradicate it in our conscious mind, its subconscious seeds will undermine the intended results of our thought. I could repeat a million times that my Cadillac will appear, and might even con-vince myself, yet it will never pop out of the air if I have the slightest disbelief lodged in my subconscious. Jesus knew without any shred of doubt whatsoever that through God *all* things were possible. That is why Lazarus rose, and that same knowing is also why the mountain *did* come to Mohammed.

Uncompromised belief in the working principle of Universal Mind creates stillness. In this belief, the mind rests like a perfectly calm body of water. If you drop a small stone into a placid lake, the effect is concentric ripples that travel great distance. The impact of this tiny mass upon the water is far-reaching; if you watch very carefully, the ever-expanding waves seem to go off into infinity. Doubt creates rough seas. If the lake is agitated, the effect of that same stone hitting the water will dissipate within a short distance. The ripples quickly become broken, deflected, and absorbed by the choppy waves. So too, the effect of our spiritual thought is minimized by the disturbance created by our doubt. When we give up our disbelief, our mind reaches the infinite and the demonstrable impact of our thought is far beyond anything we previously imagined possible.

How do we dispel our doubt? Engender faith; not some pie-in-the-sky hope, but the faith built upon our own experience. Practice spiritual thought and then notice and acknowledge the result. Suppose I am hungry and stuck at home without much around to put a meal together. I consciously apply my mind to manifest food. A few minutes later I get a thought showing how to artfully combine the shreds of a few leftovers into a savory dinner. My inspired culinary idea is the effect and demonstration of applied spiritual thought. If I recognize this connection, my faith increases, and with a deeper belief, my demonstrations may become more dramatic.

With greater faith I might open a closet in search of a jacket and find a can of my favorite chili my wife left there by mistake. If faith in my proclaimed word ("verbal thought") is strong, a few moments later the door bell might ring presenting my neighbor holding a big dish of lasagna saying, "I overcooked and just had a feeling you might like some." Each effect of spiritual thought is a demonstration that can dispel our doubt and increase our faith, if we only take notice and acknowledge that it is Universal Mind working through us.

With food on the mind, here is a story recounted by a disciple of a famous nineteenth-century yogi. A few of the master's closest disciples were gathered in his second-floor loft. The students had been in rigorous and continuous training since the pre-dawn hours. By early afternoon the increasing hunger of the devotees was starting to distract their attention. The master, not wanting to unduly interrupt their instruction, manifested lunch. As shared by his disciple, bowls of food congealed out of the air a foot off the ground, one in front of each disciple, and then unceremoniously plopped down for their repast. While I cannot say my dinner or our proverbial Cadillac has ever popped out of the air in my direct view, I have had some demonstrations that came mighty close.

A number of years ago, while flying from the northeast back to Florida, I visualized with great clarity the plane crashing. I was engaged at the time in the right-to-die case, had started my Hospice service, and had read much of the work in the "conscious dying" field. I was fascinated by the proposition that clarity and spiritual focus at the time of death held great possibilities for Self-realization. It was a fine day for flying. The sky was blue, the takeoff was smooth, and I enjoyed the beginning of the flight by looking out the window at the occasional clouds and the geography below. I felt very relaxed, centered, and extremely clear. At times like this the world almost seems transparent, as if you can see into the heart of things and sense the cause beneath the cause—matter as expression of Spirit.

About a half-hour into the journey the thought crossed my mind, *I wonder what it would be like to die right now?* The thought particularly intrigued me since I felt so "conscious" at the moment. I indulged the thought by imagining the plane starting to lose its trajectory and descend. As the nose of the aircraft headed down, I distinctly felt concern arise and swiftly shift to panic among the passengers. My visualization was extremely vivid. As we went into a free fall, I heard screaming everywhere and saw objects frenziedly flying and smashing all around the cabin. As the plane plunged, gravity pressed against my body, and I felt death grasp us. Only a few moments remained before the earth would break our fall. I turned from the chaos around me, calmly looked inside, and asked, "What is this death?"

At that moment a turn in my gut interrupted my gripping visualization. I sensed a hush and then realized that the nose of the plane had started to dip. Every passenger was instantaneously self-summoned to complete attention. The nose slowly continued to tilt downward as if the plane had run out of fuel and had nothing left to propel its lateral path against the pull of gravity. I was seized by fear as we started to lose some altitude. Like a yawning behemoth ambling a turn, the nose continued its descent and now was down fifteen or twenty degrees. Although just a few seconds had elapsed, time seemed frozen. We felt a pulse of downward acceleration, which transformed our fear to near panic. At that moment, when the rumblings of incipient screams began to be heard, the nose started to lift and the craft quickly resumed its even path.

With resumption of breathing and a few deep sighs, we soon regained our balance. The flight attendants appeared with their carts and the cabin chatter resumed its normal hum. Needless to say, the juxtaposition of my imagined death and the possibility of a real demise highlighted for me my different reactions. I assure you, my hubris in assuming that I would meet a life-ending crash with equanimity was not lost on me. "No more visualizations for me this trip," I promised myself.

About twenty minutes later as I was finishing my sandwich, the captain extended over the loudspeakers his apology for the flight mishap. He explained that for some unknown reason, the automatic pilot just shut itself off, and regaining command of the plane took them a few moments. He assured us the crew would fly the rest of the way on manual control. At that instant a clear, distinctly independent and slightly stern voice said to me, "Be careful what you think. You are more powerful than you realize." In quick succession I was startled, humbled and blessed by God's admonishment.

As once said by Nelson Mandela, our greatest fear is not that we are small, incapable, weak, insufficient or insignificant. Our greatest fear is that we are powerful beyond our wildest imagination. We are afraid to let go of our limitations, those familiar and comfortably worn shackles, and step into our majesty—our freedom. Why this case for me? Why these struggles? Sometimes we need a challenge to break out of our habitual and self-limiting beliefs. Sometimes we need adversity as impetus to plumb the depths of our despair in order to find our true power. Sometimes our self-assigned wheelchair needs to be brought toward the precipice before we can rise.

The fact was, without remembering my true nature, without the ability to access my source, I would have crumbled under the weight of my task. Is the catalyst for Self-realization always adversity, is it always this hard? Of course not. We can and do learn our lessons in a myriad of ways, including the way of joy. Often times we simply and gently ease into the experience of our truth. For me, at that time, a tough challenge was what I needed. When I could realize that this adversity was self-designed and created for my benefit, remembering became easier.

I bounced betwixt remembrance and forgetfulness on my roller coaster ride, careening through the dips and curves and plummets, shifting between fear and excitement, between despair and joy. As this ride progressed a newly found thought began to uplift me—it would soon all be over!

CHAPTER NINETEEN

# Reversing
# the Government's Torpedo

T HERE WAS NO DOUBT spring had fully arrived in the foothills
of Virginia. The pleasant sun poured upon our uplifted
faces as we rested on the courtyard bench. The birthed
flowers and leaves had quickly grown beyond their tenuousness,
and I imagined they could finally relax under the firm solar rays
that dispelled any concern the cold might return. We sat in a gray
stone yard centered by a modest fountain and bordered on one side
by a colonial-looking building of red brick, ivy walls, black roof and
white steeple. Squaring off this church or public meeting place were
tall, full shrubs that hid this enclave from the surrounding avenues.
Closing my eyes I listened to the cheerful passing sounds and
breathed in this welcomed respite. Our time for renewal was short,
but Earth's spring felt eternal.

Manny and I had arrived in Charlottesville, home of Thomas
Jefferson's University of Virginia, just two hours before. The
commuter flight from our Charlotte, North Carolina stopover
brought us to our destination with enough time remaining to enjoy
some lunch at a nicely restored basement tavern. With a half-hour
or so before expert Godfrey's deposition, we exited the tavern and
naturally seemed to gravitate to our restful cloister. Our silence was
not forced, but spontaneously fell upon us. Given the frenetic pace
of the last week, our temporary immobility had quickly moved us
into a rest too deeply sweet to disturb by chatter. And what was

there left to say? Each in our own way had resigned himself to completion of this case, and there was no point resurrecting the fact that our continued efforts probably would have little bearing on the eventual outcome.

A bit more of a breeze gently rustled the surrounding trees and signaled us it was time to go. I lifted myself, then my heavily laden black display case, and with Manny toting my attaché case we began to amble toward the court reporter's nearby office. Our load contained, among other things, copies of all my trial exhibits, which I coincidentally was required to deliver to the government by this date.

In order to prevent trial by ambush, the court, as part of pre-trial procedure, orders both parties to assemble their respective documentary evidence, number and mark it with court-approved labels, and then exchange copies. This simple-sounding task took me over twenty hours in a large conference room that had its horizontal surfaces almost completely papered. Organizing the sheer volume of materials is not the only chore that consumes time in an evidence exchange. Putting together your evidence involves planning and strategizing your case.

Trial documents and other exhibits create a blueprint for the case you are going to construct, so deciding which materials to utilize takes much thought. By listing an exhibit for trial, you waive any objections you may have to its admissibility. This opens the door for your opponent to introduce the exhibit into evidence should you later change your mind and decide not to present it at trial—an opportunity your adversary may not have had absent the exhibit's appearance on your list. Many exhibits do not weigh solely in one party's favor, and often, in deciding whether to use evidence, you must balance the potential benefit to your case with the possibility of harm. This prospective evaluation is difficult, as unexpected turns in a trial may require unanticipated shifts in strategic position. Wiggle room is limited here because, as a general rule, if you don't list and exchange your exhibit per the court's command, you are barred from introducing it at trial.

Another weighty part of our cargo had provided me with pleasant counterpoint to the arduous task of distilling trial exhibits. Manny had performed yeoman's service in scouring local libraries for books on the history and art of Chinese jade carving. His efforts yielded a few works on the subject I much enjoyed reading. I hoped that one or two, given their cogency and literary quality, were recognized as classics in the field. Not only did I wish to educate myself about the subject, I wanted Godfrey to declare as authoritative the works I now had at my disposal. One of the most effective techniques in cross-examining an expert witness is to elicit testimony on a point and then read to him the opposite viewpoint expounded in some scholarly treatise. In order for counsel to read from these independent works at trial, technically hearsay, the expert must first agree they are authoritative or well-recognized in the field.

On the morning flight I brushed up on my sources, readying to ask the unsuspecting witness about the finer points of jade. Here's one. Not many, if ever asked, would guess that the color of pure jade is white. The many hues of jade are the result of mineral impurities, emerald green caused by the presence of chromium, red from an iron compound, and so on. And here is another. Most consider nephrite harder than jadeite because nephrite is extremely difficult to shatter, while jadeite is more breakable. Actually, the relative brittleness of jadeite is caused by its crystalline structure, but it is nevertheless higher than nephrite on the scale of mineralogical hardness. I kept a number of other arcane points up my sleeve about the mineral, from carving techniques to its trade through the ages.

You might call them trick questions or minutia, but I call it fair game—after all, Godfrey was the one calling himself an expert. If the witness acknowledged that my books are authoritative and then failed at "Jadeite Jeopardy!", I would have some great ammunition to impeach his credibility at trial. If he answered wrong again at trial, I would happily share with the jury the right answer from the treatise; if he responded correctly, I would read to the jury his incorrect deposition answer.

The court reporter was housed in a well-renovated mid-nineteenth-century building that displayed enough rich timbers to satisfy even my wood-inclined tastes. I gave David my exhibits, but he had none to give me, claiming they weren't due at the moment.

We squabbled some more about Godfrey's fee for preparation time and then got down to it. I quickly discovered our witness had never been deposed, never had testified in court as an expert, and outside of this case, had never been retained to give an opinion in connection with a legal controversy. This didn't *per se* render Godfrey unqualified in our case, it just let me know I was working with a tenderfoot in the ways of litigation.

Examination of Godfrey's background revealed that the statement of qualifications prefacing his appraisal was not quite accurate. He did not receive a degree in "Oriental Studies" from the University of Virginia as claimed. The university had no department in that field. He majored in history, received his B.A. degree from the history department, and took some interdisciplinary courses on Oriental subjects. His self-presented qualification as an "internationally recognized" dealer in Oriental arts now sounded a bit inflated; a closer description of his endeavor might be "selling pieces on consignment from my New York apartment."

Fairly soon after college, Godfrey worked a few years for Christie's auction house in London and New York, and then began his independent career as consultant, "dealer," and connoisseur of Oriental arts. His involvement with the government's case started not too long after going out on his own. Listening to his testimony I could almost see the young, burgeoning-but-still-struggling Mr. Godfrey involved in the process of modestly inflating his credentials. From my own experience I easily related to the young entrant's need to arrive "fully formed" upon the field of his profession.

James had apparently done well over the years, and by his own account was now a part-time curator for a museum's Asian arts collection and had inventoried and appraised many major institutional and private collections. Mr. Godfrey was very knowledgeable about many subjects, but fortunately for me and unfortunately for him, not as knowledgeable as he claimed or perhaps believed. Hubris was something else about Mr. Godfrey I could well relate to!

"Do you know what the color of pure jade is?" I asked the expert. Although his moment of indecision was well concealed from the other participants, I instantly knew he was going to fudge: "It can be any color. Not any color, it can be a variety of colors is the correct answer." I caught him a few other times and felt the jaws of my trap close that much tighter.

Even better was the witness's answer regarding authoritative works. Without my mentioning any in particular, Godfrey named the author of the volume providing me with the bulk of my information, and attested to the writer's well-known status in the field. I then identified my other major reference, who Godfrey also acknowledged was regarded as reliable. While much of my questioning was designed to obtain grist for milling credibility at trial, I was most interested in discovering the bases for his valuation of our big-ticket items.

He claimed the incense burner and table screen were common antiques and thus relatively simple to appraise. He seemed to possess detailed knowledge of the Oriental art market of that time, having attended most of the major auctions sprinkled around the globe. His valuation of the koro and screen primarily were based upon auction sales of numerous comparable items, the details of which he would substantiate at trial by presenting catalogues he maintained for reference. I had expected to receive copies of these auction catalogues from the government as part of our exhibit exchange, and their absence limited my inquiry into his appraisal of these two pieces.

He asserted the koro was Ch'ien-Lung and adamantly disagreed it was crafted in the reign of the preceding emperor, as our appraisers claimed. We discussed how such dating was determined, and Godfrey elucidated at length the stylistic differences between the carvings of the two reigns. I failed to appreciate the distinctions he attempted to describe and was left wondering—was the subject just too subtle for my grasp, or was there nothing here to grasp in the first place?

The ivory boat told another story. Godfrey readily admitted that nothing comparable ever sold at auction. Apparently, he initially extrapolated a boat value of $30,000 from sales prices of much lesser pieces moved at auction. A short while after his initial estimate, he claimed he spied a comparable piece selling for $9,000 at a New York shop. This confirmed for him the correctness of his appraisal, which I gather he now deemed to be generous. I knew that an item that cost over $50,000 to produce in the Orient would not sell in New York at the price claimed by Godfrey. I didn't know what James saw, but it just did not add up.

While I will admit the witness appeared to have some expertise in jade, I was becoming more convinced he knew little about ivory. I had previously learned that "bridge" and "boat" were specialized terms in the ivory world, yet commonplace to anyone minimally familiar with the trade. Both describe a carving made from one complete tusk, the "bridge" crafted from a convexly mounted tusk and the "boat" from a tooth concavely fastened. Godfrey had no clue whatsoever.

The witness then sought to buttress his appraisal with information garnered from our Hong Kong escapade of two months before. Apparently, he and David had also scurried about town looking for anything comparable to the pieces in dispute. Godfrey claimed he saw two ivory boats, each at a different Hong Kong shop and each close to the size and detail of Manny's vessel. He administered the *coup de grace* by matter-of-factly revealing that both boats were selling for between $20,000 and $30,000! His nonchalance no doubt confirmed that the unerring Mr. Godfrey had been correct right from the start of our multi-decade dispute.

I didn't remember seeing any big ivory boats in Hong Kong. I guess our opponents could scurry better than we could. The witness had taken pictures of the boats for use at trial. Although the photos were nowhere to be seen at deposition, Godfrey did manage to share with us the name of one of the Hong Kong shops offering the ivory: Le Extreme Orient. Discovery is designed to uncover the strengths as well as the weaknesses of your opponent's case. Though its revelations may at times be unpleasant, at least it is better to spot a torpedo oncoming rather than have its presence announced upon impact!

Godfrey's newly found evidence left us puzzled and adrift. Manny was certain the pieces he described could not sell at the price claimed, and my recently acquired knowledge of the market offered nothing to dispute my client's opinion. How could we possibly maneuver our way out of this line of attack? I quickly ceased pondering this dilemma as the next few days engaged me in skirmishes on other areas of the battlefield.

Manny though had not deserted the problem. A few days after the deposition he called and reminded me Le Extreme Orient was one of the galleries we also had visited while in Hong Kong. With a little more discussion I remembered the shop and recalled we had dropped in on more than one occasion.

"Manny, I don't remember seeing any ivory boats. We were all in there around the same time. How could Godfrey have seen one?"

"He didn't," Manny uttered with an assured solemnity. After a brief but measured pause, he then added with an unsuccessfully concealed enthusiasm: "There was a large model boat in the store, but it wasn't carved from ivory, it was made from *bone.*"

*Wonder of wonders, miracle of miracles!* I hadn't yet grasped why, but this was obviously big.

"What difference would that make?" I inquired.

Manny chuckled and proceeded to explain to me how bone is as cheap an imitation of ivory as cubic zirconium is of diamond. Historically because of the expense and rarity of ivory, and now due to the export ban, imitators take ox bone or camel bone, stain it, and then use it to construct objects and scenes that were typically carved from ivory.

"But Manny, how do you know that boat [which I didn't even remember seeing] was made out of bone?"

"I just know. It's obvious to anyone who knows anything about ivory."

Having purchased millions of dollars-worth of ivory carvings during the years of his import business, Manny had by necessity and experience acquired the ability to distinguish the genuine from the imitation. Apparently this skill is readily and easily learned. Thus, we can fairly compare the competence of any "expert" who cannot distinguish ivory from bone, to that of a zoologist mistaking an elephant for a mouse with a glandular problem! (The previous simile courtesy of North Carolina country lawyer and Senator, Sam Ervin.)

Godfrey's blunder was so immense it approached Biblical proportion. If we could convince the jury of his error, Godfrey would be stripped of all credibility, would be left holding his bare buns, and the government's case would be destroyed. How often it is that an apparent disaster provides us with the seeds of opportunity. We weren't ready quite yet to start figuring how to seize upon this good fortune; we were still appreciating an irony just too perfect and majestic to leave at the moment. We eventually descended from this sublime plane and took to thinking. The first step was verifying from the source that the boat was bone.

Manny suggested we send his son's Hong Kong agent to Le Extreme Orient to speak with the manager. Within a couple of days we received word the boat was indeed fashioned from bone, ox bone to be exact. The store manager told the agent: this large model boat was offered for sale at the shop during the month we were in Hong Kong; it was the only large boat they had for sale at that time; it was not sold and currently was warehoused; and at no time during the period in question did they have an ivory boat displayed or offered for sale at their store. I suggested the agent try to get a written statement from the store owner confirming this information and also have the owner place on the statement a picture of the boat with a list of its dimensions. Within a week or so we received the store manager's written statement with photo. Perhaps our agent got the goods by dangling a fictitious customer in front of the dealer. At least from the match in size and price, this appeared to be Godfrey's boat—step one complete.

Now that Manny's opinion was proven correct, we next had to determine how to use this information. The manager's statement itself was inadmissible hearsay. "Hearsay" is an out-of-court statement made by a witness not testifying at trial. Such a statement is not admissible at trial because it is unsworn and the other party does not have the opportunity to cross-examine its maker. Discovery was over, and it was too late to go back to Hong Kong to take the manager's deposition.

Even if we could get the manager's statement in evidence or depose him, that would tip our hand to the government before trial. We didn't want to give our opponents any room to hedge. I could imagine Godfrey squirming out by saying something like, "I saw the boat from afar, didn't have an opportunity to inspect it, and unfortunately relied on a salesclerk's erroneous opinion as to its composition." Or perhaps, "I'm sorry, I didn't see this boat at Le Extreme Orient, it was displayed at the shop next door." I wanted *our* torpedo to strike our adversaries' blind side and sink their ship before they realized what had hit them.

One way to get around the hearsay rule was through expert testimony. An expert, in the course of explaining his opinion, can relate information received from others as long as the data are of the type reasonably relied upon by experts in his field. For instance, Godfrey is permitted to say in court he saw an ivory boat in a New York shop and the owner told him the price was $9,000. Although the owner won't testify at trial, his unsworn out-of-court statement is admissible because quotes from dealers are reasonably relied upon by experts valuing artwork. If the expert is relying on some written information for his opinion, he can read it in court, but the actual document cannot be submitted into evidence.

This was absolutely perfect. After Godfrey testified, I would recall my experts for rebuttal and ask if Godfrey's boat selling in Hong Kong for $30,000 alters their opinion of the value of Manny's boat. They of course would say no, and upon my prompting to explain why, would drop the bombshell exposing the substandard pedigree of Godfrey's vessel. And how did they know Godfrey made a boner? Here would come the statement from Le Extreme Orient. And best yet, because our experts are reading from a document *that will not be offered into evidence as an exhibit,* I wouldn't have to disclose the existence of this document to the government beforehand. We lawyers endlessly explain to our clients that the legal system doesn't work as depicted in *Perry Mason* and progeny. Despite our protestations that there are no surprise endings in the world of real trials, here was a denouement worthy even of Perry!

While my plan of secrecy and surprise fell within the letter of the rules, was I subverting the spirit and purpose meant to underlie discovery? After all, one reason for airing the strengths and weaknesses of opposing cases is to lead the parties to realistic settlements. I actually toyed with the idea of giving up the goods with the hope this might soften the government's intractable position. My clients rightly terminated this brief speculation by reminding me of

David's reaction to our prior settlement overture. A couple of months before, we had offered to pay one-third of the penalties assessed and readjust taxes based upon a one-third reduction of our values on the disputed items. This would result in a refund of approximately $300,000. But payment wasn't even demanded in this offer. We proposed that the statute of limitations issues be left for court resolution, so if the judge eventually ruled against us, the government coffers would stay shut.

This seemed to be, from the best objectivity we could muster, a pretty reasonable proposal. David certainly didn't think so. A few weeks after submitting the offer, I asked him about it during a chance sidewalk encounter near the federal courthouse in Tampa. At a distance from my face more compatible with Latin sensibilities of personal space, David derisively proclaimed that Manny and Mary had given "garbage" to the museum and assured me I was going to lose the case. We obviously were not shocked upon later receiving the government's formal rejection, nor were we surprised by the absence of a counteroffer. With settlement possibilities nil, we saw no reason to call off the ambush. I looked for any possible loophole, any way out of the steel trap I was perfecting. As I probed my snare from each angle looking for weakness, any loose parts were firmly tightened. How did the experts know that the store manager actually prepared the written statement? How did they know it's not a forgery? I had our experts call the manager for first-hand confirmation of the statement's authenticity.

What if the government claims the boat pictured on the statement is not the same boat depicted in Godfrey's photo placed in evidence? This problem was a little trickier. Since our dealer's statement was not a trial exhibit, the jury wouldn't be able to see the photo on it. Determining if both pictures depict the same boat pits word against word. Although the jury would hear from the manager's statement that only one large model boat sat in the store at the time, the jury's inability to see our photo might leave enough of an opening to create some doubt. If I could get our photo into evidence, the jury could see for themselves—but how?

I must confess I enjoyed the machinations. Here cleverness was a virtue and deviousness, within the rules, an asset. I liked watching my mind work. At times I experienced such delight in crafting strategies, I actually forgot that our case would probably be tossed out before trial on a misaddressed envelope. But that was tomorrow, and there was no reason not to have some fun today.

I discarded any plan to get the photo in evidence as part of the manager's statement. Even if I could admit it, giving up our surprise was too high a price. I got a duplicate of the statement picture and decided to introduce it as a separate exhibit that the government would get to see before trial. I had two hurdles to overcome. First, assuming David compared our picture with his and saw a match, it probably would arouse his suspicion and might expose our secret. Second, the time for listing and exchanging trial exhibits was past, and court approval would be required to add new exhibits.

To circumvent the first hurdle, I utilized a variation of the avalanche discovery technique. Our photo would be much less conspicuous among a bevy of similar pictures. I told Manny to have his agent get photographs of comparable bone boats for sale and ship them to us pronto. Our fleet-footed operative did his job and quickly provided us with the camouflage we requested. I didn't think David had exhibited enough attention to detail to detect our incendiary sailing amidst a flotilla of blanks. Nor did I think David believed it possible for him to lose this case!

Next came the court. We requested that the judge permit at trial our new evidence which, in fairness, was impossible to garner prior to the deadline for exhibit exchange. Godfrey's deposition first raised the subject of model boats selling in today's Hong Kong market. But his deposition, due to delays by the government, didn't take place prior to the cut-off date for discovery or exhibit exchange. So how could we timely find and exchange evidence to rebut a position we didn't know about? We attached copies of seven photos to our motion, and when asked, said they were, like Godfrey's boats, also examples of models currently selling in Hong Kong. Of course I did not represent to David or the court what these boats were made of, and while both likely made the erroneous assumption I was talking about ivory boats, everything I had represented was completely true.

With our photo in evidence, our experts could then make the identification: "This is a photograph of the same boat depicted in the picture taken by Mr. Godfrey and is also identical to the photograph on the statement we have received from the manager of Le Extreme Orient." Slam—dunk—case closed! I surely enjoyed visualizing this outcome. But I faced one final task. We had not yet seen Godfrey's photo of the boat. The laws of logic demanded that the model he saw at the gallery be the same one presented to us on the store manager's statement. Could some bizarre quirk of fortune here suspend the science of reason? Might Godfrey's photo have been taken from an odd angle, making it difficult to match to ours?

The acid test quickly came as the government finally had its exhibits ready for my review. I drove to Tampa to enter the insular world of the United States Attorney's office. David used this outpost of the Attorney General when litigating in our neck of the woods. Sealed doors, one-way glass, accompaniment to the rest-room—all the security you might expect when institutions of government become the target of domestic distemper. As best I could tell, the harsher public sentiments seemed to have cast no effect on the occupants of this office.

Jovial greetings and some repartee bounced between David and his occasional colleagues as he ushered me through the hallways to his temporary lodging. I felt a bit on display. Our case apparently had generated enough notoriety here to make people wonder what indeed that outrageous and scurrilous plaintiff's attorney looked like. David slowed his procession just enough to make me believe he intended to give his compadres a little more time to satisfy their curiosity. We eventually reached an undecorated cubicle filled with papers and boxes and, on a small desk, what appeared to be the government's trial exhibits. The latter might have attracted my attention had it not been for the large foamboards leaning against the walls, two of which backed massive photo blowups of oriental carved boats!

David left me to it after pointing out what was mine to look at and what was not. I kept my photo securely tucked down the inside pocket of my suit jacket, and feeling like some secret agent, waited for the right opportunity to pull it out. The room door was open, so I took to examining exhibits while carefully monitoring the flow of hall traffic past the portal. With only one or two walkbys in ten-or-so minutes, neither peering in, it seemed safe to commence my undercover assignment. With one last glance out the doorway, and with an ear attuned to oncoming footsteps, I drew out the photo.

David's two enlargements were not of the same boat. One *had* to match ours. The first took only a few seconds of comparison before testing negative. The second of Godfrey's Hong Kong rigs needed more examination. The boat was pictured from a different angle than ours. The number of masts, the decks, the distinctive dragon carved prow—*yes!* It took a little looking but this was it, no doubt about it. In my excitement I temporarily forgot how exposed my mission was at the moment. With my darting eye finding the doorway clear, I returned my photo to its hiding place and resumed my cover. Mr. Phelps of *Mission Impossible* would be proud!

Debriefing soon followed, though to my disappointment, over normal telephone lines rather than by self-incinerating tape. Manny was anxiously awaiting the results of my assignment, and I delivered the news upon returning to my office. I brought other good tidings as well. Upon examining the auction catalogues Godfrey mentioned at deposition, I confirmed another of Manny's suspicions. Of the numerous incense burners Godfrey selected to compare with ours, only one was genuine Chi'en-Lung. The rest were not definitively of that reign.

The fine print at the beginning of the catalogues revealed that when the date or reign of an item appears in bold print above its description, the auction house represents the dating to be correct. However, references to date or reign appearing within the description signifies a piece *resembling* those of the period, meaning the piece is believed by the auctioneer to be a reproduction or of uncertain date. Did Godfrey really expect that no one would notice he was trying to pass off reproductions as comparables to our antique? Or was this just ineptitude or sloppiness? And what about the table screen? I didn't see anything in the catalogues resembling our disc. Lord, would I love to get this case to trial!

# CHAPTER TWENTY

# *Bringing to Court a Show-Worthy Production*

C OURT WAS OUR DESTINATION, and we were on the express train. Whether we would get in the door upon arrival remained to be seen. We needed to prepare as if we were going on stage, and the few remaining weeks seemed too little time to get this production show-worthy. I felt like the director of a new Broadway offering. Unfortunately, I was also the set designer, costume maker, stagehand, lighting director, makeup artist, writer, production manager, talent agent, and let's not leave out my stint as a principal actor. In my spare time I was still grinding out discovery issues with David, though the end to this was in sight.

The government had requested the court to prevent our experts from testifying, and if that didn't work, wanted permission to take their depositions. David directed his primary argument at our lead expert on ivory, Robert Perlman. Now white-haired and distinguished-looking, Bob in the mid-1980s had owned and operated a modest business importing "Orientalia," as he liked to call it. Ivory carvings constituted his primary ware, many of which he purchased from the Nathan Ivory Factory. He sold from a retail shop in our part of Florida, a serendipitous location that first alerted my clients to this colleague in the trade. Bob prepared an extensive and formal appraisal of the ivory boat and declared a value of $343,000. David claimed this report was not timely furnished.

197

Experts must be identified and the substance of their opinions disclosed within a set date prior to trial. I had done so for Perleman by serving the government with a short statement of his expected testimony. After the time for disclosing experts had expired, David was alerted to the existence of Perlman's appraisal report by its inclusion on my exhibit list. He promptly called me and demanded a copy of Perleman's full appraisal. He asserted that the court's order requiring disclosure of experts mandated delivery of the report, and also insinuated I was deliberately disobeying the court's directive.

I didn't have the court's scheduling order in front of me, but told David I believed we had sufficiently complied. As I recalled, delivery of actual appraisal reports wasn't required under that order. I added that if I were wrong, I would immediately send him the appraisal, which in any event, he would later receive upon exchange of trial exhibits. David, at his aggressive best, read me the pertinent provision of the court's scheduling order, which sounded like disclosure of the report was intended. "Are you going to send me the report *now?*" he continued to push. I finally relented, and he demanded it be faxed to him that morning.

An hour or so after the appraisal was transmitted, I felt an urge to reread the court's order for myself, so I went into the file. I was shocked to find that my opponent omitted a key phrase that supported my interpretation of the provision. Had I been deliberately deceived? My God, couldn't I trust David to read a simple paragraph? Did he have the gall to pull a trick like this knowing that I would probably find him out? I stewed a bit, wondering what, if anything, I might do. The last thing in the world I wanted at the moment was another phone conversation with David.

It was a hard call to make, but sometimes you just can't let things pass unmentioned. I'm sure David knew why I was buzzing and at least give him credit for taking the call. I restated factually what had transpired between us earlier that morning and told him what I had just discovered. I asked him if he disputed any of these facts, and he said he did not. I said it appeared to me that he purposely misquoted the text to get me to send the report, and told him that unless he had some other explanation I would conclude my assumption was correct. The line crackled with silence. After a pause sufficient to confirm he had nothing to offer, I had my say. I let him know that in my years of practice I had never come across such dishonesty in dealing with an attorney. I told him he was fortunate to be in government work, because in the private sector, with his word known to be unreliable, he would find practicing among other lawyers awfully difficult. With that I asked him if there was anything he wanted to say, and upon his indication he had nothing to add, I hung up.

How are your bladder and legal ethics connected? When the latter is compromised, the former suffers. During a temporary break at a lengthy deposition or court hearing, often you and the opposing attorney are the only ones remaining after other participants have dashed from the room. Can you trust your adversary not to rifle through your file and materials should you depart for nature's needed call? When taking your stuff with you isn't practical, urinary comfort may hinge upon your estimation of another lawyer's integrity. Truly sad to say with David, during our joint appearances I was now forced to carefully monitor my fluid intake, and on occasion, grin and bear it.

Relief of another sort arrived when the court soundly rejected the government's attempt to choke off our witnesses. The judge found that our short statement of Perlman's expected testimony "meets the requirement of the Court's Scheduling Order." I found this particularly pleasing. David's back-up request for depositions was also rejected. The court declared that "defendant has failed to adequately explain why it did not move to depose these experts prior to the discovery cut-off date." I couldn't figure out why David never timely sought to depose our experts. Perhaps his overconfidence contributed to this serious tactical omission.

Time before trial was quickly ticking away, and I did my best not to commit any of my own sins of omission. I was spread thin and becoming worn attending to the innumerable details demanding my energy and attention. The uncertainty of our trial date added to the pressure. Twelve cases landed on the trial calendar for July. We were number nine on the list, which meant the cases preceding ours would first get called for trial. Sometimes many of these cases are settled or postponed, which vaults your trial to the beginning of the month. Other times the cases in front take longer to try than expected, and your turn doesn't come until the end of the month, if at all on that go-round.

Of course trial calendar vagaries provide no excuse for not being ready to go on a moment's notice. By necessity, then, you are constantly calling the court and the lawyers ahead of you on line in order to monitor the progress of the trial calendar—and at the same time fielding the steady inquiries of the attorneys behind you. All your witnesses must remain in a constant state of readiness. This proves particularly difficult for out-of-state experts, one of whom we employed, who are forced to juggle travel schedules and other commitments. It also proves expensive for clients paying to keep their experts on call.

Our office now became a communications center, issuing updated bulletins to our various cast members. As we waited for the signal, the pressure continued to mount, and my life felt suspended in time. I found myself increasingly off center. Feelings of futility returned, and my dreams took a downward turn. The theme of being trapped in a room or elevator with a descending ceiling obviously did not indicate a relaxed attitude.

My condition didn't mellow when, one morning toward the end of the month, word came down we were next up. The case currently being fought had two or three days to go, and then we were in. We made our calls, summoned our New York expert, and started to gear into our final state of readiness. I stayed so engaged that afternoon, I sat at my desk for at least three hours without budging. I took passing note of this sedentariness when I finally intended to get up to execute some task. To my shock, my intention to arise was not followed by any movement. I was unable to stand!

While our physical motion is preceded by direction of our willful mind, this connection is usually so automatic, we don't notice it. We intend to move, and naturally we move. But I still found myself seated despite *really* trying again to stand. I used my arms to push my rolling chair away from the desk. I looked at my legs. Focusing on the right, I commanded it to move, and it readily complied. The same test on the left produced neither sensation nor result.

As I wrapped my hands around the back of my left thigh and started to pull my leg up, an intense burning in the calf and ankle commanded me to immediately desist. I lifted my pants leg and to my horror beheld the outside of my ankle and calf swollen to the size of half a football cut lengthwise. The slightest touch below the knee was excruciating, as if a burning venom radiated and pulsated through my tissue. I paid the price to pull down the top of my sock and noticed a slight red mark above my anklebone. I remembered. The day before I thought I had been bitten by an insect. I had felt a prick around my ankle, scratched it a couple of times, and that's the last I had thought of it. I had never experienced any adverse reaction to an insect bite. Was this some sort of delayed response to a black widow or perhaps a tiny scorpion? Would it get worse? *My God*—what about the trial?

If someone had asked me what could displace *Fellouzis vs. United States of America* from the immediate focus of my attention, this was probably the last thing I would conjure. As I made my way to the local emergency room, with my father's shoulder serving as temporary crutch, the pain didn't leave me much room to dwell on the case. Even without placing weight on my afflicted leg, the joggle from my hopping was enough to strike grimaces. After two hours of emergency-room wait, I got a dose of Benadryl and the doctor's reasoned opinion that perhaps an insect bit me. I received the sound advice to keep off my feet and was told my disability would span a few days. I had two days before court. Would they have to wheel me in? After another hour or so to get some crutches and non-prescription pain reliever, I was finally delivered home and placed in bed.

Night slowly enveloped me as I lay flat on my back staring at the bedroom ceiling. The promise of light from a nearby lamp wasn't worth the extra pain of moving over a bit to turn it on. Nor was the allure of pain medication sufficient to get me out of bed for a dosage improvidently placed beyond reach. By now, just the passage of my breath and the micromovements of my body seemed enough to flare the constant burning. With my misery compounded by thinking and worrying about the case, I finally asked myself the question: "Why did this happen? What is this really about for me?"

I decided to meditate on the pain and did so for at least two hours. Using my sensation as a gateway, as I have previously described, I was able at times to transcend my body and experience that state of perfect equanimity and profound serenity. Like some-one who is parched, I found great joy as my thirst was relieved by the living water of Spirit.

As I came out of my meditation, I noticed the level of pain had measurably subsided. Still in a restful state, I clearly understood why this entire experience had occurred. I had temporarily become so out of touch with my spiritual self, I had moved so far off center into worry and mental preoccupation, something dramatic was needed to return my attention to God. And did I get it! Deep gratitude welled up and permeated me. I was truly grateful for the bite, my swelled leg, the pain—all of it. Thank you, Lord, for your grace and love and compassion. After all, what is it our heart truly yearns and prays for? It is not fame, power, fortune, the love of family and friends, or other external delights. Lord, I pray I may realize your presence. I pray that I never lose sight of your hand in all things. I pray that I always abide in the fragrance of your love. When this prayer is answered, through whatever mechanism, how can we not be grateful?

Here he goes again—trying to make something mystical out of his self-induced changes in brain chemistry! For skeptics, their latest trend seeks to relegate God to the functioning and experience of our more exotic biology. There seems to be little doubt that our states of pleasure, pain, calmness, agitation, ecstasy, and bliss correlate with the presence, absence, or varying degree of certain identifiable chemicals in our body. While the nature of these substances—what they are and how they work—is not fully under-stood, enough is known about them to engender their varied usage. Pain medications and mood-altering drugs of remarkable efficacy are obviously well-known and frequently prescribed. Psychotropics have been used in religious ceremony throughout human history as

a gateway to transcendent states. The connection between meditation and the production of certain brain chemicals and hormones
has been researched and documented.

Is my meditative transcendence of pain and my experience of
bliss simply the result of endorphin secretion? Is my meditation
just a skill I developed that allows me to willfully trigger these
natural opiates? As we now know, a profoundly enhanced sense of
well-being can routinely be produced by artificially increasing
seratonin levels. Perhaps the new organismic explanation of God is
an idea whose time has come—but not come for me! My experience
leads me to believe transcendent spiritual states are not chemically
determinate. Here's my empirical contribution to a very complex
and technical subject.

During my meditations in which significant pain has been
transcended, I have noticed that shifts between bliss and excrucia-
tion are often frequent and instantaneous. Dealing with pain or
bodily "distraction" is a common dynamic in meditation. In most
traditional meditation practices, the body is to be kept perfectly
still. As anyone who has meditated in one position for a long time
knows, physical discomfort can become unbearable.

On one occasion I was deep into a lengthy meditation, sitting
cross-legged on the floor, when I started experiencing intense pain
in the mid-and upper back. I didn't follow the urge to slightly adjust
my body to alleviate the sensation. Once you start to move, I find
that the temporary relief quickly evaporates under the scorching
flame of greater discomfort. As the pain in my back intensified, it
became the object of my concentration. I found I could fall into
that place of transcendence by adopting a posture of "non-interference." This means dropping any effort to have the body function
differently. It also means *completely* letting go of any desire for
things to be other than as they are.

I felt as if I were sitting balanced upon the tip of an incredibly
sharp lance. While equipoised, all my bodily sensations were
present, yet I felt a great calmness, peace, and joy. There, I observed
myself as a continual process of unfolding experience. But with just
the slightest interference, with just the slightest intention to influence the pattern of my breath or change my body position, with just

a minuscule attraction to any thought of avoidance, I pressed onto the point of the lance. While my impalement was metaphoric, my agony was not—it returned me to the intense suffering of my back pain. And upon releasing my interference, I was again perfectly resting on the tip of the spear. This balance often felt precarious and seemed as improbable as a real body and lance finding a point of equilibrium. Yet on and off I went, moving from agony to bliss and back to agony again and again. This was a play of conscious-ness, not the script of brain peptides.

When the body releases endorphins in response to pain, whether or not their effect is immediate, the relief they provide from pain is an event that spans time. If secreted in amounts sufficient to turn pain to bliss, I venture to say these flooding opiates have some lag time before their effect wears off. So the end of their salutary influence would not precisely coincide with the brain's cessation of their production. Yet I could experience a supreme bliss in my meditation for just a fraction of a second before falling back onto agony.

If endorphins were released in sufficient quantity to transport me from intense physical pain to nirvana, I submit their effect would last longer than my abbreviated ecstasy. As I moved on and off balance, I became more proficient at remaining in equipoise, and at times could instantaneously move between agony and bliss by the play of my will. Even if we argued I could, by exercise of will, immediately turn on and off the endorphin faucet, the drug's effect in space and time would preclude it from being the causative agent of my instantaneous shifts.

The transcendent non-interference I talk of is a profound letting go into the flow of life. The benefit of the meditation is not to learn pain management or to reach an enlightened state. I could end my back pain at any time by simply getting up; and what good is enhanced consciousness if you have to be seated with your eyes closed to experience it? The simple value of this meditation is the revelation that suffering is caused by our resistance to life. The way meditation integrates this discovery into the rest of our life is of much greater value. When we consciously engage our interior selves in a way that releases us from our self-made oppositions, engrams of non-interference are created. As this new way of being deepens, it profoundly changes our everyday relationship with life. The more we practice, the more we find the letting go of meditation present in all we do. We begin to surf more on the waves of life and spend less time being pounded by the surf.

My relationship with life right now meant getting out of bed to the bathroom so I could return for the night. While my pain had subsided a measure, I still had difficulty moving about. To give myself a shot at some uninterrupted sleep, I decided before bedding down again to take the Advil I had purchased. The morning brought some more relief, and although I still had only one weight-bearing leg, I made it to the office on crutches by early afternoon. I felt very happy, very centered, and very grateful to be—well — grounded! I seemed to have lost all fear, worry, or anxiety about the trial or anything else. When my leg acted up or inadvertent movement brought pain, I chuckled at the absolute absurdity of it all. I sat at my desk and felt like a general in a buzzing war room. My secretary, partner, and clients immediately followed my edicts as I, the supreme commander, directed our campaign. The next day brought me to the office sporting a cane, and I had the same fun directing the troops in preparation for the morrow's battle.

Tall majestic columns, a broad-staired entranceway, granite, marble, dark wood panels, mahogany moldings—while all routine for a turn of the century federal courthouse, its typicality made it no less grand or imposing. This working monument was no doubt meant to impress and remind locals of the authority and supremacy of the national government. Fortunately I was permitted to enter through the street level service elevator, which excused me the task of hobbling up innumerable steps. Here I was, dressed to the nines and waddling with my cane like an inebriated duck. My legion carted in our boxes of materials, and we began to assemble outside our assigned court. I slowly moved down the corridor toward the courtroom door and recognized that this must be the first time I'd ever arrived at court without something of my profession in hand.

While enjoying my release from the burden of legal handiwork, I exhilarated in my freedom from fear and anxiety. I had done all that I could possibly do and had accomplished it to the best of my capabilities. Here came the final doing, and truly, at that moment I had no attachment to any result. I was excited over the impending completion of my work, but this feeling rested upon a deep peace and joy. Of course I preferred to win and would do my best to prevail, but that was the future, and I was fully absorbed in this present moment of action. Where else but the here and now can we possibly find our rapture?

As I approached the courtroom door, my entourage nervously monitored my progress and anxiously awaited my next set of directives. We located the bailiff to unlock this portal to justice, moved inside, and staked a claim to a counsel table. The first spectator bench behind us became the resting place for our boxes. The second row held our assemblage of witnesses. While we were unloading and arranging our paraphernalia, David entered with a partner.

I was introduced to Ann C. Reid, Trial Attorney with the United States Department of Justice. Ann had lately assisted David in drafting the voluminous motions, briefs, and other papers filed by the government and now was here to help press its case in court. He who would wear the mantle of the federal judiciary this day was the Honorable Ralph W. Nimmons, Jr., lifetime appointee and United States District Judge. With everything in place we all awaited the entrance of our imperial jurist. Upon the cry of the bailiff, the courtroom quickly rose to the incoming flow of robes— though I barely made it up by the time most resumed their seats, no disrespect intended.

The judge requested we identify ourselves and our clients. Immediately after this formality, my opponents sought permission to address the court. I had little doubt my adversaries were going to ask the judge to dismiss our case. The government's pre-trial brief carefully and persuasively asserted the court's lack of jurisdiction due to Plaintiffs' failure to comply with the statute of limitations. Ann expounded the government's view, suggesting the court would be beyond its authority to do anything other than discard our claims. I eventually rose to defend our position, elucidating arcane areas of tax procedure, talking of addresses on envelopes, and appealing to the judge's sense of fairness. After all, if the law weren't an ass here and common sense reigned, our claims should be heard.

Judge Nimmons was not pleased. What happened next totally surprised us. Our pre-trial briefs, which were not "brief" at all, well explained the statute of limitations issues. The court by virtue of its own order had received our briefs a number of days ago, and we all expected either a thumbs-up or-down from the bench this morning. The judge issued some sharp words about the length of our briefs, especially mine. Aha, so that's it! Judge Nimmons hadn't gotten to the briefs in enough time to fully read them, or if he did manage to read them, he had lacked sufficient time to analyze and determine highly complex issues. So the judge gave both of us the boot. We were taken off the trial calendar, ordered to resubmit the issue to the court through another procedural format—which meant more briefs and papers—and were sent on our way. At least we hadn't lost—and now I could stay off my feet for the next few days.

Manny and Mary did not share my cheery mood. They looked devastated. It had taken them ten years to finally get inside the courthouse door, and here they were, ushered out an hour or two later. The weight and burden of their case, which they had withstood so well during last few months as we prepared for this day, now came crashing in upon them. The expense also was no trivial concern. They had two experts sitting behind them, both with meters ticking for days now. As for our opposition, they didn't score an outright victory, but did win a delay. Postponement here worked in the government's favor. Who knows, by the time this case got to trial, if ever, my clients might be dead and buried.

We submitted our new motions and briefs by September and waited, and waited—and waited. As the months passed without word, I explained to Manny that courts often take a long time to rule on complex cases such as this. As we moved through winter to spring, and spring to summer, however, I had no explanation for a delay of this length.

The time had arrived to nudge but not shove the court. I have been before more than one judge who, when pressed to make a decision, took the gambit and summarily ruled against the demanding party. We could file a motion with the court requesting a ruling, or perhaps notify the Chief District Judge of the delay. Neither prospect boded well. We opted for a letter to the judge politely reminding him this case still existed. We also pointed out by doctor's statement that Manny's heart condition was not being helped by the stress of delay. We of course did not expect a direct response to our respectful poke. What we did get was the judge's form letter refusing acceptance of correspondence from counsel or litigants. Despite its return I sensed that the judge read our letter. I also felt it served its purpose, and at the same time engendered a little sympathy for Manny.

With this we waited and still waited some more. Fourteen months had gone by, and even our letter had aged four months. While I knew the judge's pride of office would deter him from ruling too soon after our letter, I was surprised we had not as yet received our decision. When last we convened, my son was departing the second grade and now was in the fourth. In the interim: my ex-wife had remarried; I had left my home and moved in with Constance, my new love; business picked up a piece; Constance sold her digs and together we both bought a home close to, but not on the water; and the Republican "revolution" had just swept through Congress. I had done reasonably well moving on with my life while *Fellouzis vs. United States of America* was reconfiguring itself into long-term memory.

Although it was more and more absent from my mind, I nevertheless maintained a psychic connection with the case. While it was not a physical organism, the case definitely maintained its own energy as an entity formed by the thoughts, hopes, aspirations, experiences, and energies of those connected with it—and now was independent of its creators.

My predominant psychic sense of the case was tenuousness. At times my feeling would translate itself into image. Once I saw an immense battleship suspended in the air by a thread. That this strand could hold something so massive seemed incredible. Yet the bulk that was this ship—the work, effort, witnesses, investments, strategies, theories, research, writing, depositions, emperors, artwork, museums, the ivory, jade, Hong Kong, Philadelphia, Virginia, the characters, dramas, battles, victories, and tribulations—

still miraculously was attached to this slim fiber. Periodically as I touched the case, although I felt it tottering on the edge of the precipice, I knew it was still alive. *Thy will be done, not mine.* I had long before released myself from the outcome of this play with the surprise ending. Would my perfectly crafted finale explode with astonishment on the stage, or would my brilliant script of legal triumph die stillborn in dust and silence?

You'll have to wait (as I did) to find out! We now return to Mrs. Browning's story and conclude the battle for the right-to-die.

CHAPTER TWENTY-ONE

# Crusading for the Right-to-Die

P ATIENCE AND PERSEVERANCE. While the multi-decade disputes of Dickens's *Bleak House* are now the law's rare exception, success in litigation still takes staying power. The incredulity of TV's in-on-Monday-out-by-Friday fantasy version of courtroom justice makes most lawyers groan. In the real world I was seated at counsel's table awaiting the entrance of the justices of Florida's Second District Court of Appeal. Here to argue the fate of Mrs. Browning, I was full of perseverance but waning in patience. Almost six months had transpired since the local probate judge denied our request to terminate her tube feeding. While my client had become a *cause celebre* and this case the spearhead of a social movement, for me each day seemed to tick by with the unrelenting drip, drip, drip of that artificial cord.

Our nondescript courtroom aptly expressed this intermediate appellate court's near invisibility as an agency of government. Most Floridians probably have never heard of the Second District Court of Appeal, have no idea what it is, what it does, who runs it, or where it presides. And if the average person were provided this wonderful information, they wouldn't much care. For a litigant in west central Florida, however, this institution could assume monumental importance. Since the Florida Supreme Court accepted only a small percentage of cases for review, the intermediate

210

appellate court was usually your tribunal of last resort. So if your trial judge committed some grievous error in your case, and perhaps you lost your money or your kids or your liberty, this governmental phantom, for you at least, would become very real.

The Tampa branch of the Second District occupied an upper floor in a downtown municipal building. The small courtroom had a slightly elevated platform to seat the three-judge panel selected to hear the case. In front of the justices sat a government-issue table for the clerk and two additional bureaucratic slabs for counsel. No flourishes or fanfare here; just a place to do the public's business. Behind counsel was a limited spectators' area obviously intended for a small group. The only people likely to observe proceedings were the handful of lawyers waiting for the next case and perhaps a dispute participant or two.

Today was different. Television cameras, reporters, representatives of interest groups, and miscellaneous citizens were stuffed into the room, creating a buzz in the air. After the trial court's decision, we had contacted the *St. Petersburg Times,* a fairly well-respected paper with Tampa Bay's widest circulation, suggesting this was a story that would generate great public interest. Two months later, in November 1988, the *Times* followed with a front-page article in a Sunday section titled, "When Living Wills fail."

Juxtaposed were photos of Mrs. Browning, one pre-stroke showing a well-dressed and poised elderly woman, the other depicting a fetal-curled, rigid, intubated body in a nursing home bed. On top of the pictures hung my quotation: "If she is conscious, this is probably her worst nightmare." The article recited Mrs. Browning's painstaking efforts to avoid the fate that would later befall her. She had executed a living will specifically refusing artificial feeding and frequently reiterated to friends her intent to forego artificial life support devices. Her neighbors witnessing the living will quoted Mrs. Browning as saying with relief upon her signature, "Well, thank God I've got this taken care of. I can go in peace when my time comes."

The article generated a firestorm. Letter after letter to the editor decried what was perceived as a violation of Mrs. Browning's most fundamental rights. The public was not impressed with the justification the trial judge offered for his decision. He claimed Mrs. Browning was not "terminal" and perhaps, unbeknownst to anyone, might have changed her mind about tube feeding. But how could the patient have exercised any judgment regarding her treatment? The article quoted Mrs. Browning's family doctor, designated in the living will as her decision-maker, and also recited comments from the expert neurologist we had hired. The first reported extensive and permanent brain damage, and the second claimed Mrs. Browning could not meaningfully interact with her environment. Both agreed the feeding tube should be removed.

Criticism of the nursing home was even more intense. Its administrators and personnel insisted their resident chatted away, even though frequent visits from family, friends, and our doctors always found Mrs. Browning unresponsive. According to the neurologist, the nursing home staff was "hostile" during his examination of Mrs. Browning and reported implausible "progress" in her condition after his entry in her record. Being generous to the nursing home, the neurologist raised the possibility of "projective kinetic mutism," a phenomenon where automatic reflexes are misinterpreted as intentional acts. The public was not so forgiving. Prevailing opinion asserted the nursing home was venally sucking the patient's estate dry and would have no use for Mrs. Browning once her money was exhausted.

The intensity and breadth of public sentiment was not surprising given Florida demographics. This issue obviously was acutely important to the elderly. More than death, many feared loss of control over the management of their own lives. The prospect of having their wishes ignored and being subjected to unwanted medical treatments and interventions was, for many, a real and present possibility. Throughout the course of the case I received numerous letters and calls of support from strangers, most of whom were senior citizens. Some recounted "horror" stories like that of Mrs. Browning; others offered their prayers for my success in the case, and one or two advised me they would move from the state unless the "right-to-die" was won.

This constituency easily found political support. Advocates of the elderly and national right-to-die organizations joined with elected representatives in an effort to change Florida's living will law. This legislation, which would permit withdrawal and refusal of feeding tubes, was opposed by the Florida Catholic Conference, numerous "fundamental" religious groups, and "conservative" think tanks. Although these constituencies could only garner a minority of legislative support, their adherents chaired key committees and were able to box up the proposed change in the law. Even if the amendment got through the legislature, odds were, Florida Republican Governor Bob Martinez would exercise his veto power.

To proponents of mandatory tube feeding, starving to death mentally incompetent patients was the same as murder, and a cogent patient's choice to stop artificial feeding was suicide. (Actually, when sustenance is withdrawn, death is caused by dehydration, or body failure due to electrolyte imbalance.) Florida's executive branch of government apparently adopted this position through a 1986 administrative regulation mandating artificial sustenance of all nursing home patients unable to self-feed. In response to public outcry against forced feeding, the Florida Department of Health and Rehabilitative Services (H.R.S.) announced in the autumn of 1988 it would revise its previous decree. Right-to-die advocates initially hoped the administration would respond to the prevailing public sentiment. That hope was short-lived.

The new rule provided for removal of feeding tubes when the "patient is on the brink of death, death will be due to disease rather than starvation, *and* forced feeding would cause harm or be ineffective." According to H.R.S., to otherwise permit termination of tube feeding "would be sanctioning suicide." Obviously, if the patient's disease is immediately going to cause his death, nature will take its course without the necessity of removing the feeding tube. H.R.S. critics, including myself, quickly exposed the new rule as nothing more than a restatement of existing policy and a public relations ploy. With the executive and legislative branches of government closed to change, right-to-die advocates were left with the judiciary.

And here we were! While we continued to await the justices, I deflected a few butterflies by glancing at my opponent over the lectern separating our tables. I felt a slight twinge of guilt as I saw

Marie King, the Assistant State Attorney, still a bit flustered over the seating arrangements. I had pulled a little dirty trick, which I can reasonably claim was anomalous to my otherwise unsullied legal persona.

A couple of weeks before, I had found myself at a lunch counter next to an acquaintance who was a colleague of Marie's when he previously worked for the State Attorney. He asked me about the case, and I queried him about my opponent. He casually mentioned Marie was an adherent of astrology who closely followed her daily horoscope. I had arrived in court before Marie and normally would have selected the table to the right of the lectern. According to the custom of the tribunal, this position is taken by the appellant, the party seeking to reverse the lower court's decision. With a spontaneously mischievous impulse I placed my materials on the left table, staking my claim to this territory. When my opponent shortly followed into the room, she naturally headed towards my side until I intercepted her with, "Marie, my horoscope says staying on the left is advantageous today, so I took this table!" I knew I was bad—but my dab of guilt wasn't enough to disrupt the enjoyment I felt tweaking Marie and gaining a minor psychological advantage.

Perhaps my rebellious nature or anti-establishment attitude got the best of me. More likely, though, it was Marie's heavy-handed prosecutorial demeanor during trial that provided the disincentive to resist my vexatious astrological impulse. As we rose in deference to the incoming procession of robes, rebellion was the last thing on my mind. I had overcome my early professional combativeness by eventually learning that the most effective way to sway a court was by advocating your position politely and with respect. This doesn't mean you can't be firm; it does mean you can never *argue* with the judge.

"If it please the court. . . ." With that, off I went into my oral argument. Each side is allowed twenty minutes to convince the court why the decision in question should be reversed or upheld. Each party has previously submitted extensive briefs (that's a legal oxymoron) to the appellate court, which we hope is now well aware of the facts and legal issues of the case through the written advocacy. Ninety percent of most appeals are decided on the basis of written submissions, and few cases will turn on oral argument. Yet this is a party's only opportunity to directly face the phantom court and one of the very few times skillful oration may just carry the day.

And this date had a particular significance, it was Mrs. Browning's birthday:

On March 14, this very day, in the year 1900, Estelle M. Browning was born. Who, witnessing the birth of Estelle Browning, so long ago, could possibly have foreseen that eighty-nine years later this newborn, now an elderly lady, could be kept alive through devices which supplant her lost bodily functions? And we, at this point in time, as we glimpse into the future, perhaps can barely conceive how science and technology will be able to perpetuate our physical existence long after the body's innate capacity to sustain itself has ceased.

This case, in its broader sense, is the field in which the conflict between human values and the value of technology takes place. The human value at stake here is liberty. The liberty to be let alone. The liberty to control one's fate. The liberty to control one's bodily integrity. The liberty of free will and self-determination, to make decisions concerning yourself and about yourself, so long as they do not harm others.

This argument held the stuff of every lawyer's dream. No arcane point of contract law being argued here. This case affected lives—not just Mrs. Browning's and those similarly situated, but all of our lives. Even if we never faced Mrs. Browning's particular predicament, this case would define our freedom by declaring to what degree and under what circumstances the State was permitted to intrude upon an intimate area of personal choice. But it was also important not to leave this case in the abstract. These three men had to be put on the hot seat—to look (at least in the mind's eye) upon Mrs. Browning's face before deciding her fate.

To better enable me to paint that picture for the court, or perhaps because *I* needed to take this case out the abstract, I had visited Mrs. Browning the evening before. Entering the nursing home felt, as usual, unpleasant. To the staff and administration I was *persona non grata,* and they took little effort to conceal their sentiment. I had not seen Mrs. Browning for a couple of months and found her condition no different from that of previous visits. Perhaps she did look more worn and a bit thinner.

As I always did, I looked into her eyes and shouted to her, hoping for some response or sign. After a minute or two I sat in the chair by the foot of her bed, closed my eyes, and started to meditate. Having "soulspoken" with Mrs. Browning when we first met, I decided, with a measure of earnest self-inflation, to purpose-fully initiate such contact. I settled into my breath and noticed all the passing sounds move through my consciousness. As I deepened my relaxation, I reached out with my awareness to see if I could touch her soul-presence. From deep inside I repeated, "Mrs. Browning, it's okay to leave your body. There is no reason to stay in this body. It is all right to die now." A few minutes into my meditative encouragement, I was jarred by a high-pitched sarcastic cackle and the words, "*You're* telling me to drop my body—and *you* can't even get out of your head." Apparently Mrs. Browning had a spirited sense of humor!

There wasn't much of an opening for levity before the court of appeal, so I stuck close to my solemnly persuasive delivery. Con-vincing appellate judges that they, in the seat of the trial court, would have decided the case differently will not win your case. An appeal is not a new trial. No new evidence is introduced. A reviewing court presumes the trial judge was correct in his decision, and may only upend the lower court if it misapplied the law or had no evidence to support its factual conclusions.

Facts that can be interpreted two ways provide no grounds for reversal. If the salient fact in an auto injury case is whether the light was red or green at the time of the accident, and one witness says it was red and three others saw it as green, an appellate court has no legal authority to overturn a trial judge's conclusion it was red. That is why appeals that challenge the factual findings of lower courts have a very slim chance of success.

So in addition to arguing the broader constitutional issues, I resolutely sought to cast the hard conclusion of the trial court as one of law rather than fact. The trial judge had concluded Mrs. Browning was not terminally ill because she may continue to exist with artificial sustenance for months or years, although removal of the feeding tube would result in her death within four to nine days. Since Mrs. Browning's living will predicated refusal of artificial feeding upon her suffering a terminal condition, denial of our petition was consistent with the judge's logic.

Whether or not Mrs. Browning was "terminal" was a *legal* conclusion reached upon undisputed facts. If a patient's medical condition is to be judged assuming artificial life support is in place, Mrs. Browning clearly was not terminal, given her extended life expectancy. With a life span of a few days absent such artificial support, however, it was undisputed that by this measure she was terminal. The trial court's determination presented an issue of *law* wide open for appellate consideration.

Mrs. Browning's underlying condition—the stroke leaving her unable to swallow and take in sustenance—made her terminally ill, I argued. The feeding tube artificially prolongs an otherwise imminent death and creates the exact situation Mrs. Browning intended to avoid. Adopting the trial judge's logic means an underlying disease or condition, no matter how severe or death-producing, would never be terminal so long as there was some medical technological intervention able to hold off death. Such an analysis raised the grim specter of diseased persons involuntarily wedded to sophisticated machines that stave off death, keeping people minimally alive until the natural aging process or some other factor ends life. Such a prospect is as undesirable as it is dehumanizing. "It should not and cannot be the position of this court..."—at least when I put it that way!

Being a crusader, especially for a client and a cause in which I deeply believed, was exhilarating, heady, humbling and fun. I still got a kick that evening seeing myself on the TV news, notwithstanding my frequently displayed countenance in the media of late. If this case were hot stuff now, it would soon intensify with the decision of the Second District. On April 10, 1989, the appellate court issued its opinion and the next few days were spent behind

TV cameras and on the phone with reporters, attorneys, and national interest groups. The case wasn't over by a long shot, and it looked as if we were heading for the Florida Supreme Court.

In a broad sense the decision delivered a smashing victory. The court declared that an incompetent patient such as Mrs. Browning had the right, under the privacy clause of the Florida Constitution, to terminate artificial feeding. The court also found that such a decision could be made for the patient by a guardian or close family member, outside of court and without judicial review. The need for promptness mandated an informal decision-making process, because as the court acknowledged, "The list of cases in which courts 'grant' a right of privacy only after the patient has expired, grows longer every day."

These lofty words were significantly tempered by the barriers the District Court required the guardian or family member to traverse prior to making a decision. The surrogate must have clear and convincing evidence of the patient's intent. This decision is to be that which the patient would have made, not the surrogate's or "the decision which a public referendum or a benign leader would reach." In addition to considering the patient's living will, the surrogate must also investigate the patient's oral statements, her religious beliefs, and evidence of her character and life style, all of which may be relevant to the decision she would have made.

Next, the surrogate had to obtain affidavits from three physicians describing: the patient's current medical condition, including the level of mental and physical functioning; the degree of pain now and in the future expected to experienced by the patient; the benefits, risks, invasiveness, painfulness, and side effects of the medical treatment that is to be withheld or withdrawn; the prognosis of the patient with and without medical assistance, including life expectancy, suffering, and the possibility of recovery; and whether it is medically ethical to withhold or withdraw the proposed treatment. Now that's a mouthful. Have you ever tried to get an affidavit from a physician? I have found doctors to be quite a risk-averse group and not prone to giving sworn written statements.

When you have completed your investigation of the patient's intent, received and considered the medical affidavits, you're finally ready to make your decision—aren't you? Not quite. The court then requires the surrogate to determine whether the patient's right to forego medical treatment is outweighed by the interests of the State. How's that again? How is the average family member supposed to make this Delphic determination? While the Second District may have taken these decisions out of the judicial arena, the court certainly kept lawyers in the game. I couldn't see how a surrogate could negotiate this minefield without legal assistance. Although I was disappointed the appellate court insisted on such an arduous procedure, my mood was easily displaced by the significant victory of removing the judiciary from the decision-making process.

A mood harder to buoy was my frustration over the court's application of its newly pronounced standards to the particular facts of Mrs. Browning's case. The judges refused to overturn the trial court's decision. Although neither faulting me nor the trial judge for failing to follow procedures not yet enunciated, the Second District told us to start over again consistent with its new guidelines. And our appeal court proved decidedly unhelpful by carefully skirting the question of whether Mrs. Browning was terminally ill per the provisions of her living will. I felt the appellate justices had copped-out, just as I felt the trial judge had punted in making his decision.

Neither court apparently had the courage to stamp its approval upon and sign their names to an order that would directly result in Mrs. Browning's death. I strongly believed we presented evidence at trial legally sufficient to prove our case, even by the more exacting standard now prescribed by the Second District. I acknowledge the issues in the case were multi-tiered and highly complex, and I do not minimize the difficulty encountered by these courts. Yet I am convinced that at their source, the decisions of the trial judge and the appellate justices were generated by fear.

# CHAPTER TWENTY-TWO

# *Collective Consciousness and the Fear of Death*

J UDGES DON'T STOP BEING INDIVIDUALS upon attaining the bench, and therefore may be subject to various apprehensions. For instance, they are not fully insulated from the political process and, especially the trial judge who is subject to direct electoral challenge, may be reluctant to offend a key constituency. The State Attorney exerted a powerful force in local judicial politics, and I was not pleased to see how chummy and deferential the trial judge acted toward my opponent. Of course each judge brought with him his own morals, religious beliefs, family history, and psychological shadows about death and dying. What repeatedly struck me in the course of this case, however, was not so much the influence of personal motivations on behavior but the effect of collective consciousness on individual thought and action.

On that deeper level, I sensed how some opposition expressed in this case by the legal participants and their social and political allies was unconsciously generated by societal fear of death. Sometimes I experienced my psychic sense visually. In the trial court, as the judge was forming his thoughts and preparing to speak or make some decision, I felt the transpiring events as surface manifestations of larger underlying forces. In a way, I could see the judge's individual consciousness as a thin membrane or film floating over vast currents, taking its shape from the upsurges and swells.

Sometimes I saw all of us as if we were in a small boat on a vast ocean, thinking we were deciding our course but being moved by forces beyond our comprehension.

This collective fear of death and dying was no small force. We had relegated death and the dying process to an unspoken-of closet. Doctors and hospitals became our new shamans and death was the enemy, the scourge to be fought at all cost. Losing your patient meant defeat. Death became sanitized and disjoined from human touch. When the patient died she was discreetly and silently removed until miraculously reappearing—reprocessed and embalmed—now fit for human eyes and appropriate societal exit.

This fear-based dehumanization of the death process impelled the modern Hospice movement. Appearing in the late 1960s and 1970s, Hospice was not formed just to facilitate dying at home. The movement was about retrieving death from the profane and returning it to the sacred. I learned this first hand upon becoming a Hospice patient volunteer after the conclusion of Mrs. Browning's case.

Such a volunteer visits the patient once or twice a week for an hour or two. Depending on the wishes of the patient and his condition, sometimes you converse, read to the patient, watch television together, hold his hand, or sit by the bedside in silence. The visit also serves the important purpose of giving the primary care giver, usually a spouse or other family member, a welcome chance to get out of the home for a spell.

My first gig as a volunteer sent me to the mobile home of an engineer in his mid-seventies suffering from congestive heart failure. He and his wife had retired to Florida from the Midwest about ten years before. I visited every Saturday morning, and the first few weeks found my bed-bound patient alert and conversant. He was gray-haired and very thin, but I could still easily see he had been lean and fit in his prime. It was also obvious he was afraid to die. His keen mind that had served him so well was insufficient to provide him respite, and he seemed unable to tap into his emotions, which were evident to everyone around him. We related intellectually, and he enjoyed having someone with whom to exercise his mental prowess. Probing his emotions fell outside my province.

One of the first things you learn as a volunteer is that your role is to facilitate the death of the patient, not the death you think is best for the patient or the death you envision for yourself. If a patient gives you an opening, even subtle clues, to explore other areas, fine. Otherwise you remain within the limits of the patient's invitation and comfort. My patient, by his behavior, clearly defined what he wanted from me, and that's what I provided. Within a few weeks his condition deteriorated, and I usually found him asleep or semi-conscious. He was agitated and often hand-clenched, as if desperately holding on to life. His psychological pain distressed his wife, and during much of these visits we sat together and talked about how she felt.

After about two months with the family, I appeared at their door at my usual time, but on this occasion found the wife waiting for me. "I—I think he might be dead. I'm not sure."

I wasn't quite prepared for this. The odds of your patient dying during your weekly visit were slim—and this my first assignment! "Well, why don't we go in together and see?" I reassuringly said after a measured breath.

We slowly walked together into the bedroom and stood by her husband's side. His body was tense and supinely arched, with head tilted back, mouth open, and eyes lifted towards the center of the forehead. We watched carefully, and after a bit were barely able to discern some very shallow intermittent breaths. Within a few minutes we clearly could tell that breathing had permanently stopped. I continued to hold his hand while she stroked his hair. We left the room a few minutes later and sat in silence. We returned shortly after and decided to say some prayers. The body, even though it had ceased to function, seemed to subtly glow with the presence of his Spirit. After prayers we left the room again, and she called family members and notified the Hospice nurse.

In my Hospice training, I learned that the grief process was lessened in length and severity when survivors had the opportunity to be with their loved one's body immediately after death. I was therefore instructed to encourage family members to remain with the deceased and have physical contact, such as cleaning and dressing the body, before calling the mortuary. We continued going in and out of the room until the nurse arrived about thirty minutes later. The three of us then washed, groomed, and dressed her husband with care. At that, when she was ready, she called the funeral home, which took about an hour to come and remove the body.

We experienced a sacred process. Each time we returned to the room, I noticed a slight difference. I saw the body transform as I sensed his Spirit slowly exiting, first from the extremities into the center then out through the mouth. Where spirit remained the body seemed luminescent; where it had left was just dead flesh. Both of us felt him leave, a process that took about an hour after his physical death. During this time we naturally and spontaneously treated the body with reverence, as if it were a temple. What the funeral director wheeled out a couple of hours later seemed like refuse—wasted remains to be plowed under as fertilizer.

The force that created today's Hospice also propels the right-to-die movement. We sense that keeping one alive against his wishes—artificially perpetuating the body once the spirit is ready to depart—is a defilement of life's final rite of passage. It appeared so obvious to me that the ability to die with dignity, as that term is defined by each individual, is an essential personal right.

At first I couldn't quite fathom why the opposition in the case and in segments of society was so intense. Critics publicly vilified Mrs. Herbert, and we received no small amount of hate mail, some of it threatening. I understood the political, economic, and moral interests driving some of the opponents, but those concerns just didn't explain the intense reactions displayed. This case did not really make sense until I began to tap into the collective fear of death.

For those of you disbelievers, tread with me a while and I'll do my best to argue that "collective consciousness" is more than just some science fiction writer's fancy. As a starting point, we all recognize we are influenced by the people around us. We find uplifting our contact with some people, and with others we feel brought down. We also recognize that groupings of individuals can have a predominant feel or character. Thus we find that some neighborhoods or communities are enhancing and others definitely are not. We discover this not only from physical surroundings, but also sense it from the consciousness of the people creating their environment. As we expand our focus, we recognize that national groups have different characteristics, and depending upon our proclivities, we feel more "at home" with one than another.

We often recognize how individuals and small groups affect us, but how are we influenced by larger masses of people? Since our minds and bodies are part of vibratory creation, we tend to vibrate at the prevailing frequencies we encounter. We intuitively know this law of synchronicity to be true. No matter how awake and refreshed you feel, if you walk into a room of a hundred sleeping people, in a short time you will start to experience drowsiness. If you keep the company of thieves, it's not too long before you have larceny on your mind. More objectively, research has shown that when a group of women start living together in close confines, their disparate menstrual cycles eventually fall into one common rhythm. If a number of clocks ticking out of phase with each other are placed together they will eventually modulate into a common beat.

If the beat of my thought is different from the beat of yours, it is relatively easy to see how each of our ideas may have influenced the other. If the pulse of my thought differs from the rhythm of a thousand, million, or billion minds acting in concert, who is going to influence whom? If a drop of red dye is released into a swimming pool, not only is its effect negligible, it loses its individual aspect of "redness." Such is the controlling power of the collective mind. Individual thoughts and beliefs contrary to those prevailing in society are often discounted and dismissed by both the society and its wrong-thinking member. But even deeper than this, strongly held collective beliefs act to inhibit an individual's formation of contrary ideas in the first place.

Consciousness *is* vibratory. Individual consciousness, which is a part of the Universal Mind, has access to the infinite. What forms into our conscious mind from this infinite source depends upon the quality of our mental vibrations. If our minds are fixed upon the refined vibrations of the Divine, we will generate thoughts of love, compassion, and abundance, and perceive ways and ideas to manifest in the world these higher thoughts. If our minds vibrate in lower realms, our thoughts will be filled with greed, jealousy, lack, and fear. And if a billion minds hum at this lower vibration, what chance do I have to maintain an individual vibration at a higher frequency? For that matter, if a billion minds resonate with the frequency of one belief, how can my mind possibly avoid vibrating at the same frequency, thus pulling into my consciousness the thoughts and ideas that support this belief and suppressing those in opposition to this stricture?

Please, don't fret or despair if you've reached the conclusion you're just an automaton hopelessly subject to mass whims. Although many societal beliefs are prevalent, they are rarely universal or monolithic. Therefore, we have the opportunity to align our minds with those who share similar beliefs to ours or who possess ideas and beliefs we aspire to. This principle is exemplified in the old spiritual admonition that company is stronger than will power.

When I lived at the monastic community in Massachusetts a number of years ago, I was struck by the uplifting effect of the collective energy. There can be incredible power generated by a group dedicated to unfoldment of God-consciousness. Living there during a time of personal crisis did not end my negative thinking, emotional distress, or psychological pain. However, the community energy did significantly lessen the depths to which I sank. I felt as if my afflictions were encased in a buoy I was tied to; they couldn't submerge me, and even if I wanted my troubles to pull me under, the upward force counteracted any downward push.

It is no surprise then that most religions and spiritual traditions urge their adherents to seek the company of holy persons—preferably, of course, the revered of their own particular persuasion. The primary value of being with such spiritual masters is not derived from religious education or the intellectual transmission of spiritual principles, although significant benefit may often result from this instruction. The consciousness of a true holy person, which is significantly aligned with absolute truth, powerfully vibrates at highly refined frequencies. Being in the presence of such a person naturally raises our own vibrations and can profoundly affect our lives. No matter how much time might be spent with the learned Pharisees, any benefit is insignificant compared with one touch of Christ's robe. For that matter, what is the value of a well-versed priest or minister who is not more spiritually evolved than most of the congregation?

This practice of spiritual "energetic transmission" or "vibratory upliftment" is prevalent in Eastern religions, but largely absent in conventional Christianity today, although found in historic Christian esotericism. This guru/disciple, master/pupil relationship, although minimized and trivialized by Western estimation, still remains a sacred and essential part of Hinduism and other spiritual traditions. I have had occasion to spend some time with men and women professed, usually by others, to be "holy" or spiritually mastered. Most of them say the same thing. Anyone sincerely interested in leading a spiritual life, who is reasonably studied, probably won't hear anything they haven't heard before.

Yet after being with some "masters," I found my life markedly changed. Whether I might have slept through a weekend program or listened attentively, for weeks after, I found myself naturally more energetic. My meditations became more effortless and the quality of my thoughts improved. My negative tendencies did not seem to affect me as much, and I found myself measurably more productive in practical areas of my life. For a period of many years early in my spiritual growth, I could feel my higher energies wane after a time and often felt the need to "recharge" by again spending time in a "master's" presence.

This dynamic obviously has potential for dependency, and worse, exploitation of the unwary or vulnerable. The true spiritual teacher seeks to establish the strength and clarity of the disciple's own vibration, so ultimately the pupil is self-sufficient and no longer in need of the master. Some followers refuse to be kicked out of the nest, and no doubt many teachers encourage their devotees' continued fealty. Many dynamic and evolved spiritual leaders, even though they genuinely care for their students, unconsciously may engender their dependency. Even the exalted may carry the unperceived seeds of ego desire that unknowingly manifest and magnetize followers towards adulation of the master. Not so benign are the charismatic spiritual personas who calculatingly cultivate the worship of their flocks for personal gain and aggrandizement.

For me I derived a definite advantage from my contact with various spiritual teachers. It served me well at that particular stage of my life. We all need assistance at various times in our spiritual progression. I met some teachers and groups I spent much time with and others I knew I had no use for. Intuition and a rigorously skeptical mind serve one well when deciding whether to associate with a spiritual teacher or organization. Even so, it may be very difficult to see deeply into a dynamic spiritual leader.

At times when I was unsure, I remembered Christ's admonition, which answers the question: "There are many teachers. How can we tell which is true?" He said in essence that although two trees bore fruit equally appealing to the eye, the product of one may be sweet and the other bitter. The genuineness of a spiritual leader may often be judged best by the quality of his or her close disciples and associates. Are they self-sufficient, open-minded, pleasant, respectful of others, and good humored? Are they people you really would want to intimately associate with? If not, odds are the brilliant and appealing visage of the master conceals darkness you want to avoid.

One truly illumined soul can uplift all of humanity. No matter how degraded the collective mind, the clarion of Truth can lead all to resonate with the glory of God. The lives of Jesus and the prophets and seers are testament to this. The consciousness of one individual *can* affect the mass mind. Although changes in collective thought most often result from the accumulated efforts of many, that is not always the case. The Cold War ended not because we outspent the Russians, or because internal forces collapsed our enemy. The Cold War was won when Ronald Reagan *believed* it could be won. While I voted for his opponents on both occasions and never had much fondness for this president, I heartily acknowledge that his consciousness primed the dissolution of this earth-threatening impasse.

As an early adolescent growing up in the mid-1960s, I remember the arms race as an inevitable and permanent fact of life. "Why doesn't each side stop spending all this money on weapons and use their resources to clothe, feed, and educate their citizens?" Ideas like that were dismissed as pie-in-the-sky foolishness. *Everybody knew,* like it or not, this was the way it had to be. The acceptance of this belief was so predominant it became glaciated in the collective consciousness. No wonder the number of missiles kept skyrocketing. When Reagan first expressed his belief that the Cold War could end, the intelligentsia as well as the average person dismissed it as quackery. Yet the persistence and strength of his belief, amplified by the power of his position, eventually altered the collective opinion on this planet. His seed crystal caused the glaciers to fissure and melt.

I most keenly felt the existence of a collective consciousness while driving to court late one afternoon. I was cruising on Edgewater Drive, a beautiful little stretch of two-lane road between my office in Dunedin and the courthouse in downtown Clearwater. A few feet off the west edge of the road, Clearwater Harbor shimmered under blue sky, gliding pelicans, and soaring ospreys. I don't recall what I was thinking at the time, but whatever filled my awareness at that moment was interrupted by a stupendous feeling of joy. As the sensation started to subside and I began to ask myself, "What was *that?*" another massive wave of joy hit me.

What I felt was not internally generated, but seemed to be emanating from elsewhere. Like cosmic or gravitational forces moving through space, the successive pulses of bliss felt almost like the shock waves of some immense explosion passing through the planet. This joy and bliss was profound, intense, sweet, exhilarating, and expansive. I stopped trying to figure out what was happening and for the next few minutes just relaxed into my seat and enjoyed each successive stroke. Like standing on the shore of some massive ocean, I allowed each endless wave to pass through me, one after another caressing, purifying and enlivening every cell of my body and part of my being. Within a short time I approached downtown Clearwater, and by then the waves had subsided to ripples. Upon entering the courthouse they either had ceased or I had stopped noticing them.

I spent that evening quietly at home. I was in one of my "retreat" phases, during which I rarely watched television, listened to the radio, or read newspapers or magazines. My afternoon experience had been, for me at least, extraordinary, and as I reflected on it I tapped into a warm feeling of well-being.

The next morning I was walking by my office and saw the front page of the newspaper through a vending machine. My body involuntarily halted as my gaze fixed upon the picture taking up most of the page. Hundreds of people were dancing, cheering, drinking, and waving banners and flags on top of the Berlin Wall as masses of people celebrated in the streets below. I instantly and absolutely knew this was it! This had emanated the waves of joy I had felt. I had generally known events in Eastern Europe were moving rapidly, but had not followed current events in any detail the past few weeks. I read some fine print and discovered that the Berlin Wall, or more precisely, the control and suppression associated with it, had formally fallen at Berlin's witching hour the night before. I roughly calculated the time difference and realized that this monumental event had transpired in real time at the same moment of my bliss experience. Hundreds of millions all around the world must have been watching this scene on television. This global joy was birthed by freedom—a bright new light shattered decades of fear, oppression, darkness, and limiting beliefs.

The fact is, such waves of joy—whether you call them mass mental emissions, electromagnetic pulses, gravimetric ripples, etheric currents, pranic discharges, psychic transmissions, or sub-physical phenomenon—not only exist, but also affect every one of us. Their effect may be more subtle if unconsciously experienced. Had I not been directly aware of these waves, I might have just noticed an unspecific feeling of well-being. Everyone discerns on occasion a feeling that seems to arise out of nowhere. By the same token, and not so uplifting, societal currents of fear, limitation, and lack likewise affect our thoughts and emotions.

Many might disagree that the consciousness of Ronald Reagan ended the Cold War. I readily admit even the great are found standing on the shoulders of others. No doubt if enough drops of red dye enter the pool, we eventually will start to see pink. Our cause for death with dignity was no different.

The Second District's ruling further galvanized public opinion, and the majority chorus favoring right-to-die increased their volume and ranks. Their voices and cries bombarded the legislature that was again considering whether to permit withdrawal of feeding tubes under Florida's living will statute.

At this time I received from a stranger in Orlando a copy of his thoughtful letter sent to every state legislator, urging each to support the proposed change in Florida law. Although his eloquence was directed to all, he recognized his best chance to change a vote was to influence a mind now receptive to a different vibration:

> My hope is to contact members of the legislature who have been close to the problem, by personal experience, and therefore will be better able to evaluate what I will say here. I do not intend to imply that a special intelligence is needed  to understand this problem; but I do believe that a special experience is needed.

Remarkably, his insight was borne out. The proposed bill came out of committee and could now be voted upon by the entire legislature. A powerful state senator from Jacksonville made the difference, as I recall. He was a declared member of the "religious right" who previously had managed to kill the amendment. He had recently experienced the death of his father, who suffered through continued medical treatment the family had been unable to terminate. Although diametrically opposed politically to the prior attempts to amend the law, his position changed because his "special experience" indeed enabled him to "understand this problem." The bill was now open for passage. If enacted, Mrs. Browning didn't need the courts. She would be entitled to relief under the new law.

Her cousin and I didn't care how the tube was removed. Any legal method allowing us to terminate Mrs. Browning's artificial feeding would suffice. Back in the courts, the Second District had certified our case to be one of "great public importance." This gave the Florida Supreme Court jurisdiction to hear the cause, assuming one of the parties made such a request. The appellate court's decision was not everything we had hoped for, but we surmised it gave us enough to proceed with removal of the tube. We therefore were in no rush to decide whether to take the trip to the Supreme Court. While we were ruminating, the State Attorney made the call for us. They filed their request for review, and for me it meant more brief writing. My job was now to get the highest state court to definitively declare that Mrs. Browning was entitled to die free from intubation.

So we were now waging war on three fronts. In addition to preparing for Supreme Court and legislative battles, we were also heading back to the local probate judge. The Honorable Thomas E. Penick, Jr., Circuit Court Judge, had requested I inform him of the guardian's decision when reached under the Second District's new guidelines. By the end of May we had jumped through all of the appellate court's hoops, and I advised Judge Penick that Mrs. Herbert intended to bring Mrs. Browning home on June 9, 1989, in order to remove the feeding tube.

The State Attorney, anticipating our move, had previously requested the Second District to postpone application of its decision until the Supreme Court finished with the case. I argued that, "Mrs. Browning may never be the recipient of the relief afforded her," should the court stay its decision. The Second District agreed and refused to delay implementation of its ruling. The prosecutor then claimed Mrs. Herbert "does not have the best interests of Mrs. Browning in mind" and turned to Judge Penick to block her intended action. With a hearing set for June 7th, we prepared for a showdown on one of our three fronts.

# CHAPTER TWENTY-THREE

# *Battling on All Fronts*

"THE SCHTROWBERRIES—the schtrowberries" clicked through my mind as we waited outside the chambers of Judge Penick for a numbingly early seven-thirty hearing this June morning. Not too early though for the local TV crew, whose members I recognized, by this stage in the case, on a first name basis. Bogart's "the schtrowberries—the schtrowberries" continued its play as I saw Captain Queeg involuntarily and incessantly manipulate three metal balls in his hand. For those of you who haven't seen the classic 1950s film *The Caine Mutiny*, Humphrey Bogart played a mentally unbalanced World War II captain. Paranoia finally sent our skipper over the edge, and the object of his obsession was a can of strawberries supposedly stolen from the ship's mess. Oops! Was that Judge Penick talking berries and massaging ball bearings? Fair or not, my mental fancies portrayed our jurist a wee bit out of kilter.

The tall, fit, and ramrod straight judge had attained a rank of Brigadier General in the Air Force Reserves. His rigidness appeared to contain an insecurity; to me, Judge Penick didn't seem to bend very well and on occasion appeared to crack. He had been appointed to a lower level court in the late 1970s and was quickly selected to move up to the Circuit Court.

Judging is an awesome responsibility. People's fates and lives are often on the line, and an error in judgment can have devastating consequences. The decision to be made is often unclear. Especially for a new judge, these responsibilities of office can become burdensome if not crushing. A judge's ability to relax under this pressure and feel comfortable with his uncertainty is a great asset. The imperious judge who always must appear to be right and in perfect control places himself under tremendous stress.

Judge Penick was no stranger to me, as I had appeared before him many times over the years. In moments of particular stress, the judge would sometimes exhibit, what I considered to be, unusual behavior. At a crucial turn in a trial or hearing, or at a time when the judge appeared to be under intense advocacy, he simply took an exit. Out of nowhere he would stop the proceedings by calling in his secretary or assistant and then start conversing with her about some trivial matter that had nothing at all to do with the case, as if no one else were present. A room filled with attorneys, litigants, the testifying witness, the stenographic reporter, and court personnel sat in silence. Most of us, in our disbelief, discreetly peeked around just to see if anyone else thought this was strange. After a few minutes with his escape valve open, the judge, as if we were an afterthought popping into his mind, resumed the proceeding as suddenly as it had been stopped.

We all have personality and behavioral quirks of some degree. For most of us, toleration of our peculiarities is not forced upon others. Not so with the judiciary. They hold their audience captive. That is why judicial demeanor and temperament are so important. Those with external power have that much greater responsibility to behave soundly and treat others with dignity and respect. Unfortunately for me and other lawyers, we too often walk out of court apologizing to a client startled by the rudeness or insensitivity of a judge. I'm not here to engage in judge bashing. I know of numerous jurists of exceptional professional and personal stature, and I have had the pleasure of appearing before some of them. A majority of judges earnestly do their best to conduct themselves well and reach the appropriate decision. As for Judge Penick, he usually gets an "E" for effort, and every once in a while, especially when ruling in my favor, may actually earn an "A."

If evidence and the rule of law were to be the focus of the morning's hearing, I should have been brimming with confidence.

Our "investigation" to comply with the Second District's guide-lines was extensive and bore favorable results. We located many long-term friends of Mrs. Browning and obtained their written statements. These close acquaintances fully corroborated the testi-mony of Mrs. Herbert and the witnesses to the living will regarding Mrs. Browning's medical treatment wishes. After signing that document she told one friend it "guaranteed she would not be kept alive by any artificial means." To others Mrs. Browning proclaimed she was "confident her wishes would be carried out" and now would "be able to die with dignity."

Local friends also rebutted the nursing home's estimation of her abilities. "I often visit Estelle . . . but see no difference in her condition since she had the massive stroke." According to another, "Never is there a response of any kind." A good neighbor added, "I have visited her in the nursing home many times, she has never recognized me or understood me. . . . Every time I visit I leave in tears." Many gave unsolicited opinions about the course of events: "it is a crime to keep her breathing in this condition;" "she's been reduced to a breathing corpse;" "sue the nursing home for the money they obtained . . . because of ignoring her wishes. . . ."

We also marched into ecclesiastical territory, propelled by the Second District's suggestion that a patient's religious beliefs "may influence" the surrogate's decision. Mrs. Browning was a long-term member of a Dunedin Presbyterian Church. I eventually found the Church and Public Issues office of Presbyterian Church (USA). The office director graciously provided me with the church's position on withdrawal of life support as adopted by its 174th and 195th General Assemblies. The church "Affirms the right of older persons to stipulate that technology shall not be used to prolong biological functions when there is no medical hope of restoration to meaningful existence. . . ." Closer to home, I spoke with Mrs. Browning's minister, who told me a decision to remove life support "is a matter of individual conscience for the patient, and the patient's family if the patient is unable to make such a decision." A memorandum of the minister's statement and the National Director's letter with transmitted Assembly minutes were all now part of our arsenal.

Medical evidence was shorn up with the addition of a well-respected board-certified geriatrician. All of our physicians again examined Mrs. Browning, and their extensive affidavits more than satisfied the appellate court's requirements. But what about the court's demand for a Solomonic pronouncement that the patient's right to forego medical treatment is not "outweighed by state interests"? I had enlisted the services of a law school professor and a physician-lawyer who had recently co-authored a law review article on right-to-die issues. They provided a detailed legal analysis of the competing personal and state interests in our case. Their report concluded that Mrs. Browning's right to terminate tube feeding indeed outweighed the state's interest in preserving life. Of course I could just as well have gone through this legal exercise, but since when has Judge Penick listened to me?

If reviewing my evidence did make me a bit chipper, the feeling was dispelled by another look at the State Attorney's opposing motion. Marie King had reached into the slime bucket to put this together. First was the suggestion of impropriety with Mrs. Browning's funds. Mrs. Herbert, like countless guardians, had been late in filing certain financial documents. Listen to Marie and you'd think a mortal sin occurred.

Next, Mrs. Herbert apparently committed the crime of using guardianship funds to replace the air conditioner in her cousin's home, the expense fully disclosed in the guardianship accounting. Many years before, Mrs. Browning had asked her cousin to move from Rhode Island to Florida to reside with her as her companion. For over two years since the commencement of the guardianship, the court never raised an objection to Mrs. Herbert's continued residence at the ward's home. Now it seemed awfully sinister. The Second District explicitly approved family members as surrogate decision-makers. Obviously that court did not consider the expected financial relationships between patient and family surrogate to constitute a conflict of interest.

Worse still was the charge that Mrs. Herbert and I were conspiring to cause Mrs. Browning discomfort. The nursing home had requested Mrs. Herbert to consent to the replacement of the nasogastric tube with a gastric counterpart. This would involve a surgical procedure requiring Mrs. Browning's transport to a local hospital. The staff claimed their patient's nasal tissue had been degrading and was causing discomfort. Mrs. Herbert, under intense pressure from the nursing home administration, consented to the switch before discussing it with me or our doctors.

I was immediately shocked and disgusted and saw the intended surgical procedure as further degradation of Mrs. Browning. After a bit, slightly cooler heads deliberated upon the contraindications. Mrs. Browning had experienced problems with her previous gastric tube, would likely suffer the stress of transportation and surgery, and there were reasonable prospects of terminating artificial feeding in the near future, which would obviate the need for surgery. We revoked consent and now were faced with Marie's innuendo we were harming Mrs. Browning.

Still on the subject of Mrs. Browning's medical condition, the State gratuitously inserted some double hearsay. One of our doctors supposedly had told an unnamed nursing home employee that he "was quite surprised to find such a lively, alert patient." I worked very closely with all three of our physicians and believed with a certainty no such statement was made by any one of them. I doubted I would ever see or have the opportunity to cross-examine a person daring, under oath, to attribute this statement to our doctor. If this were the State's best attempt to overcome our medical evidence, they had lost on that issue.

The State's bottom line proclaimed that Mrs. Herbert should be removed as medical surrogate and replaced with a special guardian appointed to make the decision. The Second District did permit the trial judge, *upon presentation of evidence,* to review the "good faith" of the surrogate. I wasn't concerned about hard facts, but did lack confidence in the trial court's inclination to look past the State's innuendo and hearsay. If Judge Penick wanted to avoid making a decision, Marie was doing her best to provide him some cover.

I tried to dispel my lingering pessimism by reminding myself we were exceptionally fortunate just to be here this morning. After the Second District had denied Marie's request to stay the case, she made the same pitch to the Supreme Court. As I was completing my response in opposition, a deputy Supreme Court clerk called to tell me the court had already granted the State's motion. How's that for listening to both sides? The June 7th hearing before Judge Penick was canceled, and we were sorely disappointed to be waylaid after coming so close to a chance for victory.

Bouncing right back I entered the rarefied echelons of Supreme Court practice. I immediately filed my motion with the court along with a letter politely opining that "fundamental fairness would suggest that such a decision be made by the Court *after* receipt and review of the guardian's response in opposition." Much more direct was our assessment of the ward's condition: "Mrs. Browning . . . is subject to pain and torment each day her life is artificially prolonged against her will." An appellate court rarely reverses itself, especially in short order. But here, apparently, a change of heart took place. Three days later the Supreme Court threw out its previous order and summarily denied the State's motion to stay the proceedings. The newspaper headlines gyrated, our temporary fortunes revived, and June 19 now became the date of our meeting with Judge Penick.

Our resuscitation was short-lived. We were ushered into chambers and the judge proceeded with some opening remarks. Within a minute or two the judge started to stammer, and I realized he had caved. Slam—bang! No evidence, no hearing, no witnesses—the court was appointing another guardian. Judge Penick had no interest in hearing about medical opinion, patient intent, religious doctrine, or the contest between individual and governmental interests. Nor did he require the State to prove any of its allegations. The only thing we were allowed to do was place our objections on the record. The judge concluded with the high sounding: "I want every possible legal procedure utilized for the protection of Estelle Browning's right to privacy and to protect the best interest of Estelle Browning." Mrs. Browning would likely be dead by the time "every possible legal procedure" was utilized, and the only thing protected as a result would be the judiciary's ability to avoid its responsibility.

The decision was a bitter pill to swallow. It took most of my determination to restrain from excoriating Judge Penick in the media, although with me on television decrying his decision as a "direct attack on family values," the judge may have had a different opinion of my self-control. I venture to guess he was a tad displeased with my recitation in the morning paper: "The court didn't even give us the opportunity to present evidence . . . and went beyond the bounds of the appellate court opinion." I was getting pretty good at trying my case in the media and shaping public opinion. For example: This court "says you have to have strangers make these decisions. How many courts and guardians must Mrs. Browning go through in order to have her desire carried out?" Developing a good "sound bite" helped, but so did the media's support of the cause. Some of my best quotes appeared on the editorial pages.

In the following days I tried to see if anything could be salvaged on Judge Penick's front. I fully cooperated with the attorney the judge had appointed as special guardian and sent him the materials we had compiled in our "investigation." I quickly learned he intended to conduct a formal inquiry and planned to depose Mrs. Browning's friends, including those residing out of state. When I pressed a bit, the attorney admitted his investigation would take months, and he seemed impervious to my suggestions that time was of the essence.

I could always bring Judge Penick's decision back to the Second District for review, and thought well of my chances of convincing the appellate court to mandate an evidentiary hearing. This route would take just as long as waiting for the special guardian. Either way, I probably could get in and out of the Supreme Court within the same span of time. And the legislation still offered hope. The bill narrowly passed and now awaited the governor. No one expected him to sign it. But if he didn't veto the amendment within the next two weeks, it would automatically be enacted without his signature. As our other two fronts showed more promise, we accepted defeat before Judge Penick and moved on.

I found it difficult not to blame the judge and Marie and the special guardian. I felt angry and frustrated. Have them trade places with Mrs. Browning for one day, and then let's see if they disregard her personal liberty interests. I knew my reactive emotions and blame were symptomatic of my attachment to the outcome of this case, but that didn't seem to help very much. Sometimes, though, simply choosing to take a different perspective can lift our energy and change the way we feel.

A few months into my marital separation, when I had just started to get my bearings, I went to pick up my son from his swim lesson at the local pool. His mother had brought him, and I found her sitting on the metal benches with other parents as they watched the kiddies finish their strokes. I warily sat down next to her. After a minute or two, she hesitatingly told me that perhaps she had made a mistake and was considering the possibilities of reconciliation. Shocked, I didn't say too much, but at the same time didn't close any doors. By the time I got home I was livid. *After all the pain and torment I've gone through, do you think I'm going to jump on that bandwagon again? She's lying—she's just trying to manipulate me while we're negotiating a property split. How vile!* Well, how's that for some defensive mental gyrations?

After a couple of hours of this, I had a vivid image of standing on a busy railroad platform. Two trains were ready to depart, one on each side, and I was free to choose which one to take. I then realized I had a choice to make regarding my wife. I could believe she was operating from ill motive, wanting to harm or take advantage of me, or I could consider her sentiment genuine. The consequence of the first kept her in negative energy and placed me in the weakened position of a victim. In the second, she was held in a place of integrity and courage, and I was in a position of being well-regarded. I did not know for a certainty what her true intentions were, so I had the option of adopting either belief. On the left platform I could take the train of pain and negativity, or on the other side I could board the transport of empowerment. I turned to my right, entered the train, and we pulled from the station. I immediately felt uplifted and noticed my anger was gone.

Although the move toward reconciliation was transient, I held to my choice and as a result continued to feel all right about that aspect of our dissolution. This power to choose our reality is available to all of us all the time. I am not suggesting you disregard what you perceive to be the facts or truth of a situation. But since we experience so much of our lives through the stories and dramas we construct, why not create one of empowerment?

I read a book many years ago on "rebirthing," a type of energetic breath work, in which the authors claimed that every "negative" occurrence in human history could, at least in our imagination, be recast in an uplifting light. The authors were not promoting historical revisionism, but touted this exercise as a way to expand the view of our personal pasts. I tried it with the most horrendous examples human history could offer, and sure enough, I was able to do it. It took a while with the Holocaust, but I eventually came up with: "The human race, driven by greed and lust for violence came, with the impending advent of nuclear weapons, upon the verge of annihilation. Only the most shocking example of human debasement, only an unimaginable cruelty could waken humanity before the hovering doom descended. The Jewish people, long ago in their collective consciousness, agreed to play the role of the lamb whose slaughter was necessary to shock humanity into a new moral consciousness. Their sacrifice saved humanity at the brink of extinction and propelled us into a new age."

If our minds can conceive of an uplifting Holocaust, can it be so difficult to look another way at the slights and injuries and abuses we perceive were inflicted upon us? Can we be so certain our memories accurately portray past events? What actually "happened" to us one or five or fifty years ago may bear little resemblance to the ensuing judgments and beliefs now deeply etched by repetition in our neural pathways. Choosing to see things differently is not about running from the truth; it's about recognizing and abandoning those beliefs that no longer serve us. Perhaps I should follow a little of my own advice, and after nine years now, finally usher Judge Penick, Marie, and the special guardian aboard the station's empowerment train!

But wait—let's also grab a seat for the Governor. After intense lobbying from both sides—this legislation setting the Executive's record for incoming mail—on July 3, 1989, Bob Martinez vetoed the revision of Florida's living will statute. I had done my part by sending the governor a lengthy letter explaining Mrs. Browning's case and detailing, among other things, her physical torments. I also called his General Counsel, an acquaintance, in an effort to assure my letter would be read.

In the governor's veto message, conveniently released right before the holiday to minimize attention, he passed the buck to the court rather than attribute the decision to personal conviction. He claimed the Legislature "prematurely" acted because it lacked the complete "guidance" of the state Supreme Court, which was now reviewing the Browning case. How's that for a professed "conservative" whose doctrine espouses separation of powers and disdains intrusion by the judiciary into legislative matters? I certainly was not alone in considering the veto an act of political cowardice. A couple of days later the *St. Petersburg Times* lambasted the governor in its editorial, "The right to suffer." The paper, to my particular pleasure, not only spotlighted Martinez' flabby backbone, but also criticized "officious prosecutors" for interfering in the Browning case.

The editorial did make me feel a bit better, as did the ensuing letters hostile to our opponents, published shortly thereafter. But there was no denying that our options were again narrowed. The state Supreme Court was our last hope.

# CHAPTER TWENTY-FOUR

# *My Supreme Court Appearance*

With only one front now left to pursue, I toiled feverishly on the giant task of my Supreme Court brief. I was working a two-or three-week string of twelve-hour days and still had a week or two to go before I could enjoy a much needed respite. A network television crew found me at my office on the Fourth of July to get my reaction to the governor's veto. They ended up coming over for some taping, and there I was on the holiday news—Mrs. Browning's white knight, stalwart at his covered desk, intently crafting her plea of last hope to the Supreme Court. Did I love it! And given my strenuous effort, I much appreciated the positive reinforcement.

A few days later I received a call from Lois West, Mrs. Browning's primary physician, and was told her patient had begun "Cheyne-Stokes" breathing, an irregular respiratory pattern harbinging a hastened death. If I could have redoubled my efforts I would have, but I was already working as quickly and diligently as I thought possible. We finished the brief on Friday, July 14th and had it copied and readied for Monday filing and service. Although the State would prepare a reply brief, I expected we could orally argue the case in August and get a decision in September. Right now there was nothing to do but wait. I started to decompress. That Sunday I attended a party and felt relieved and satisfied with an effort well done. How quickly sentiments change. Midway through the evening I received word of Mrs. Browning's death.

> In a way, for each of us, a part of our liberty of choice, a part of our freedom to control our own body and our own fate, died along with Mrs. Browning, or perhaps was taken from us. . . .

> It is hoped that the Florida Supreme Court, in its final determination of this case . . . removes the government from the patient's deathbed and leaves decisions in these matters to be made by the patient and the patient's family. Perhaps then, Mrs. Browning's prolonged tortured death will not have been in vain.

With these words I completed my recitation of Mrs. Herbert's prepared statement and the noonday press conference began. Crammed into my closing room were numerous television and newspaper reporters along with their cameramen. Our emotions were mixed. Both Mrs. Herbert and I expressed our relief that Mrs. Browning's torment had ended. But for my client, this solace was flooded with a deep guilt and sadness. Mrs. Herbert had promised her cousin she would not allow her to suffer the decrepit existence and lingering death Mrs. Browning had most feared.

Had I done any better in keeping my soul's promise to Mrs. Browning? Had I done *everything* in my power to release her from that artificial cord binding her to continued life? I did my share of hindsight ruminating. Perhaps I could have chosen a slightly different course or strategy along the way, but I genuinely believed an altered route would have brought us to the same destination.

Mrs. Herbert and I agreed to pursue the case to its final decision, and we used the conference to press our cause in the court of public opinion. I pointedly expressed my frustration over the legal system's inability to cope with these cases. Whether this failure is caused by a judge skirting a hard decision or a structure unsuited to prompt deliberation, the result was the same. Mrs. Browning's forced manner of death trampled upon her personal liberty, and only the Florida Supreme Court could prevent countless other Floridians from suffering the same fate.

This was grist for the story now front-page news in Florida and well covered on the national wire services. Mrs. Browning's picture and account even appeared in the *New York Times* national edition. Although our voices were dominant, other opinions were also heard. Widespread was Marie King's contribution to the national debate: removal of feeding tubes in cases like Mrs. Browning's "should not be allowed because it actually constitutes genocide of the elderly." If this case were to be won on the field of public opinion, Marie's incredible offering was a delight.

Even more outlandish were arguments presented by some in the religious right. A talk show broadcast on a well-known Christian television network featured a guest Bible "scholar" who asserted that tube feeding was scripturally mandated! This sure captured my attention while channel grazing. I intently waited to learn how I managed to miss this in my reading of the gospel.

As stated by the pundit, because a Roman soldier gave Jesus fluid while he was dying on the cross, it is God's will that today's dying be intubated. According to his twisted logic, had our technology then existed, Christ should have been tube-fed on the cross. Why not indefinitely delay the Lord's death with some artificial sustenance? But wasn't the purpose of Christ's death his resurrection and *our* salvation? Oh gee, might as well postpone that too! And by the way, wasn't that *vinegar* offered up by the soldiers (Luke 23: 36)?

Itching to dispense a stern dose of critical thinking as hopeful cure for "expert" idiocy, I called the station the next day in an attempt to get myself invited on the show. I got to the assistant program manager, explained who I was, told her I had seen last night's show, politely suggested there were differing points of view, and offered to appear on the program if she felt her audience might be interested in another look at this complex issue. She was incredulous. I don't remember her exact words, but the gist of her response was: "Buddy, don't you know this is propaganda? We don't care about other points of view."

I don't intend to demean the contribution made by religious groups to this public debate. While I often thought their positions uninformed and theologically suspect, I respected the offerers, since their opinions seemed to arise from sincerity of conviction. I guess though, in the case of our "scholar," the image of a glop bag nailed to the crucifix above an intubated Jesus exceeded even my sensibilities.

The debate lasted longer than expected. With Mrs. Browning's death, the court was no longer compelled to accelerate its consideration of the case. The State filed its final brief, and oral argument was eventually set for January 1990. In the interim, I continued to receive numerous inquiries and cases regarding removal of feeding tubes. The Second District's ruling currently declared the law in Florida, so I assisted families in meeting the court's cumbersome requirements.

Substantiating the decision was easy compared to implementing it. The Department of Health and Rehabilitative Services refused to modify its nursing home feeding tube policy, even though its regulation was rendered unconstitutional by the Second District's opinion. Pending the Supreme Court's pronouncement on the subject, I fought some pitched battles with health care providers and their regulators. Convincing a nursing home that the H.R.S. rule was no longer effective was an enormous struggle. In many cases the family's only recourse was to bring the patient home to die.

It took more than convincing to get H.R.S. to back off. The agency often threatened nursing homes with licensure problems should the patient's tube be removed. More menacing were threatened charges of elderly abuse made against surrogates. I did some bullying of my own. Agency operatives were informed that their continued actions would result in a suit against them personally for unlawful interference with the constitutional and civil rights of the patient. With the law unsettled, institutions find it particularly difficult to set and implement policy. But that was their problem. At least at this moment my clients had a constitutional right-to-die, and I would prod—and if need be, push *very* hard—to make sure corporate confusion and bureaucratic obstinacy did not prevent exercise of that right.

If resistance and confusion were to be eradicated, it would have to occur here. I sat in the third or fourth gallery row of the Florida

Supreme Court in Tallahassee. This court was everything the Second District was not. The marble walls, classic columns, lofty ceilings, deep mahoganies, imposingly high judicial platform, and cavernous interior all echoed the stature, pomp, tradition, and solemnity befitting the pinnacle of this branch of government. The surroundings were not lost upon me as I firmly held the transcript of the oral argument I had spent two months perfecting.

Amidst talk of turtles and shrimp, I wondered which part of the large gallery attended the case now being argued, and who had braved the chilly January morning to hear of death and dying. Florida now required commercial shrimpers to use nets rigged with T.E.D.S., an acronym for "turtle extraction devices." I gather since sea turtles are bigger than shrimp, enabling the escape of our hard-shelled friends also provided the latter a substantial means of exit. The question now before the Court was whether this crimp in garnering shrimp impermissibly restrained the seafarers' right to ply their trade and earn a living.

As I looked about, I at least knew which case had drawn the adjoining spectators. My wife and parents were here for what easily constituted the apex to date of my legal career. This was one of the very few times, if not the only time, I can truly say my wife was enamored with me. I suppose power and success really are potent aphrodisiacs—as my spouse had made particularly evident our previous night at the Governor's Inn. It goes to show the mind *is* the premiere erogenous zone. (Neither hair had I grown nor iron had I pumped of late.)

I received a marked demonstration of the mind's role in sexual arousal after my initial visit to the Kripalu Center. As I mentioned before, a loss of interest in sex was one effect of my experience there. What I actually lost was the mental overlay priming my sex drive. The visual imagery I previously found sexually stimulating no longer provoked that automatic result. But my natural physiological drive remained. With my physically and mentally generated urges separated for the first time, I was astounded to see that the latter was responsible for approximately ninety percent of my sexual desire. Lest any spiritual aspirants be discouraged from pursuing their transcendent goals, let me assure you I suffered no loss from my experience, but gained a large dose of sexual *freedom*. It is liberating to decide when and how to use your mind for sexual stimulation rather than being left to the mercy of mentally stoked cravings.

If any part of me were musing in the previous night's glow, the phrase "next case" surely brought me to attention. Marie and I took seats at our respective counsel tables, and after a pause the chief justice gave us the signal to begin. With the archival tapes now recording, the State, as initial petitioner, went first. This gave me an opportunity to size-up the mood of the court. Sometimes appellate justices sit stoically silent, leaving the attorney an opportunity to methodically present her argument. On other occasions the court is animated, peppering counsel with questions designed to flesh out the weaknesses or inconsistencies in your case. Therefore, the ability to deftly move with and about the court's inquiries is as much a necessity for the appellate practitioner as is a well-prepared argument.

If preparation were to be the measure for today's success, victory was doubtlessly assured. I find it easy to speak contemporaneously in public forums, and almost never use a prepared text. Even with a demanding subject, as long as I'm familiar with the material, I do very well with just jotting down a few key words or phrases. Arguing before an appellate court I leave nothing to chance and work from a modestly detailed outline. Here I had written and practiced a speech to end all speeches. Although I didn't expect to get up and read my argument, I knew most of it by heart and hoped at least to fit my more compelling oratory amidst the court's probes.

The seven justices were giving Marie a wide berth. Perhaps I'd get to sow more of my legal seed for jurisprudential posterity. Regarding the right of privacy, the right to be let alone, the right to control your own body and fate:

> This court has recognized that it is difficult to overstate this right of liberty, because it is the very bedrock upon which this country was founded. This is so because, given to us by our creator, this right of liberty is unalienable. It is inborn and inseparable to our nature, and cannot be conferred by any

government, or taken away by any government or institution of man. It is the function of government to protect and defend and act in consonance with the expression of this liberty. Governments that do not must eventually fall.

In recent weeks and months we have borne startled witness to the fact that no matter how hard governments may try to eradicate this liberty, it can never be extinguished, but only suppressed, temporarily. We have borne witness to millions of men and women throwing off the yoke of tyranny in the flowering expression of their liberty, even at the cost of their own lives. In this case it is the exercise of free will which is at issue, which is perhaps worth more than life itself.

Thomas Jefferson would have been proud. Unfortunately, except perhaps for the roaming spirit of our founding father, no one heard this argument or any other part of my prepared remarks. No sooner did I arrive at the lectern and utter my name when, out of the blue like a one-two punch, the justices unleashed their interrogation. I took a moment or two to shake off the jolt and get my legs back. I was composed, direct, swift, and firm in conviction, yet the shaking of my left foot and calf betrayed my apparent sure-footedness. Luckily the lectern hid this localized repository of nervousness from the court's view.

One justice couldn't wait for another to finish his question before she started to ask her own. "Yes, your honor . . . that's true, your honor . . . but—" Again and again I brought the justices back to the essential elements of the case. I addressed each concern, each misgiving, until the querying justice was satisfied with the appropriateness of my position. I felt so fully present in our exchanges I had no idea how time progressed; and I was too engaged to then realize how joyful and exciting this experience was.

The questions finally stopped. Turning to the timekeeper, I was shocked to discover only slightly more than a minute left of my twenty-minute allotment. I also noticed my lower leg had sometime before stopped shaking. Glancing down at my prepared speech on the lectern, I realized it was not to be used this day. My necessarily brief closing remarks were not particularly stirring. I knew this oral argument had really ended after my answer to the final question.

Upon thanking the court I looked at the chief justice and saw in his eye, recognition and appreciation of a job well done. Next came the media gathered by the exit. A bouquet of microphones and another round of questions, this time asking me to divine the court's ruling from the remarks the judges had just made.

We had to wait nine months to see how our predictions fared. I was delighted my prognostication proved a bit faulty. The Supreme Court's landmark opinion rendered more than even I had hoped for. Starting with the premise that "everyone has a fundamental right to the sole control of his or her person," the court concluded that "a competent person has the constitutional right to choose or refuse medical treatment, and that right extends to *all relevant decisions concerning one's health.*" Most expected the court to limit its decision to terminal patients, yet the court found a person's right to refuse treatment exists "regardless of his or her medical condition." To make absolutely clear the scope of its ruling, the court added, "the right involved here is one of self-determination that cannot be qualified by the condition of the patient." Floridians now had a breadth of choice exceeding that of other citizens, as most states required a terminal condition as predicate to ending life support.

Not only was prognosis irrelevant to this right, so was the type of medical treatment involved: "We see no reason to qualify that right on the basis of the denomination of a medical procedure as major or minor, ordinary or extraordinary, life-prolonging, life-maintaining, life-sustaining, or otherwise." And finally laid to rest was the argument that artificial provision of sustenance should be treated differently. The court found "no significant legal distinction" between supplying food and water through a tube and other forms of medical treatment.

The court rejected the State's call for judicial intervention. It agreed with the Second District that medical treatment decisions for incapacitated patients should be made by family members or friends, upon consultation with health care providers, in a private setting. The court also greatly simplified the decision-making procedures promulgated by the lower appellate court. At my urging, the justices also clarified the legal interpretation of "terminal condition." The court agreed that patient prognosis should be determined as if no artificial life support were being administered.

Without a doubt this was a stunning legal victory—but there was more. At the very end of the court's lengthy opinion it added:

> We are satisfied that clear and convincing evidence existed to support a finding that Mrs. Browning suffered from a terminal condition. Under these circumstances, the surrogate was correct in instructing Mrs. Browning's health care providers to discontinue all life-sustaining procedures in accordance with Mrs. Browning's wishes.

I was deeply pleased with this vindication, more for Mrs. Herbert than for me. My client had been excoriated by segments of society, maligned by the State, disregarded by the lower court and emotionally battered by the nursing home. We were right. Our critics were wrong, Judge Penick was wrong, and the Second District did avoid its hard choice.

The justices, by virtue of Mrs. Browning's death, were not required to make this determination, and likely that was the reason they made it. Was this an act of graciousness, or was it, perhaps, an expression of atonement for the judiciary's failure to fulfill its duty to Mrs. Browning? No matter—either way, we much appreciated the gesture. It didn't take away all the sting of Mrs. Browning's manner of death, but it sure helped.

One thing the ruling didn't help was the right-to-die portion of my practice. The court's broad and clear opinion established relatively simple procedures. The legislature eventually followed suit and revised the living will statute in accordance with the court's decision. Within a year or so, families were routinely able to remove feeding tubes from patients like Mrs. Browning. Lawyers weren't needed, so my success happily proved to be the bane of my newly developed specialty, though I still do get the occasional right-to-die case that stretches the envelope.

In the first few months after the decision, the H.R.S. feeding tube regulation still caused difficulty for some patients and families. Everyone knew the rules were unconstitutional, but because they hadn't been amended, nursing homes were reluctant to disregard them. Word was, the state agency was in the process of revising the rules, and many suspected it would try to circumvent the Supreme Court with some regulatory legerdemain. One afternoon I received a call from a *St. Petersburg Times* reporter I knew, asking my reaction to the H.R.S. morning announcement. I had not heard the news that H.R.S. had scrapped its regulation without offering a replacement. Apparently the State Attorney General had informed the agency that its duty, as well as that of its regulated providers, was to safeguard nursing home patients' constitutional right to refuse tube feeding.

After giving the reporter a few quotes for his copy, I rocked back in my chair, took a deep breath or two, and closed my eyes. As I inwardly smiled, I felt a deep sense of well-being. I knew the suffering of countless patients and their families would now be relieved. Like winter's frozen river giving up to spring, I felt the last ice jam, the final obstruction, being swept away. I enjoyed the inner glow and then heard my mind say, *If not your case, the court would have eventually reached the same decision in another case.* Perhaps so—but it was this case, it was this decision, and I was the lawyer who had argued it. A profound satisfaction welled up. I believed I had made a difference. The result of my efforts would touch many lives, now and in the future. I felt proud to be an attorney and was grateful to God for this extraordinary opportunity. I still am.

# CHAPTER TWENTY-FIVE

# Successful Cryonics—
# The Big Case Resuscitates

OW IS A BLOWFISH connected to witness cross-examination? Through creativity, of course! More than eighteen months before this New Year 1995, I was slowly pacing my office—my steps only interrupted by an occasional glance at a desk carefully littered with the materials I needed to prepare my cross-examination of James B. Godfrey. I was well-versed in the facts, intimate with the issues, and knew all the points that had to be made through my questioning of the government's expert on Oriental antiques. Organizing my materials and presentation would take some careful thought and planning, but this is routine work for a legal tactician. Why, then, did I continue my deliberate, rhythmic-paced rumination? There was a seed thought, some germ of an idea, that held the key to unraveling Godfrey's effectiveness as a witness. I could feel it and almost touch and taste it, yet it eluded the grasp of my conscious mind.

The slower I moved the more I receded from my outer vision. Facts, issues, trial techniques, past examinations, and the like all rapidly moved about me as if I were in a wind tunnel surrounded by flying bits of paper. At times the wind stops, everything comes to a rest, and something from within starts to emerge. *What is it I'm looking for?* Seemingly out of nowhere I saw the image of a small blowfish swimming. These puffers, to deter potential attackers or perhaps to entice a mate, will suck in air or water and inflate themselves to a much greater size. My fish looked like a little balloon, comically bobbing with cheeks ready to burst. Yes, of course—this was it!

Our little blowfish gave rise to the most delightful word, "puffery," which means exaggerated praise or commendation, especially for promotional purposes. I had facts to show the young Mr. Godfrey had inflated his credentials when dealing with the I.R.S. I chuckled inside as I saw the tiny blowfish, now with Godfrey's visage, puffing out his cheeks to look bigger. What an image—and what a wonderful way to commence my examination of the witness. This key wouldn't unravel Godfrey's effectiveness, it would decimate it. Who says there's no room for creativity in legal work?

Blowing the dust off of my Godfrey file and reviewing past inspiration was not solely an academic pursuit. Two months before, the mighty Federal District Court had finally issued its edict. As expected, the Court declared that the statute of limitations barred my clients from recovering the $300,000 they paid in 1985. As to the $422,033 payment—whose refund claim was mailed on the last day of the limitations period and received by the I.R.S. past the deadline—the Court determined that the taxpayers were entitled to the benefit of the timely mailing/timely filing statute. Although the claim was addressed to the District Director instead of the Atlanta Service Center, "the Court finds that the fact that the Plaintiffs' claim was received at the correct location in two days gives rise to the inference that the claim was 'properly addressed.'" *Hallelujah!*

Our celebration chorus felt mighty good, though I was relatively quick to advise Manny and Mary that the government really did have the best of the law on this issue and might very well win an appeal. Nothing like a lawyer to douse a good time. Some brief work at the calculator stoked our enthusiasm. Interest on our recoverable payments brought our possible award to around $800,000—a significantly plump turkey to shoot at.

We didn't even have to score a bull's-eye to enjoy Thanksgiving dinner. If the jury found the value of the donated items to be less than that claimed by Manny and Mary, my clients would owe some tax for the years in question. But, although we couldn't recover the first $300,000 paid, I saw no reason why that sum couldn't be applied toward any taxes later determined to be due. Of course the government might see this a different way. More involved calculations revealed that we could still lasso the $800,000, even with the jury splitting the difference between our valuations and those of the government. As long as the jury agreed we were not responsible for any penalties, $300,000 looked to be enough to pay the I.R.S.'s tab on a compromise verdict. Pass the stuffing, please!

There may have been a small measure of confidence in our good cheer. Mostly, though, we were enjoying the resuscitative warmth of a cryonic experiment that, at least for the moment, appeared to be successful. Our case was out of the deep freeze and there were indeed robust signs of life. We could lose at trial (I didn't think so) or be overturned on appeal (a more likely bet), yet right now, all the work and effort wasn't for naught—and that felt really good. The court, having quickened the case by its decision, apparently did not want delay in bringing it to term. Another pre-trial conference was promptly set for January 18, and our trial was placed on the calendar for the week of February 6, 1995. We were close to the top of the list, and apart from some natural disaster, expected this case to be tried in the coming month.

So did the Honorable Ralph W. Nimmons, Jr., although our jurist doubted he would preside over the shindig. He informed us at pre-trial our case would likely be heard by Anthony A. Alaimo, a visiting federal judge from the Southern District of Georgia. Federal courts often temporarily assign their judges to help relieve another district's congested trial docket. I was sorry and a bit dismayed to hear that our punctilious Judge Nimmons would be busy elsewhere during our trial. We obviously enjoyed his favorable (albeit tardy) decision, and for us he was now a known commodity. A job guaranteed for life can breed in its occupant anything from disdain to tyranny. I knew nothing of Judge Alaimo, but David's reaction to the news suggested otherwise for him. Although he had never appeared before Alaimo, David unhappily relayed to me our visitor's reputation for being extremely tough and rough with attorneys. There's nothing like common dread of a judge to bond opposing counsel.

I hadn't seen David for a year and a half, and from what I saw at pre-trial, my opponent looked no worse for the wear. The conference with Judge Nimmons went smoothly. Our primary topic of conversation was the offbeat method of reaching a judgment peculiar to tax refund cases. In most contests, all the jury is finally asked to do is check a box or write a number on a verdict form. In criminal cases, the jury checks the "guilty" or "not guilty" box. In a civil monetary dispute, the jury either puts an "X" where the verdict form says "we find for the defendant," or it enters a number on the line "we find for the plaintiff in the amount of $____." The Court then issues a simple judgment based on the jury's verdict, and the trial phase of a case is concluded.

In a tax refund case, the amount the plaintiff ultimately recovers first depends upon the taxes, penalties, and interest actually owed by the taxpayer for the years in question. Once the taxpayer's initial liability is set, this amount is deducted from payments made, and any excess, plus interest thereon, is refunded to the plaintiff. The first step in computing Manny and Mary's initial tab would be to determine the deductions from income for the donated items. Second would be to decide if they are liable for any penalties. Third, my clients' tax returns for the years in question would have to be reworked with the data from steps one and two in order to compute the actual amount owed. The jury could perform the first two steps, but obviously could not tackle the third. This is why juries in tax refund cases should just make factual findings, and leave to the parties' accountants the calculation of tax liability and resulting refund amount.

In our case we had the added complications of unused deductions carried over from one tax year to another and the possible application of the $300,000 payment to any taxes found due. The thought of having our jury compute the taxes and refund made both David and me shudder. How would we ever instruct them? Would we have to call accountants as expert witnesses? But what good are accountants *prior* to the jury making its initial findings? Although Judge Nimmons appeared thoroughly unfamiliar with tax refund cases, he was swayed by counsel's rare unanimity. He consented to the jury's limited role and also agreed the court would resolve any dispute should the parties fail to concur on the refund amount after verdict.

Judge Alaimo apparently was not as accommodating in nature as was our local jurist. A week or so before trial we were summoned for a status conference. Before entering temporary chambers I was treated to courthouse scuttlebutt that Alaimo had fined an attorney five hundred dollars earlier that day for arriving at a hearing five minutes late. Manny and Mary accompanied me into chambers, since the judge had ordered each side to show up with someone authorized to settle the case.

Our visiting jurist sat at a conference table in a large office filled elsewhere by his hard-at-work retinue. In a display of old-world charm, he immediately rose upon seeing Mary and graciously led her to a seat. The small and fit Judge Alaimo looked to be in his late sixties or perhaps early seventies. He reminded me of my immigrant maternal grandfather: Mediterranean-featured and completely bald except for some short gray hair at the sides. He may be rough and tough with attorneys, but his pleasantries with my clients revealed someone cognizant of and well-skilled in personal relations.

When we got to business, it didn't take long to discover our judge was mentally nimble and already familiar with the case. His directives were promptly issued: Our proposed jury instructions and verdict forms shall be submitted on computer disc so the court can adjust the differences and make any other changes it deems necessary. The court shall initially introduce expert witnesses to the jury. Standard fare so far. Experts shall not be permitted to sit in on the trial, and counsel shall not, outside of court, reveal the testimony of other witnesses to their expert. This was a bit unusual. The modern trend allows an expert to follow the trial proceedings so he can be sure his opinion conforms to the evidence.

His next edict was even more unusual. The judge informed us he would not make rulings at trial regarding the introduction of documentary evidence. Each of us had a list of exhibits a mile long and an even greater tally of objections to the other's evidence.

Normally, such objections are raised and ruled upon during trial at the time a party seeks to introduce the written or photographic exhibit. Judge Alaimo didn't like "to spend time" doing this at trial, so he ordered all of our exhibit disputes to be resolved beforehand by one of the local magistrates—someone who is like, but not quite, a federal judge. Such a directive raises a double-edged sword. On one side it makes trying the case much easier. The attorney knows what's in and what's out and can plan his presentation without worry it will be upset by an unexpected ruling. On the sharper edge is the possible loss of admissible evidence.

The use of evidence is very context-specific. A subject or issue one party can't directly raise may inadvertently be opened up by the other party. If an unexpected answer given by the opponent's witness touches a subject previously off limits to you, or a sloppy question asked by opposing counsel does the same, the subject becomes fair game. Thus an exhibit that may not be relevant at the start of trial may in fact become pertinent as the case develops. For instance, if Grandma is suing her stockbroker for selling unwanted risky investments, she can't get into evidence a previous judgment against the broker for swindling another customer. But if the broker blurts out while testifying, "I've always been honest with my clients," the prior judgment becomes admissible. Trials are not always linear, and you can never anticipate all the bumps and curves along the way. I didn't envy the magistrate's job. Exceptional foresight would be required to properly sort out our evidentiary disputes.

The judge asked us how long we expected it would take to try the case, and I gave my "just short of a week" estimate, with David not far behind. As if he didn't hear us, and without mentioning his surfeit of cases, the judge told us we had two days—tops! Some judges are notorious for pushing along their dockets. Trying cases is not an exact science. Our promise to move as quickly as we could appeared inconsequential to Alaimo and his decreed timetable. And of course if we could settle the case, look how much more time the judge could save.

David was directed to step out for a minute, and we were asked how much it would take for the government to buy peace. My clients' bottom line was up to $400,000, although I thought the prospect of an appeal on statute of limitations should push that figure down a bit. A few minutes after trading places with David, we were ushered back to find a noticeably displeased judge and unnerved attorney.

David seemingly lacked authority to offer us anything more than a pittance. Apparently some Justice Department bigwig was needed to authorize the bucks reasonably required to settle this case. To Alaimo, the government had violated his settlement conference order. To David, top Justice Department brass were too busy and important to be at the beck and call of mere federal district court judges. My adversary had obviously said it more politely. He argued there were very few officials in the department with this type of authority, and given the great number of cases litigated by the government, such officials couldn't perform their mandated duties if forced to attend these conferences. Thus, requiring an official with sufficient settlement authority to appear in this case would "impermissibly interfere with the functioning of the executive branch of government."

The judge was not amused with talk of separation of powers. He scheduled a new settlement conference, specifically ordering the government to produce in person someone authorized to settle this case in an amount up to plaintiffs' maximum possible recovery. This was David's problem and of no consequence to me. We didn't care if the Attorney General or anyone else from the Justice Department showed up, since we knew the government had no interest in settling the case. I was no doubt happy David had managed to irritate the judge and felt no sorrow over my opponent's necessitated diversion of attention to this extraneous issue. Ignoring the judge's order was not an option, since that would constitute contempt of court and could lead to sanctions against the government, such as the dismissal of its defenses.

Back at the office I managed to set our evidentiary hearing before the Honorable Elizabeth A. Jenkins, United States Magistrate. Given the proximity of our trial, we were able to get a morning later that week, one day before the rescheduled settlement conference. We had enormous amounts of hearsay evidence we wanted admitted. "Hearsay," you remember, is an unsworn out-of-court "statement" usually excluded from consideration at trial.

Our magazines and catalogues showed pieces, that we claimed were comparable to the donated items, selling at prices to our liking. We had appraisals from numerous "experts" and quotes from dealers who would not be testifying at trial. These hearsay materials were clearly inadmissible to prove fair market value of the donations, but could properly show that my clients reasonably believed their deductions were valid. But what was the relevance of Manny and Mary's beliefs and whether those beliefs were reasonably formed? Just because my clients believed they were right didn't entitle them to the deduction; however, taxpayers' belief is highly relevant to the issue of penalties.

The I.R.S. imposed two penalties against my clients, one of which was for negligence. This penalty is not for getting your taxes wrong, but for taking a position whose impropriety would have been revealed by reasonable effort. You can't do your taxes with blinders on and expect not to be penalized if found to be in error. The Service claimed that since the deductions taken by Manny and Mary so vastly exceeded the real value of the donations, *ipso facto,* the taxpayers' belief as to the value of their donated artwork was not reasonable. Therefore, any information my clients were privy to that supported their belief should be admissible to prove they were acting reasonably.

Attorneys love it when they can get evidence in on one issue, even when the judge instructs the jury the same evidence can't be considered on another issue. If the jury sees my clients' old magazine showing a jade table screen selling for $100,000, they get to hear my obvious argument that Manny and Mary had good cause to believe theirs was worth $90,000. The indirect message survives the court's cautionary instruction. With a like screen selling for 100k, the jurors can't help but think our screen really *is* worth what we claim.

While readying for our magistrate's hearing I was startled to receive the government's emergency brief to the Federal Circuit Court of Appeal. The appellate division of the Justice Department sought reversal of Alaimo's order mandating the corporeal presence of someone authorized to settle the case. This effort kept a couple of lawyers up all night and would have cost a hefty sum in the private sector. Another prudent use of public resources, I chuckled. Even though I wasn't going to respond to the appeal, I enjoyed the department's brief. It certainly was convincing, since by the end, I readily believed the government would fall if forced to send a bureaucrat to our settlement conference.

It took some doing, but I finally got all my exhibits, giant photo blowups and such, into a handcart and over to the federal courthouse in Tampa. In a modest hearing room, Magistrate Jenkins appeared and judiciously informed the world she was not fond of being on the butt end of Judge Alaimo's peculiar predilection for resolving evidentiary disputes. A magistrate's job is to do the judge's bidding, and that in itself didn't seem to bother the hardworking Ms. Jenkins. I think she realized, as well as did counsel, that rulings on the evidence could better be made at trial. Despite all our misgivings, we got into it—hours in the trenches, and a good portion in hand-to-hand combat. No prisoners taken here—each exhibit was a fight to the death.

As we proceeded, Jenkins allowed us to sit but David, in the fever of combat, couldn't restrain himself from bolting up in attack. With my opponent vigorously arguing from a standing posture, it didn't take long for me to arise. Although the magistrate's reminders seated us for a spell, the lust of battle again propelled David upward and forward leaning, with me close to follow. Each of us was behind our own table, with the bar separating us from Jenkins's elevated station. Given the magistrate's distance and power of office, I was surprised to hear her say, upon David's latest vertical thrust, "Please sit down. I find your stance intimidating." You would never get the same from a male judge, even if he felt the same as our magistrate. I found Jenkins' sensitivity to herself and honesty of expression refreshing, and definitely more powerful than the angry or threatening remark one might expect from the bench in this type of situation.

When the hearing ended I checked my lacerations to see if immediate attention was required, and finding no heavy bleeding, took stock of our position as the dust began to settle. We had lost some good men, but the troops and our position were, for the most part, intact. (Okay—enough of these battlefield analogies for now.) I admired David's stamina as I wearily drove back to the office. At the end of our encounter, he appeared to lack the fatigue that prompted me to delay our marking of evidence. Each of us was ordered to physically inspect and initial the others' original exhibits so there would be no question of their authenticity at trial. We were going to be at court the next morning for our rescheduled settlement conference and agreed to mark exhibits after meeting with Judge Alaimo. But before our next go-round, I hoped for the rest that David apparently could do without.

CHAPTER TWENTY-SIX

# *Becoming an Empty Vessel*

THE DECOR HADN'T CHANGED since our last get together and neither had the personnel. That morning I was informed that the Circuit Court had denied the government's emergency appeal, and I wondered whether my opponent had the chutzpah or bad sense to show up without a settlement figure. Perhaps some unseen department potentate was waiting in the wings. David, upon entering chambers, was quick to announce to the court his expanded stature as authorized government settlement agent. David's mantle descended from the highest echelons of the Justice Department, so he said, and Alaimo either took him at his word or simply lacked interest in pursuing the matter further.

The judge already knew what we wanted, so he spent some time with David to see how tightly the government had sealed its coffer. As we waited I thought how wonderful it would be to spend the next week counting settlement dollars instead of trying this case. I enjoyed only a glimmer of this fantasy, as I firmly knew the odds of settlement were close to zilch. Judge Alaimo confirmed reality by explaining to Manny and Mary that the government had put no credible proposal on the table.

It was Friday, and we were told there was one case in front of us. We could start anytime next week and had to be poised on a moment's turn. I said good-bye to my clients and followed David to the U.S. Attorney's office to mark evidence. We found a room, sat across a table, and began to initial the tag found on each exhibit offered by the other. One of the first items were copies of plaintiffs' tax returns for the years in question. We each had listed the returns as exhibits, and David proposed using my set as a joint exhibit since my copies were better quality than his. The I.R.S. apparently had lost the original returns, and its copies were unsigned and had pages missing. I refused David's logical and practical suggestion. Although David didn't understand why I wanted the poorer copy before the jury, he was convinced I was posturing for some advantage—and he pressed me on it.

There indeed was an object behind my obfuscating obstinacy. I saw a tactical advantage that I was not inclined to share with my opponent. It involved the other penalty assessed by the I.R.S., which was for "substantial understatement" of taxes. Intent or reasonableness was irrelevant to this punishment. Here, if the taxes you paid were a certain percentage less than the amount really owed, you were fined. However, the underage wouldn't be penalized if the taxpayers "adequately disclosed in a return or in a statement attached to the return" the position they were taking.

This particular penalty supposedly promotes disclosure of questionable items and deters taxpayers from trying to hide or mischaracterize deductions. If we could prove that the appraisals of the donated items were attached to Manny and Mary's returns, we could avoid the penalty. Since our copies of the tax returns were arguably self-serving, I also wanted the government's version before the jury. Even though the I.R.S. copies had no appraisals attached, because they were so shabby and otherwise incomplete, I could argue they were poor indications of whether appraisals were actually attached to the originals.

Oh the lawyer's mind at work! A trial attorney's mind never rests, never stops—it is always percolating and churning in its ceaseless pursuit to find an opening to improve a position, a way to advance the case. This ability is a boon to clients, but often a plague to attorneys. Unfortunately, most practitioners can't shut off this engine at their own bidding. As the sorcerer's apprentice discovered, the willing servant he conjured soon became a demon forcibly occupying his every moment. And with a case, it not only occupies your attention, you seem to eat, breathe, and sleep it. As astutely observed by Sri Ramakrishna, our quotable nineteenth-century Indian saint, "If one is to realize God he must think of the Lord incessantly, like a lawyer does with his cases." Imagine what we lawyers could accomplish if we devoted our minds elsewhere with such fervor.

What David was passionately dedicated to at the moment was exposing my cover. He repeatedly asked why I wouldn't agree to the joint exhibit, and my unconvincing answers stoked his effort. I finally just refused to talk about it further. As we continued with the exhibits, David became more overbearing and obnoxious. His initials on my successive exhibit tags changed from letters to lines and then became smaller and smaller until they were two barely discernible dots on the paper. I became concerned. At trial David might claim that he hadn't seen or marked the exhibit and try to have it excluded. He enjoyed my consternation and obvious irritation, and grinned widely when I asked him to increase the size of his initials. The dots became lines for a while until dwindling again. I summoned up the energy and repeated my graphological request. I was still feeling yesterday's fatigue, now much compounded, and felt as if I would be bowled over by David's continued aggression.

At the end of our session, David asked if he could take my set of tax returns out of the room for a moment. It's a little hard to explain to a layman, but a lawyer's original trial exhibits are kept very close until received by the court. A little mark or alteration on an exhibit can change its meaning, and sometimes an altered or lost exhibit can severely damage or destroy a case. You want your jewels kept inviolate, and the last place you want to put them is in the hands of an opposing attorney you don't trust. David was already up and reaching for my returns when I asked why he wanted them. He said he'd like to show them to someone, and with weariness overcoming the exercise of my better judgment, I agreed. After a few moments turned into several minutes I left the room, walked down the hall, and spied David in the copying center reproducing my exhibits, which were unstapled and scattered around desks and chairs.

What my fatigue did not impede was the generation of anger. I was mad as hell. The man had lied and was tampering with my exhibits. I didn't know if I was angrier at his unabashed demeanor, his severe breach of legal and civil morals, or my failure by allowing this outrage. I grabbed my exhibits, packed up my materials, and headed home. Driving back to my office and away from David's grinning face, it was easier to look past my anger. This left me with what my anger had concealed—fearful feelings of harm and violation.

The logical mind might say, *C'mon George! It's only a game. You weren't hurt. There's no sensible reason to feel that way.* Our fears come in all shapes and sizes. If we recognize them and respect their invitation to insight instead of avoiding or minimizing them, we come much closer to our true fearless nature. At some level all of us are afraid, whether it's about a seemingly trivial challenge in our practical day or the disintegration of self at the heart of meditation. God-realization requires courage. Transcending fear, releasing ourselves from its illusion, is an unavoidable process as we progress on our journey to the Divine.

Somehow our fear is released by experiencing what lies behind it. For me, by resting in the vulnerability of feeling harmed I was soon overcome by a deep wave of peace. "Resting in vulnerability" means allowing myself to experience the sensations associated with the "harm," rather than avoiding them in (expressive) anger or the (suppressive) mental and quite logical belief that my feeling was non-sense. In this peace I felt fully supported and nurtured by everlasting life, and I experienced the joy of knowing that nothing—no *thing*—can ever remove or sever that source. With this arose a genuine and profound sense of love and gratitude for David. He had again fulfilled his role in catalyzing for me a fear that needed to be released. I can be a pretty hard guy to push and therefore create my foils well.

I don't want to belabor what you've heard me say before. We attract to ourselves those persons and situations necessary for us to transcend our limitations, to unmask what is unreal. If we don't notice and learn, we play it out in the same or perhaps a different setting again and again. If we recognize our "antagonist" as the deliverer of a gift, we can truly appreciate and love this messenger. That is why Jesus entreated us to turn the other cheek—not for us to suffer more of the world's indignities, but to realize that every part of life, every bit of our experience, is a gift from God.

But even when we think we've learned our lesson, why does it seem that we repeatedly go through the same stuff? Why did my flare-ups with David continue after I plumbed the deeper issues triggered by our interactions? These are fair questions. Our growth is not linear. One way is to see it as an ascending spiral, like a vertically stretched Slinky. It may appear we're traveling in circles, and indeed we are, but each revolution brings us to a spot slightly ascended from the same location on the prior go round.

When working on an issue, especially in the beginning, it seems we frequently get caught in the same pitfalls. After a while, when we believe we have resolved the matter, we unexpectedly fall flat on our face. "Darn it. I thought I learned how not to get hooked into my co-worker's sarcasm, and here I am just as angry as I was a few months ago." Although the scenery looks familiar and you think you haven't progressed, the fact is you are not who you were those months ago. There is a qualitative difference. Your unwanted reaction may be less intense and of shorter length; you may feel more compassion for yourself and your antagonist; the incident may be accompanied by a greater insight or wisdom than before. Some deeply held areas of unconsciousness are brought into light by degree. As we ascend the spiral, we may visit the same issues over and over and even come to see our more elevated responses as a measure of our growth. Some of our shadow parts, when brought fully into the light, finally drop away like withered leaves.

Another, less Newtonian, way to look at spiritual growth is through the model of quantum physics. Electrons have defined orbits around a nucleus, but don't travel between orbits; they leap. When enough energy enters the atomic system, an electron assumes higher orbit. It travels no distance, since there is "nothing" in the space between the orbits, and the "leap" is instantaneous, since it took no "time" to get there. With a loss of system energy, the leap is reversed.

Sometimes in our growth we suddenly realize we are different, that we have transformed into what we were striving to become.

We know our place in the world has changed, yet can't fully understand how we got there. It is like being on the second floor of a building and wanting to get to the next but not seeing a way up. Then, without warning, we find ourself on the third floor, and as we look back down we don't see any stairs or elevator or ladder and wonder how we ascended. As with the electron, we might soon take a downward leap and find ourself back on the second floor. In a system that is energetically unstable, the leap between levels may be frequent. So for us, in times of transition as we move into higher energies, we often fluctuate between our newly experienced expansive way of being and our old, restrictive patterns.

This quantum model fits well with the anciently described chakra system. The latter identifies subtle energy centers in the body, starting beneath the base of the spine and rising to the crown of the head. The lower centers govern survival and procreative and ego/power needs, while the higher pertain to love, compassion, wisdom, and ultimately God-realization. As our relationship with the world moves from one of greed and control to selfless love, as we become less absorbed with our own circumstances and more cognizant of and responsive to the needs of those around us, our energy starts to reside in the higher chakras. When are we most susceptible to falling back into our lower centers? When we feel lacking or depleted in energy—as does the electron. How many times have you heard yourself or another say, "I know if I go visit my mother [or go in to see my boss, or talk with my ex-wife, etc.] feeling tired as I do, we'll end up having an argument, and I'll feel hurt and say some things I'll regret later."

Acutely aware of the upcoming week's energetic demands, I was careful not to allow work to intrude upon the weekend time I had set aside for some rest and renewal. Although the case had been prepared for trial in 1993 and I had been intently working on it for the past two months, there were still a thousand things to do, and another million just to make better what was done before. More and more preparation could easily have filled every available second. Exercise, good nutrition, yoga, and meditation were a well-heeded necessity for me. Monday morning brought word on the progress of the preceding case, and on Tuesday came our green light for Wednesday morning.

While doing yoga on the eve of trial, I deeply knew the case was a watershed event in my life. I started to become contemplative and even felt a bit solemn. Then I felt a burst of energy that carried a distinct sensation that *I* wasn't going to be doing anything. I felt like an empty vessel, a vehicle through which Spirit does its own work. I felt deep gratitude for being endowed with the abilities that allow this work to be done through me. In a sense I lost, at least for that moment, a personal agenda. I became an agent and God was the principal. All I needed to do was permit the work to come through me. All I needed to do was act while remaining unattached to the results of my actions. Victory was no longer mine to win— but then again, neither was defeat mine to bear.

CHAPTER TWENTY-SEVEN

# *My Kingdom for a Nap*

B RACING FOR THE COLD was going to take some extra doing this February morning. Constance departed from our house well-insulated, but I didn't realize until the tail end of our forty-minute drive to Tampa that I had left my suit jacket hanging in our closet. Before such an embarkation, I usually take pains to remember to place this parting remnant of lawyer's dress on the back seat of the car. Only once in seventeen years had I been guilty of this sartorial omission. If Judge Alaimo fined an attorney for being five minutes late, how would he greet this transgression? It was too late to turn back now.

My uniform deficiency proved not just a formality. I was truly shivering by the time we managed to unload Constance's Land Cruiser and get inside the lobby of the courthouse. Once we arrived at the courtroom I called the office and asked my mother, who was filling in for my secretary, to arrange for prompt delivery of my suit half. Meanwhile, Constance and I, along with Cindy my secretary, put our heads together, and the invention mothered by this necessity was to transfer the suit jacket off of Constance's back on to mine.

"Would counsel please introduce themselves and their clients to the prospective jurors?" Judge Alaimo began.

"Yes, your honor. I'm George Felos of the firm Felos and Felos and [looking like a complete jackass in a frock with no buttons, and sleeves up to my forearms] would like to ask my clients, Manny and Mary Fellouzis to stand and face the jury box."

269

Actually, my self-consciousness soon evaporated as I discovered to my astonishment that no one noticed my peculiar taste in clothing. It goes to show we are much less the object of everyone's attention than we think. Of course it also helped that Constance was wearing navy blue instead of pink that morning.

We proceeded with jury selection, where cases are sometimes won but often lost. In state court, counsel conduct extensive voir dire, questioning of prospective jurors, to ferret out potential biases or background information that may prove a juror hazardous to their case. This must be done though with maximum politeness so you don't offend the sensibilities of the jury panel.

The process is much more of a crapshoot in federal civil trials. Here, for the most part, the judge asks the questions, and most are directed to the panel as a whole rather than to any individual juror. That, along with the questionnaires the jurors fill out beforehand and your gut feeling, are about all you have to go on in making your selection. Judge Alaimo was at his gracious best in questioning the panel and did permit counsel to ask a few questions of our own. Instead of selecting six jurors and two alternates as we do in Florida state court, we were to pick a full jury of eight. If we lose a juror or two, there are no alternates; the remaining jurors then decide our case.

None of the candidates presented any legal cause for removal, so we were left with our three peremptory challenges. This means we could boot up to three jurors from the panel, without explanation, and take the next three in line. Of course, so could the government. Our most favorable juror, I thought, was a highly educated attractive middle-aged professional woman from Sarasota. Not only did I feel a connection with her, but believed she had a plaintiff's bent, as she had litigated a major claim arising from an airplane crash. I could tell she knew what it was like battling against an intractable and obnoxious defendant.

After huddling with Manny and Mary and consulting with Constance, I approached the bench with David and we made our initial challenges. I was very surprised that David kept my favorite on the jury. We went back to our respective tables and in whispers reviewed with our clients the newly composed panel. The chosen representative of the government seated next to David was William Reddy, the I.R.S. agent who had investigated Manny and Mary for fraud over ten years before.

We had one challenge left, and if we used it, the next juror in line was an insurance adjuster. This usually is the last person in the world you would want to have meting out dollars on a jury. Even more than accountants, insurance adjusters are notorious for maintaining a tight purse string when assessing damages. Who on the jury was so horrendous I might risk replacement with an adjuster? She was a perfectly harmless-looking legal secretary who happened to have worked many years for a tax attorney. For some reason I feared her as a juror. Either she hated the I.R.S. and would be the best juror in the world, or she had seen so many tax scams pulled by her boss's clients, her view of the case would be too jaded. If she did possess either bias, I thought the former more likely—yet why hadn't David booted her?

We spent too much time thinking, for the judge's liking. He summoned us back to the bench and asked for our final calls. David accepted the jury and at the last moment I went with the adjuster—*fates protect me!* Was my decision unfortunately consistent with the old and uncomplimentary adage that lawyers don't want intelligent persons on juries? Maybe so; but my call wasn't a vote against brainpower, it was an exclusion of specialized knowledge.

My opening statement was nothing special but certainly adequate. It seems in all my preparation I omitted to compose one beforehand. I knew everything there was to know about this case and had no difficulty speaking extemporaneously.

"Imagine over two-hundred-fifty years ago in the court of Chinese Emperor Yung-Cheng, a master artisan holding a piece of rare jade—peering into its luster—waiting for his discerning eye to capture from it the image of the figure he will carve. Imagine this treasure, painstakingly crafted and created from those hands, carefully passed down through the ages until it finally rests in the palms of my clients."

I don't remember if I said it that way, but you want to spark the interest and imagination of the jury. Opening statement is an opportunity to explain to the jurors your clients' story and lay out a map showing what you expect to prove during trial—and it does not have to be boring. It also is the essential place to reveal all of your warts. The weaknesses in your case will be exposed and exploited by your opposition, and it is imperative they be introduced by *you* in order to soften and minimize their impact. I obviously used the occasion to explain to the jury how an ivory model boat worth $380,000 in 1980 could be purchased for $17,000, less than three years before.

David's opening was also adequate, although I knew that his stiff and somewhat awkward demeanor resulted from this, his baptism into the realm of jury trial. I was delighted to hear him extol at length the virtues and stellar accomplishments of James B. Godfrey. David assured the jury they would have, by the conclusion of trial, no doubt whatsoever that Godfrey's appraised values were correct. Ah, yes—the bigger they are the harder they fall. The government had just pinned its entire case on their expert's lapel, little knowing I had a ticket to send him to the cleaners.

In a civil trial, since the plaintiffs have the burden of proof, they get to present their case first. "Burden of proof" in the non-criminal arena means presenting evidence which, when compared to the evidence of your opponent, shows your version of the disputed facts "more likely" than the rendition offered by the defendant. This differs from criminal proceedings, where the state's burden of proof "beyond a reasonable doubt" is significantly greater. In a civil case, a little tip in the scales toward the plaintiff is all the protagonist needs to win. But if the evidence on each side weighs equal in the eyes of the jury, it is required by law to find for the defendant.

Before getting to my first witness, the judge had us submit en masse our exhibits into evidence to avoid the delay of piecemeal introduction. There were no surprises, since these submissions had all been previously ruled admissible by the magistrate and marked, more or less, by counsel. Yet I felt a surge of excitement seeing our small photo of Godfrey's bone boat stamped by the clerk into evidence. Our well-prepared and concealed fireworks were close to detonation.

Manny was sworn in, and we were off! It took a while for him to overcome his nervousness and for us to build up a head of steam.

Manny is best when lecturing—or pontificating, some might say—and really started to crank up as we walked through the twenty donated items. Each had an interesting story of its own—perhaps the way it was acquired, the historical or cultural significance of the piece, or a lesson about its fabrication. As I held each picture in front of the jury, Manny did his stuff. It went something like this:

"That group of pieces is an amberina punch bowl set created in the late nineteenth century in the eastern Ohio/western Pennsylvania area. This region was famous for the production of decorative glass, 'art glass,' and flourished as a center for that art form through the first third of this century. 'Amberina' describes the color of the glass, which is created by adding molten gold to the liquid glass at a critical point as it is formed." How's that for sounding authoritative?

Manny's expertise respected no borders. The Chinese temple or "tomb" figures were particularly intriguing: "These four, solid wooden painted figures, ranging in height from eight to thirty-six inches, are depictions of deities or perhaps high court officials. Two have been dated to the Ming Dynasty, 1368-1644, and the other two are apparently eighteenth century. Upon the death of a wealthy individual, his family might donate the figure to a temple as a remembrance or perhaps bury the sculpture with the deceased."

"Mr. Fellouzis, what is the significance of the hollowed-out compartment found in the back of some of these figures?"

"They were designed to hold scrolls of writing. The deceased, before his passing, may have composed an eternal message for the gods or perhaps reflected upon his earthly life. The scroll was placed in the compartment and a block of wood was then put in the hole to fill it and cover the scroll."

Fascinating! And there was more.

"Mr. Fellouzis, what effect, if any, would the presence of these scrolls in the figures have on their value?" Oh yes, it was money we were talking about!

"Tomb figures are not common, but those with intact scrolls are particularly rare, and therefore, of course, much more valuable. Scrolls are lost or destroyed over time and may purposefully be discarded. A lazy son might purchase a figure from a grave robber, remove the old scroll, and place the stolen sculpture in the temple to honor his dearly departed father."

"Mr. Fellouzis, did any of the figures you donated contain intact scrolls?"

"Two of them have scrolls, and one of those two is particularly significant. It has a petrified sea horse on top of the scroll. This was meant to deter someone from later removing the writing. A candidate for earthly departure, knowing his fellow Chinese to be very superstitious, might place on the scroll an item whose disturbance was believed to cause bad luck. It is extremely rare to find not only the scroll, but also the dried remains of its protector. The only other one I have seen intact remains in my personal collection. That one has a small snake coiled on top of a scroll, which has never been removed. And if you knew how the Chinese felt about snakes, you'd know why!"

You can't help but be impressed by Manny's expertise and find likable his enthusiasm for his preferred art—two wonderful qualities you want your client to exude to the jury. Things were going reasonably well, but we'd see how he looked after cross-examination.

David took his turn at the lectern and fumbled his papers about until they were either arranged to his liking or the awkwardness of the pause prompted him to begin. Specialists who are in court much more than me probably have a better-polished trial demeanor, but compared to David's anxiety I definitely appeared and felt smooth and relaxed. His initial questions barely concealed the nervousness exhibited to me via my view of his shaking left leg. Remembering my own Supreme Court palpitations first gave rise to compassion for my legal colleague and then the recognition that yes, experience does count for something.

Of course my fleeting sentiment toward David did nothing to deter me from exacerbating his unease. David tried to impeach Manny's credibility by presenting supposedly conflicting deposition statements. I immediately rose and objected. I asserted that the deposition was consistent with the witness's testimony and started reading those portions of the deposition aligned with Manny's challenged trial statements.

Perhaps I overstepped a bit. The deposition probably contained some minor conflicts that David could bring out. Proper procedure would permit me to read the consistent parts of the deposition during my re-direct examination, which follows completion of cross. But my self-confidence and a nod my way from the judge left David nonplused and effectively scuttled his impeachment effort. My opponent did score a few points during cross-examination, but never hit his stride, thanks to some well-made objections placed at just the right times. Day one ended with Manny intact as a witness and still left with the opportunity to do himself some good during the next day's friendly re-direct examination.

We conducted the day's post-mortem over some rich Italian food, which did well to warm the evening chill and fill my deep hunger. Trials are so energy intensive that, despite a good lunch and the figs and almonds usually stocked in my file case, I feel ravenous by day's end. During trial week I make a point of eating lots of fish, the most concentrated protein source I am willing to offer my vegetarian-tuned body. I gave Manny and Mary my assessment of our efforts so far, and did my best to bolster their spirits. I am the last person to inspire over-confidence, but by the same token, a winning attitude is favorably picked up by a jury. And it was the jurors in whom I was keenly interested. They were the only group whose opinion of our efforts ultimately counted.

Constance and my clients had been assigned the job of observing the jurors' reactions to the proceedings. During much of the trial, especially when questioning witnesses and interacting with the judge and opposing attorney, the jury is outside my direct view. Although I have a feel for what's working and what's not, it is valuable to have someone else with me to unobtrusively watch our decision-makers. I went round the table for my jury reports and made some mental notes for the following day.

One of our jurors, a very young woman, seemed to me somewhat unhappy and a bit distracted. I asked if anyone else picked this up, and Mary mentioned she thought this juror had something bothering her. We tossed it around and came to the conclusion that our case was not causing her disturbance. I got the strong feeling the young woman was experiencing some personal distress and simply did not want to be physically present in court or on the jury.

The evening had waned by the time I got home. Determined to give myself over to yoga and meditation, I allotted less than an hour to arrange my materials and review the next day's plan. Keeping connected to my Source was far more important to this endeavor than honing more details. I was stretched past my usual limits, faced with innumerable demands on my energy, and under tremendous pressure. My wits and abilities and resources were significant—but not enough. The situation demanded the secular's alchemization into Spirit. Failure to heed that demand does not necessarily mean a "result" cannot be obtained; but the price of fear or ego-based "success" exacts a horrible toll. Withstanding, rather than transcending, the enormous stress presented through this work destroys the body, fries the mind and emotions, and deadens the spirit. Why challenge myself like this? Why choose such a harrowing path?

The beautiful story of the Hopi Indians comes to mind when pondering these questions. A Hopi elder once was asked why his nation settled in such an arid and inhospitable place as the desert cliffs of the southwest. He explained that the Hopi, before finding their permanent home, lived and roamed for many generations in other parts of this immense land. They previously settled in lush valleys and on the fertile plains of great rivers. What they planted burst abundantly from the rich soil, and they enjoyed close and plentiful game. But the ease of their lives weakened the Hopi's connection to God; they did not find it *necessary* to rely upon the Source for their sustenance.

The elders, knowing that forgetfulness of Spirit would lead to the ruin of their people, kept moving the nation until they found a place where survival depended upon their conscious reliance upon the Divine. When they came upon their present home, they knew that the scant water, meager soil, and harsh environment could barely sustain them. There, the nation could only flourish by being centered in God's living presence. If there are always more loaves before me than I can possibly eat, how might I realize and remember that man does not live by bread alone?

This story particularly resonates with me. Sometimes too much comfort leads to my complacency, then indolence and inertia. The resulting sluggishness obviously is not conducive to spiritual practice. Well, if I need a challenge to keep me spiritually alert, I had surely given myself a good one here.

Morning two of this stimulus for spiritual awakening broke through my groggy cry for additional rest. I had spent more of my night falling into sleep than actually participating in slumber. I could hardly tell whether my insomnia was rooted in nervousness or excitement, but because the two are quite close in many respects, I ascribed my sleeplessness to the latter. Why not make the more empowering choice?

All but one assembled for the start of day two. The young juror who had seemed so distracted the previous day was nowhere to be seen. The bailiff eventually received a call informing us that the lady had been in an automobile accident, and although not physically injured, was too shaken up to come to court. That's one way to manifest your desire. We proceeded with our jury of seven.

Manny was up again to finish his testimony and seemed more confident after the previous day's practice. Re-direct examination is not an opportunity to have the witness repeat his story. Counsel can only seek clarification or further explanation of what was covered on cross-examination. Fortunately, I had enough material here to keep Manny in front of the jury for a while, which given his laudable performance, pleased me much.

We had our two experts to hear from today, along with deposition testimony to read. First to testify was Arthur Horowitz, New York City-born and-raised, now in his late forties or early fifties and getting pudgy. Within a year or two after graduating from high school, Arthur began work in his father-in-law's import and wholesale business, which specialized in Chinese and European fine arts. His twenty-eight years with the company he eventually acquired gave Arthur some good practical credentials.

Manny, when starting his own business in Chinese arts, had become Arthur's customer. Within a few years Manny's Chinese import operation eclipsed Arthur's, and they switched roles as vendor/customer. My clients' former attorney had engaged Arthur, along with other appraisers, to value the donations during the I.R.S. administrative proceedings. Our expert had visited the

Carnegie Museum in 1985 to inspect the items, and his resulting appraisal served as the basis for his testimony.

Arthur was administered the oath of witness, and his simple "I do" unmistakably proclaimed his New York accent. Even setting dialect aside, he was not my first choice in experts. Number one on my list would have been Samuel S. T. Chen, Distinguished Professor Emeritus, Ph.D. Harvard University, advisor to the United Nations and Representative of the National Palace Museum, Taiwan. Dr. Chen had performed his appraisal in 1988, and although his numbers were lower than Arthur's, his stellar qualifications more than made up for the difference.

One danger in an old case is the occasional infirmity or death of a witness or party. While Dr. Chen was still with us, his battle with inevitable aging made him reluctant to travel or expend the energy necessary to proclaim and defend his prior opinion. Much as I tried, I couldn't convince him to testify. Of course, I waited until the last possible moment to inform David that our likely choice of expert would not be appearing. When you inherit a case you're sometimes bequeathed a hand you would have preferred not to play.

This is not to say that Arthur Horowitz was chopped liver! Though somewhat nervous on direct examination and tentative under cross, he came through without major blunder. As for David, he, like Manny, performed better with a day under his belt—which also contributed to the lessened effectiveness of our witness. But to the government's surprise, we had one salient fact that significantly and irrefutably buttressed Arthur's credibility. His only other stint as an expert witness involved a shipment of contemporary and antique Chinese jades.

"Mr. Horowitz, who hired you to appraise that shipment and testify in court?"

"Why, it was the United States of America." The Customs Service had impounded the cargo and presented Arthur in Federal Court as its expert to establish period and value. Did I have fun with that!

Our Philadelphia and Hong Kong witnesses had their say via deposition testimony. Nothing else induces jury somnolence like reading from depositions, so counsel has to break it up and keep it short, if possible. Some judges prefer to have the court clerk play the role of the witness. The attorney reads the deposition questions and the clerk mouths the transcribed answers from the stand. Even the most dramatic testimony will be rendered interminably boring by the clerk's usual monotone, mispronunciation, disinterest, and lack of understanding of the subject matter. Here we replaced the absent witness with my father. His prior review of the depositions and command of public speaking enlivened the printed testimony more than I had expected. Not only was snoring banished, we even seemed to hold the jurors' attention.

Of even greater surprise was our ability to present Dominic's deposition in the first place. David never tried to strike the testimony. I surely thought he would object at some stage in the case. He failed to raise the issue at any of the pre-trial conferences, was mum before the magistrate, and uttered no cry as we commenced our reading before the jury. I was truly bewildered. David *knew* Dominic's failure to answer questions on cross-examination gave the government strong legal grounds for having the entire testimony excluded.

Not only did I think the deposition was highly favorable, I believed it was essential. It provided our only corroboration of Manny's storied purchase of the ivory boat. Maybe something here was too obvious for me to see. Did David think this deposition helped his cause? Was his failure to object an oversight on his part? For whatever reason, all our transcontinental anguish and machinations over the Dominic affair turned out to have been needless expenditure of energy. Sometimes events in a case curiously but happily turn out differently than you expect. Getting to use Dominic's deposition fit this adage well—or so it seemed at the moment.

We closed our case with Robert Perlman, our man of ivory. Bob concealed his nervousness better than Arthur and proved a more convincing witness. Knowing his stuff also had something to do with it, as did his love of the tusk. Bob had not actually seen Manny's boat, but relied on photographs for his appraisal. Most appraisers will agree that a credible valuation usually requires actual inspection of the item. Bob didn't disagree, but asserted that the ivory boat presented a special case. He was well familiar with the producer's quality of workmanship, as he had visited the Nathan Ivory Factory and had imported a substantial number of their carved pieces. Bob had also been offered this particular boat for sale prior to Manny's purchase, and therefore had firsthand knowledge of its value.

In 1978 a U.S. importer had shown Bob pictures of Manny's boat, still owned and displayed by Nathan Ivory, and tagged it at $158,000 delivered net to purchaser. Factoring in the importer's customary ten percent cut, along with the freight, insurance, and duty charges, confirmed for our expert a $125,000 Hong Kong wholesale price. This corresponded with both Manny's and Dominic's estimations. Now how does that price inflate to over three hundred thousand? Bob tacked on twenty percent for the increased price of raw ivory from 1978 to donation year 1980, then calculated dealer markups to the ultimate retail purchaser. This brought us a $425,000 retail dealer-to-customer price, and a tab of $345,300 if sold by a wholesale importer direct to the consumer. To be on the "conservative" side, Bob proclaimed the latter amount as the boat's 1980 "fair market value."

That sounded good to me. I thought we had locked in pretty well the Hong Kong wholesale value of the boat. But how far the jury would walk down the path of dealer padding remained to be seen. Bob also testified about an ivory model boat *he* had purchased in China in the early 1980s. Manny's boat dwarfed the witness's four-foot junk, but the two models were stylistically similar. Bob purchased his for $80,000 and claimed it had a U.S. wholesale-to-dealer price of $180,000. This also sounded great. But is there really a retail customer out there who will shell out such astronomical sums to justify these dealer spreads?

Ann Reid didn't ask this or get much of anything else during her cross-examination. David's dark-haired, diminutive, and seemingly younger companion got hopelessly mired in trying to figure out how the witness had computed the dealer markups. While merchandise pricing may be a bit arcane to the layman, Ann's befuddlement suggested lack of preparation as well as inexperience.

To our delight, Bob came out of cross-examination with his credibility enhanced.

What would really, *really* enhance and delight me was some sleep, any sleep. Day two ended with me longing for bed. My meager slumber the night before was starting to impose its effect. Dinner, preparation for tomorrow's finale, yoga, and meditation were all necessary, but each just one more thing to do before night's rest. To my horror, "excitement," now combined with over-tiredness, conspired to make sleep even more elusive than the prior night's holy veil. Search as I might, no relaxation technique, breathing method, calculated indifference, or other strategy brought the respite I craved from my fitful fatigue. Tomorrow was it: the big day; my shot at Godfrey; the denouement—and I'd be too tired to stand, let alone think!

# CHAPTER TWENTY-EIGHT

# *Barbecuing the Government's Expert*

M Y BATHROOM MIRROR REFLECTED A SORROWFUL VISAGE. Not until sometime after four o'clock had I finally conked out, granting me only a couple of hours of sleep before my painful shove into day three. I had long ago recognized that adequate sleep was critical to my successful performance of a demanding task. I never pulled all-nighters in school—at least not for purposes of studying. Rest usually garnered me more points on exams than did information crammed in the wee hours. After mentally uttering some lamentations, I realized this was a propitious time to change a long-held concept.

"I am not my body," I declared to my likeness with the energy I could muster. "This flesh, these bones, these hands and feet, this mind, are all God's creation. They are imbued with Spirit. They are always Divinely impulsed at their source. God knows no fatigue. Spirit is never tired. As a child and expression of God I fully know that I now and always have all the energy I want and need. Since all is God, fatigue is an illusion. I now banish it from my consciousness. Thank you, Lord, for this knowing. And so it is!"

If this didn't get me pumped up, nothing would. Whether I was activating subtle but powerful spiritual laws or just giving myself a pep talk, it seemed to be working. I arrived at court feeling a bit precarious in the physical realm, but firm in my resolve. I rested in a strange sort of concentration as I practiced conservation of energy—no needless talk, no unnecessary movement, and no gratuitous action or thought

First up was David's direct examination of our man Godfrey. The judge greeted the witness and unintentionally gave us a point. Godfrey's still youthful appearance, combined with the long years since his appraisal, led Alaimo to comment that the witness must have been of tender age when commencing this effort. I made a mental note to reinforce the jury's likely belief that blossomy youth and inexperience are firmly connected.

Fostering that notion would have to wait for cross-examination, since Godfrey was now testifying with substantial authority. He came across as well-bred, well-schooled, well-learned, well-spoken, and well-qualified. But as direct examination proceeded, I sensed he was coming across, well—*too well.* There crept out a condescending attitude of erudition as Godfrey now seemed to be lecturing down to his audience rather than testifying to the jury and court. The effect wasn't particularly overt, but certainly enough to register on my ego eruption meter, which has been finely calibrated after so many personal readings. The witness finally was turned over to me. I brought my notes and needed exhibits to the lectern, took a deep breath, and dove in.

"Mr. Godfrey, please tell us what the word 'certified' means to you."

This immediately displaced the relaxation and comfort the witness had acquired by the end of direct examination. His posture straightened as, by my estimation, he momentarily tried to figure out what the heck this question had to do with the case. Starting cross-examination with an unexpected and seemingly extraneous query is a great way to rattle a witness.

With a bit of uncertainty came, "It means to swear to something."

*Exactly!*

"Mr. Godfrey, your appraisal"—which I now prominently displayed—"begins with the words 'This is to certify,' and after your *certification* you list your credentials and then describe each item and give your opinion of its value."

No argument here from the witness.

"Sir, in your appraisal you *certify* you're a 'qualified appraiser ... have received a B.A. degree in the field of oriental studies from the University of Virginia,' and 'have been engaged ... as an internationally recognized professional dealer.'"

Another assenting nod from the witness.

"And in your appraisal you endeavored to be as accurate as possible, as careful and precise as you could be because you were certifying, you were *swearing* to the truth of its contents. Isn't that so Mr. Godfrey?" (Let's distinguish this *sworn* document from idle cocktail party chatter.)

Still without a clue, the witness concurred.

"Then, sir, why did you state in your appraisal you received a B.A. degree in Oriental studies from the University of Virginia, when that is *not true?*"

We were off! The dimensions of the witness box instantaneously constricted, my favorite juror smiled along with one or two of her compadres, the judge stopped his paperwork and lifted his head, and the courtroom crackled.

Godfrey angrily asserted the authenticity of his educational pedigree. This happily led me to his deposition, where there was no mention of a degree in Oriental studies. There he *swore* he was a history major taking courses in "Asian studies," a field for which there was no major or degree. Upon hearing his pre-trial testimony read back to him, Godfrey claimed there was no real difference between his appraisal and deposition statements.

The jury wasn't buying it. He had proclaimed just a few moments ago that his certified appraisal was as careful and as accurate as it could be. In the eyes of the jury, this was a hair definitely large enough for me to split; so I continued to dissect, and the subject kept squirming.

"Not only was there no degree offered in 'oriental studies,' you didn't even concentrate in that area. Your deposition says you specialized in 'Asian studies.' Mr. Godfrey, you weren't telling the truth in your appraisal, were you?"

Godfrey started to look even more ridiculous with his bristled assertion that Asia and the Orient were the same. This led to a discussion about geography. I finally departed the venue of his education with:

"Well Mr. Godfrey, do I now understand you to mean that Pakistan is part of the Orient?" I suggested that the reports of Americans' abysmal deficiency in geography really are true.

Though we left the University of Virginia behind, we certainly weren't done with his credentials. I had a few words to say about Godfrey's position as "head" of Christie's New York Chinese department, a dominion basically consisting of him and his secretary; and let's not leave out his status as an "internationally recognized professional dealer," which mostly meant moving consigned goods from his New York apartment.

"Mr. Godfrey, do you know what the word 'puffery' means?"

With our witness bereft of definition, I happily supplied the particulars.

Referring to his appraisal, I asked, "Was there some self-inflation going on here for promotional purposes, Mr. Godfrey?"

Although the witness huffily denied his puffing, I don't think the jurors, or anyone else in the courtroom, saw it his way. My little blowfish worked its stuff. As we moved on to substance, the witness now seemed to be traveling light—not too much credibility left for Godfrey to tote along.

Our first stop among the donated items was the wooden tomb figures. Here was a good place to discuss the relationship between a piece's condition and its value. As I expected, Godfrey generally agreed that condition has a significant effect on an art object's worth. The auctioned tomb figures he used in valuing Manny's pieces were cracked, chipped, worm-eaten, and had hands missing.

"Why, then, Mr. Godfrey, would you use inferior catalogue pieces to ascribe a value to my clients' better-preserved figures?" I asked.

He claimed the donated and auctioned items were comparable.

"But sir—no cracks, chips or holes were listed in your appraisal description of the wood figures, and you *certified* you 'carefully examined the articles.'"

"Just because an item is carefully examined, doesn't necessarily mean damage will be noted in its description," he countered.

Good point Mr. Godfrey.

"But, Mr. Godfrey, why in your appraisal would you note a three-hundred-dollar snuff bottle is 'chipped' but not describe the alleged damage to a twenty-five-hundred-dollar tomb figure?"

In his frustration Godfrey blurted, "Well, one of your clients' figures had a hand missing."

This gave me pause. Do I challenge the statement? This was one of those moments in a trial that tests how well you know your case. Sitting on the clerk's table with the rest of the evidence were numerous photographs of our four wooden figures. My word had bettered Godfrey's up to now, and I didn't want to force a point and end up on the bottom side. The figures all looked sort of alike. Darn it, I didn't remember any missing hands. My steps towards the clerk's station brought: "Mr. Godfrey, I'd like to see this missing hand."

Without time to look I gave him the photos and commanded him to "show me." As he examined the pictures, I waited to be proven right or wrong. Just when enough time had ticked for me to conclude that Godfrey had erred with his absent extremity, we heard: "This one—this figure is missing a hand."

I took the outstretched photo, gazed at it a moment, smiled serendipitously, retrieved a copy from my files, gave Godfrey the copy, and walked in front of the jury box holding the photograph before them.

Our demonic deity was handily intact. One appendage did have only the thumb and pinkie extended, and at first blush, it looked as if the three middle fingers were missing. But quick scrutiny revealed the middle digits were tucked into the palm. Our god of the dark realms was displaying a *mudra,* a ritualized hand gesture found in Indian art and dance. I was well familiar with mudras through my practice and study of yoga. Certain intricate hand positions are believed to be natural and spontaneous manifestations of spiritual ecstasy. These known hand positions are often deliberately as-sumed by aspirants while meditating and are used during various yoga exercises. Mudras should be as familiar to an Oriental art scholar as the attributes of saints are to a Western art historian.

"Mr. Godfrey, please tell us, where on this picture is a missing hand?"

He made his expected choice.

With my finger on the picture to show the jury, I countered, "But, Mr. Godfrey, you can clearly see in the picture that the *hand* is not missing. There's the thumb and the pinkie."

"Well, there are three fingers missing," he testily muttered.

"Mr. Godfrey—do you know what a mudra is?"

Godfrey appeared shocked by my display of Eastern esoterica. The blood seemed to exit his face as he muttered a "yes." Godfrey agreed with my definition of the word and reluctantly admitted the figure's hand formed a mudra.

Having now lost his claim to missing fingers, you'd think he'd leave it alone. But no—

"The pinkie is cracked" he mumbled.

I brought the photo even closer to the jury.

"We don't have a magnifying glass here, Mr. Godfrey, but I don't see any crack."

With giggles about to erupt from a couple of jurors we now heard the witness sourly say, "Well, there's a chip on the end of the pinkie."

From a lost hand to missing fingers to a cracked pinkie and now a *chip*. Wait—I suppose there was a little flake off the end of the digit. I guess if you practice reductionism *absurdum,* you can always eventually be right!

The rest of Godfrey's cross-examination didn't fare much better for him. It didn't seem as if he had reviewed his deposition or, if he did, had bothered to check the accuracy of his statements. He gave the same erroneous answers to my questions on the finer points of jade. This time I hauled out my learned volumes on the subject and read to the witness and jury the correct and truly expert word on the subject. Godfrey unsuccessfully tried to split hairs or simply disagreed with the published works he had previously admitted were authoritative. His auction comparables for the incense burner further discredited him. He was forced to admit that the fine print at the front of the catalogues showed his items to be of disputed or recent date. With this the witness shuffled. The fact that Manny and Mary's koro was a genuine eighteenth-century piece was no longer a significant valuation factor in his opinion.

We finally got to the ivory boat. Godfrey admittedly did not deal with large ivory pieces as frequently as he worked with jades.

"Mr. Godfrey, is it fair to say then that your expertise in ivory is not quite what it is in jade?"

"Absolutely not. I'm as much an expert in ivory as I am in jade."

How did I know he was going to say that? I continued my set-up.

Placed on an easel right next to the witness box was the government's massive foam-board blow-up of Godfrey's photo from *Le Extreme Orient*. We established it was Godfrey who, through his trained eye, determined this boat was ivory—no dealer representation to rely on here. This model, which was selling at *Le Extreme Orient* for up to $30,000 just two years earlier, certainly confirmed for Godfrey that his $30,000 appraisal of Plaintiffs' boat was correct. I did my best to bind Godfrey as firmly to the mast of his bogus vessel as was possible before ending my turn. Hopefully both Godfrey and the government would go down with their ship.

I'd be lying if I claimed I didn't enjoy roasting James. No doubt most everyone else in court, except for the witness and his counsel, also found the experience pleasurable. We all delight in the prick of an inflated ego or the exposure of some hubris, as long as it's not our own. While a good part of me was an actor playing my role another part of me identified with my scripted persona.

Godfrey's inaccurate appraisal had played a large part in a decade of suffering for my clients. I believed the appraisal was close to inept, and my clients asserted it was deliberately in error. Yes, I felt good about my performance; yes, I was satisfied with my effort; yes, I largely remained a spectator to my actions. Yet a small part of me reveled while I grilled the witness and dined on the result. Sure, this was a meal of Godfrey's own making. He provided the ingredients, and I was just the chef. Although I was perfectly professional and wouldn't have changed a word of my examination, I wondered whether my motivation held a tinge a vengeance. In order to enjoy your dinner is it sometimes better to overlook what goes on in the kitchen? Perhaps you have to wait to see how digestion goes before answering that question.

The government called only one other witness, Mr. Reddy the revenue agent, its representative at trial. He was asked to recite the statements made to him during his fraud investigation well over a decade before. He wasn't relying on written notes and wanted us to believe his memory was sufficient to recall the details of ancient conversations from one investigation among the hundreds he conducted. His primary target was the Weissman's, whose favorable deposition testimony conflicted with the statements they allegedly made to Reddy.

"Objection your honor, this is hearsay," I asserted.

In response, Ann Reid claimed that the statements were proper exceptions to the hearsay prohibition because they were inconsistent with the Weissmans' deposition stories. Generally, a witness's prior out-of-court statements are admissible to show a conflict with his sworn trial testimony. Up we went for a bench conference.

My research confirmed what I had concluded during the Philadelphia depositions. A witness's prior avowals are only admissible if the witness is questioned about them first. David had to ask the Weissmans about these prior statements and give them a chance to explain or adopt them, before Reddy could utter this hearsay in court. The judge firmly agreed, graciously tried to dispel Ann's confusion by explaining this evidentiary point, and sent us back to our tables. The ruling basically scuttled Reddy's use as a witness to the government and made my cross-examination brief. With its two witnesses out of the way, the United States rested.

## CHAPTER TWENTY-NINE

# *The Denouement*

"MR. FELOS, ANY REBUTTAL?" Before my mind could form a word to utter, my body felt as if it were imploding, all its energy sucked down a drain leaving nothing to support its form. A siren went off and my corpus delivered a clear message: "Unless you get me some rest, *now,* I'm checking out of here!"

"Your honor, may we have a short recess before commencing our rebuttal testimony?" Some brief but deep conscious relaxation would pacify my physical counterpart and promote a temporary revival. Ten minutes seated on a quiet bench with my eyes closed was all I needed.

The judge routinely denied my request. It was late morning, rebuttal in a case like ours is rarely lengthy, and the judge wanted all the testimony concluded before the lunch break.

"But, your honor, we only need a few minutes." With Alaimo waving off my pleas, I was pressed on.

*Well, body, at least I respect you enough to heed your voice. I did try my best to get you what you wanted.* If you're about to abuse your faithful servant, you might as well be as polite about it as you can!

Our relationship with our bodies is fundamental to our well-being, yet woefully neglected. Because mind controls matter, we may choose to disregard the body's requirements and good sense. Your body didn't want a piece of cake after a filling meal, or crave a midnight movie or saturation in drugs or alcohol. It was you wanting to have more "fun." The body's real needs for nutrition,

290

rest, exercise, and relaxation are constantly signaled to us. We habitually override and ignore these natural requests and stop hearing the signals. This desensitization to the body may not be felt in the short term, but the chronic result is ailment, disease, and breakdown.

What we call the "natural" messages and workings of the body are really impulses of the Divine. You don't have to read a book or study nutrition to discover which foods your body requires. You don't need to calculate how much sleep is best for you or what type of exercise to get. When your body is injured or an organ damaged, you don't have to instruct the cells how to perform their healing tasks. Your respiration and digestion efficiently and continuously transpire without your personal oversight. Where does this knowledge, inherent in the body, come from? While science has done reasonably well to describe how the body works, it can't explain *why* it works. If not impulsed by Spirit, the body ceases to function. When the soul departs the body, see how well science can make it work.

The importance of the body in our quest for spiritual realization is also often ignored and neglected. While we are told in Western religions the body is the "Temple of God," you don't hear too much exposition about this from the pulpit. In contrast, many Eastern paths place great emphasis on physical health. In yoga, for example, purification of the body is considered fundamental to the development of mental clarity, and such clarity is thought essential for the realization of subtle spiritual vibrations. Many religions recognize that an unhealthy body hampers meditation. How often will you see Spirit in your temple if the floors are dirty and the altar left unattended? And in the more practical realm, how can you fulfill God's work on this Earth if the vehicle given you to perform your service is in disrepair? Disregard for the body may be a sin of omission, but contempt for the body is blasphemy.

Attendance to the *real* needs of the body is acting in consonance with Spirit. It is an act of Self-love. Most of us, to some degree, are in conflict with our body. Whether it is a matter of neglect, or dislike or hatred of our physical form, the result impedes God-realization. Self-love is the foundation of spiritual life. The first and greatest commandment is to love God completely, with all your heart, soul, and mind. How can you begin to love God if you neglect, dislike or abuse the physical temple in which God dwells? How can you possibly love your neighbor if you reject yourself? Jesus said, "Love thy neighbor *as* thyself." Isn't your capacity to truly love another limited, then, by your inability to love yourself?

Many years ago I decided to see for myself whether attending to the body really is a form of spiritual practice. I was determined to switch places and become the servant of my body. For two or three days I intently listened to the internal signals and gave top priority to the body's wants. If I had to urinate, I didn't wait until the next commercial, I immediately got up and went. If hunger began I asked my body what it wanted, and its response governed my choice of food. I was extremely diligent about ending a meal at the exact moment my body communicated it was full. If my eyes were tired I shut them, even if it meant abandoning temporarily the newspaper or office file in front of me. On the first urge to defecate I left for the bathroom rather than making one more phone call. If I sensed a need for motion, I got off that chair or bed. An urge for rest was met with the interruption of my activity.

The yogis call this "following your *prana*" (innate energy). As I got into the practice I found it very enjoyable and self-caressing. I quickly became much more sensitized to my body and discovered I could "hear" messages and sense signals that I routinely missed. This sensitivity soon expanded beyond my physical body, and I experienced heightened emotional and mental awareness. Paradoxically, although I directed much of my attention inward, I also became more conscious of my environment and the people around me. Any activity we engage in, if it is consonant with Spirit, will reveal to us both our interior and exterior worlds.

For me, consciously attending the body was a worthwhile exercise. Obviously, it is not something you can do with the intensity I have described when certain practicalities of life demand otherwise. If I'm conducting Beethoven's Fifth Symphony in concert, I'm not going to stop the orchestra and walk off the stage during the fourth movement just to take a tinkle. But our shortcoming here is body disregard, not an excess of sensitivity or attentiveness—so you might want to try this experiment, as external situations permit.

"Your honor, my body demands a respite, so I'm going to have to depart the courtroom now for a bit!" My fancied plea would have earned me a couple of hours in a holding cell. Judge Alaimo left little room to contest his decrees, so onward I went, running below empty and hoping I wouldn't stall before the lunch break.

"We call back to the stand Mr. Robert Perlman." I had led Bob through the program more times than I could remember. *Just get it right one more time.*

"Mr. Perlman, next to you is a picture of a ivory model boat which the government's expert, Mr. Godfrey, testified was selling in Hong Kong for twenty or thirty thousand dollars just two years ago. Does this information, sir, alter your opinion that the Plaintiffs' comparably sized boat was worth $343,000?"

"No sir, it does not."

The follow-up had to wait for the completion of my perfectly timed bewildered pause. "Why doesn't it change your opinion Mr. Perlman."

With rising cadence and arm stretching towards the blow-up beside him, Bob crescendoed, "Because *this* boat is not made of ivory!"

The jury didn't need my tasteful display of astonishment to move to the edge of their seats. The judge, clerks, and bailiffs popped up, knowing this would be far different than the usual rebuttal testimony. The next question and answer revealed the boat's bone constitution.

"But, Mr. Perlman, why would a bone model be valued differently than an ivory counterpart?" I queried.

"Ivory is a prized and valued substance; bone is refuse. Ivory sells for hundreds of dollars a pound, bone for nine cents a pound. Works of art are made from ivory. You make soup with bone."

I could have hugged Perlman on the spot. The jury loved it, and the clerks and bailiffs puffed with restrained laughter. As for David and Ann, they looked too shocked to move. We got to dollars, and Bob's analogy of ivory and bone to diamond and cubic zirconium was enough said on that subject.

How did Bob know the boat was made from bone? He had never seen Godfrey's boat, and the detail needed to be tied down.

"Mr. Perlman, how do you know that . . ." *Ouch*—some muscle popped in my neck, and the back of my head and neck were shouting in pain. *It'll have to wait.* "How do you know that Godfrey's boat is made from bone?"

Here came Bob's conversations with the manager of Le Extreme Orient and reference to the manager's confirming written statement. Next was Bob's positive match of our photo in evidence with Godfrey's picture and the photo on the manager's statement. Still not a peep from the government.

We were not done yet. Happily for me, Perlman had authored a couple of articles on the subject of telling ivory from its imitators. He well described how bone carvings proliferated upon the skyrocketed price of ivory and the later import ban. Carvers predominantly used either camel or ox bone for their imitations, and Bob explained how the bone was treated to make it appear like ivory. And let's not leave out "ivoreen." This product consisted of ivory dust, ground from the scrapings and discards of ivory carvers, combined with a plastic and then poured into molds of traditional pieces. "Ivoreen" contained minimal amounts of ivory, and all it did was provide unscrupulous dealers some cover from fraud while they misrepresented this product as the real thing.

"Mr. Perlman, is it difficult for someone to tell the difference between an ivory carving and one made from bone?"

Keeping a straight face he countered, "For the layman it might prove difficult, but for someone with *any* expertise in ivory, it's child's play."

With enough fun under our belts, I turned Bob over for cross. David and Ann, coming out of shock, were now slumped in their chairs and had the look of two small children missing their clothes. A few inconsequential questions may have been muttered on cross-examination. I was surprised we got through our performance without a whimper from the other side. I could think of numerous objections I would have made in their place. Even if they couldn't stop the juggernaut, at least they could have interrupted its pace.

We trotted out Arthur and Manny, who gave their similar spins on the bone boat, and then we rested our case. The government had one last bite at the apple, and that meant bringing Godfrey back on the stand. David requested a moment to consider the option, and Alaimo let him exit the courtroom. After a minute or two my opponent entered and announced that the United States had no further witnesses or evidence. The judge sent us to lunch, and our side exuberantly spilled out of court. We all sensed our case was won. We converged in the hallway, and Manny, Mary, Constance, my secretary Cindy, and Bob all bubbled in the rush of this stellar performance. I, of course, cautioned that the trial was not over yet.

Bob, who had left the courtroom after his testimony, provided us a tasty tidbit. A few moments before, he overheard David tell Godfrey that we claimed the boat was bone and then ask Godfrey whether he wanted to go back on the stand to refute this. Bob said Godfrey declined the offer with the claim of an impending flight, then grabbed his tail between his legs and scampered down the hall.

After waiting for the chuckles to subside, I shared my surprise over Bob's revelation. If Bob got it right—and I had no reason to believe he didn't—David had violated the court's pre-trial order. Alaimo had specifically prohibited us from discussing with any witness, including our experts, the testimony of any other witness during the course of the trial. Calling Godfrey back to the stand was David's decision to make *without* boning up his expert. Although this was a serious offense, my surprise appeared to be unshared. In Manny and Mary's view of David, his behavior was par for the course. I guess I still thought more of my adversary than did my clients.

With the retinue dispersing, I clued Constance in on my physical condition. The throbbing pain was substantial and unremitting. We found a quiet place, and I tried my ten minutes of closed eyes without much success. Unfortunately, while some brief but timely work may secure the latch on the barn door, once the animals have escaped, getting them back in can take days roaming the countryside. I did my best, and we left to join the others for lunch. We still had our final arguments to make to the jurors, and the judge would give his legal instructions before their deliberation. Alaimo had yet to resolve the differences between the jury instructions and verdict forms each side had submitted. Without some unforeseen catastrophe, I believed the case was ours. All I had to do was keep standing.

And stand I did as David and I waited beside the bench to receive the judge's rulings on jury instructions. These directives explain the legal issues in the case and the process by which the jury should reach its decision. Most instructions become so technical—presumptions, permissible inferences, burden of proof, and so on—many think they do more to confuse than assist the jury. Though there has been a movement to simplify jury instructions, it still has not firmly taken hold.

The differences in our proposed instructions were not great enough to warrant upset by either David or me over any of the judge's decisions. What came next, though, had us both spinning. Alaimo handed each of us a copy of *his* proposed verdict form. On this paper the jury records the results of its deliberations. Judge Nimmons had agreed at pre-trial that all the jury would do is determine: whether the items were part of Plaintiffs' personal collection; if that were so, their value when donated; and whether Plaintiffs were responsible for any penalties. Calculation of any refund was deferred for the number crunchers.

Staring us blankly in the face was a verdict form with two alternative lines: "We find for the Plaintiffs in the amount of $_____;" or, "We find for the defendant."

"The jury can't enter a refund amount for the Plaintiffs . . . they have no ability to make this determination . . . there's insufficient evidence for them to calculate a refund." We fielded our protests and reminded Alaimo of our stipulation approved by Judge Nimmons.

Alaimo would have none of it. He said our proposed verdict forms were much too complicated and the jury would never understand them or get through them. Granted, there were twenty donated items and the jury would have to reach separate determinations for each, and then move on to the penalties by separate tax year. My verdict form was streamlined compared to David's, but even mine would be a chore for the jury. But there was no other way around it. Going with the judge's form would render a nonsensical verdict that would have to be thrown out after trial.

The more we argued—I was now principal spokesman—the more Alaimo hunkered in. Finally he had enough, sent us back to our seats with his verdict form, brought in the jury, and commanded we proceed with our closing arguments. At my station Manny and Mary wanted to know about the ruckus, and I barely had a second to explain when the judge piped, "Mr. Felos, your closing argument please."

What the heck was I even going to tell the jury to do with this verdict? I couldn't believe it—we'd come all this way for a mistrial. There would be no surprises left in our bag when we re-tried this case next month, or next year, or whenever—if ever!

Under the barrel of Alaimo's gun I paused, reached deep down for some Truth, and came up with, "Your honor, may I *please* approach the bench?" I hoped I was approaching the judge's good spirit rather than a citation for contempt.

"All right, Mr. Felos, but the time is coming off your closing argument." Up again we went.

"Your honor, we have all worked very hard these past three days to finish this trial. The court has done its best to assure that each side has been treated fairly. I know that your primary concern here is that justice be served. Your honor, if we proceed with this verdict form, all our efforts will be wasted. We *will* have to retry this case. I know you don't want that to occur. I feel so strongly about this, I would rather use the defendant's verdict form than proceed as we are going. I respectfully urge the court to reconsider."

If this isn't what I said, I came pretty close. I wasn't begging, arguing, or trying to manipulate the judge; I was expressing what was true at that moment. Alaimo turned to David, and my opponent harmonized. With a sigh as if he resigned himself to an irresistible impetus, the judge acceded.

As we headed back for closing arguments, I considered the action of my adversary. Alaimo never would have shifted had David uttered the slightest opposition to my plea. David likely knew he had lost this case and could have easily scuttled the trial. His prospects would significantly improve by forcing another go-round. Why did David choose as he did? From one side you could argue that, having just gone through three days of nerve-wracked misery, David would do anything to get it over and avoid a replay. On the other hand, we could suggest that as an officer of the court interested in promoting justice, David was propelled to do the right thing. Another choice of trains to take at the station. I ascribe the lofty motivation to my opponent. Why not think the best of someone when given the opportunity?

The best I could think of for closing was a fairy tale. I told the story of the Emperor with no Clothes. It seemed a clever way to state the obvious: the government and its expert were naked, shorn from their pretense and exposed, left with no case at all. We all knew it, and somebody had to point the finger. I spent most of my time explaining to the jury how to fill out that monster of a verdict form.

But there was a point when I felt I really reached them, a place where communication came from the heart. I picked up a two-by-three-foot blow-up of the jade table screen, the one that displayed the side with the gold-engraved nature scene, and walked to the jury.

"You don't need any experts to tell you whether this is art. Look at this. It is exquisite. It is extraordinarily beautiful." And it truly is. I stood and took a few moments for myself to appreciate the splendor and subtle beauty before my eyes. The situation momentarily disappeared and the trial was gone. Isn't that what art is supposed to do? I believe the jury shared a similar experience. I then looked over to the government's table and found inspiration for my final remarks.

"Our government is extremely powerful. Its agency, the Internal Revenue Service, can take your money, seize your property. But we don't live under some communist or authoritarian regime. There is a rule of law and day of reckoning. Eventually, even if it takes years and years, the state is forced to have its actions scrutinized by you. You are the bulwark and the arbiters of our freedom. No matter how much power the state holds and no matter how hard it grasps, it must yield to your decision. That is the greatness of our country." This could have been gifted grandstanding, but it wasn't. It truly sprang from my heart, and I believed what I said. The jury can tell the difference, and I felt they resonated with this message.

David gave an excellent closing argument; it was his high point of the trial. Although he didn't have much to work with, he skillfully burnished the chinks in our armor and did his best to conspicuously project the flaws in our case. Jury instructions took about a half-hour, and our panel exited about three-thirty.

Finally—just the wait—nothing to do, nothing to think of, no matter or thing or person requiring my attention. The relief a trial lawyer feels when that jury walks out of the courtroom is hard to describe. I let everyone else take to the vigil while I tried to find a wave of decompression to ride. The search was not easy. Attempting to relax around my spasmodic neck musculature was the best I could do. Minutes turned to more hours than we thought would be necessary for the jury to get through the verdict form. Figuring out what a jury is doing and how they're leaning is about as accurate as palmistry or reading tea leaves; absent real divination, it's little more than a parlor game.

We started to worry. At seven o'clock or so, the bailiff summoned us to chambers with information that the jury had sent a message to the judge. I guess visiting Federal judges don't work past five on Fridays, since we were met with Magistrate Jenkins who read to us the jury's note. Our group of seven was unable as yet to reach a verdict and asked whether they could break for the weekend and return Monday morning to resume their deliberations. What was so hard for them to resolve? David expressed no opinion and deferred to the court's wisdom. I asked to consult with my clients.

I formed our powwow. We started in on the guessing and ran by some pros and cons. We didn't want to keep the jurors here against their will and possibly force an unfavorable decision. On the other hand we were reluctant to send them home for a couple of days and by some quirk have the entire trial unravel. (Stranger things have happened.) Anxiety compelled our decision. Manny and Mary simply could not bear the stress of waiting through the weekend, so they said. The magistrate was inclined to keep the jury, so she easily agreed with our decision. We all concurred on the wording of the return note, counsel departed chambers, and we resumed our wait.

I had just started to settle back in with my clients when the bailiff burst into our room with the announcement we had a verdict. Well, we forced their hand—let's see what we got. We reassembled in the courtroom and carefully watched the jury procession. As my favorite juror walked by me toward her seat she projected a marked glumness that seemed to say "I'm sorry." The next bad sign was the rise of the insurance adjuster. He had been selected jury foreman and now was going to read the verdict.

"Yes . . . yes . . . yes . . ." These successive affirmations answered the question whether plaintiffs held each item for a year prior to donation. More yeses to the question whether each piece was a "capital asset." These two inquiries were David's convoluted way of having the jury determine if the donations were part of Manny and Mary's personal collection. We had made it past the first hurdle. Next came the numbers: "A blue covered jar—twenty-five hundred dollars; a moulded snuff bottle—eighteen hundred dollars; a blue and white snuff bottle—thirty-two hundred dollars."

As I scribbled the bucks it seemed the jury was giving us exactly what we asked for on each item.

"A jade koro—fifty thousand dollars . . ."—a little more than half our request.

As the numbers poured in, all of the smaller items were on our mark, but the jury cut the table screen and ivory boat: $42,000 for the jade disc and $158,000 for the emperor's yacht. Next came the penalties. No negligence and no substantial understatement—Manny and Mary were penalty free.

The outcome was a victory to be sure. There were the hugs, exclamations of gratitude to the jury, and the offer of a handshake to David, although I declined to add the customary, "Nice working with you."

Oh, those insurance adjusters! Reading the jury proved easy in hindsight. My favorite juror, with, I suspect, a majority following, was ready to give us one hundred percent on our big-ticket items.

The adjuster, true to his color, and perhaps with a supporter or two of his own, just couldn't bear to fully open those purse strings. That apparently was the jury's impasse. I think my juror, rather than award us less than what we wanted, was willing to come back after a weekend and work more on her opponent. But with the locked-in jury unable to pry more out of the adjuster, our champion reluctantly agreed to the reduced amounts. Thus the glum face. And it wasn't hard to figure out where the jury got the $158,000 for the ivory. That matched the amount the importer quoted when trying to sell the boat to Perlman.

Hopefully the jury's struggle and compromised numbers would prove inconsequential. My quick addition and rough calculations seemed to show that the first $300,000 my clients paid would cover their tab with the I.R.S. If we could fully apply that barred payment to their tax liability, we had about $800,000 coming to us, assuming, of course, we also could stave off the expected appeals—another succession of minefields to traverse. But after years of the army clawing for territory inch by inch, it was time for a breakthrough. Things don't have to be hard—really.

# CHAPTER THIRTY

# *Off into the Sunset*

SOME OF THE BEST SUNSETS ARE THE UNEXPECTED ONES. Over the summer Gulf the early evening skies often display the moisture-laden blacks and grays that are simultaneously the remnants of the last tropical downpour and the makings of the next. As the covered sun sinks toward the horizon, sometimes a small cloud break occurs and a shaft explodes into the dusky canopy, wildly illuminating part of the amphitheater with tawny oranges, reds, and pinks. Sometimes only the horizon is layered with wide brush strokes of cloud and haze. Will the circle of fire be obscured at the final moments of its descent? As the sun falls to meet the water it slips behind a curtain, but then a few seconds later reappears, miraculously setting in front of a more distant backdrop of gray. When it unexpectedly emerges at the last moment in a wet charcoal sky, occasionally it radiates a red or pink that is so otherworldly, you are surreally transported as if you were now watching this spectacle from Mars or perhaps some place in your dreams. And just as startling, you may see no sun or glow at all where it has set, but later behold rivers of crimson streaking across improbable parts of the horizon.

A poet would add the gentle play of dolphins to these sunset surprises. But it is usually the morning hours that bring these lovely creatures in view of our dock. Sometimes they glide through St. Joseph Sound with supple grace, and other times they display intense bursts of power, as when churning the water in pursuit of

302

mullet. When the tide is up a bit they occasionally come right up to the end of the dock. Once, a large dolphin, swimming parallel to the sea wall, went right under the planks as I stood two or three feet above. I exhilarated in the sound of the air streaming through its blowhole as it swam beneath me.

And then there are the manatees! Most often their presence is betrayed by a ripple in the water followed by barely surfaced nostrils. Just sighting a speck of their immense form is enough for a thrill. Sometimes you may spot a dark gray back momentarily curve out of the water, and only after it has submerged do you realize the lack of a dorsal fin made this a manatee rather than the dolphin you first assumed you saw. A close encounter with sea cows is rarer than with the Sound's dolphins. One sunny morning I was slowly pacing the dock, customarily spying for mullet with cast net in hand and teeth. I caught sight of a pod of at least fifteen manatees a couple of hundred yards out, moving in a long line to the north. A few moments later a huge area of clear water in front of me turned brown, and I knew that one had broken from the pod to feed on the tasty sea grass around the dock.

Where would he surface? The water kept roiling until I saw his back about thirty feet to my left. *What a giant.* Then with an effortlessness seemingly inconsistent with his bulk, he circled to the front of the dock and displayed his full form just a whisker away from my cemented legs. There must have been at least ten or twelve feet in front of that flat tail and near half that much in width. If this weren't enough, about twenty feet away on each side of the behemoth a youngster popped up. They seemed to be standing straight, with their heads and shoulders out of the water. Perhaps this was a mom after all.

Constance and I have experienced many joys on our new-found perch facing Caladesi Island and the Gulf of Mexico across St. Joseph Sound. For me, the greatest joy has been the one I didn't anticipate. Even more than the sublime sunsets, playful dolphins, majestic manatees, and all the various water birds and other wildlife are the *mullet*. Considered a junk fish out of the Gulf region, mullet is commercially pursued primarily for roe that is sold in Japan at astronomical prices. Floridians know and enjoy the wonderful taste of these beautiful blue-hued plant eaters and most prefer their mullet smoked. The cast net led me to mullet love. Since there is nothing you can put on a hook to compel this vegetarian to bite, a net is demanded if you wish to transfer mullet from the water to your plate.

Though I haven't exactly been transformed into a hunter/ gatherer, I have spent long and happy hours on the dock peering through the water in search of mullet, studying their movement and habits, and becoming familiar with their life cycle. My neighbors most often see me sporting a pith helmet and sunglasses with net ready to spread. And coming up on two years in our new home, my casting proficiency has yielded admirable quantities of my fish. On occasion I might come home from work, see nothing in the fridge worthy of dinner, and walk out and hear a big splash. Mullet are proficient jumpers. Fifteen minutes later there is a fish in my net, and in less than an hour it is in my stomach. In some small way I can understand why the ancients honored the spirit of their prey and ritualized the hunt. I won't go as far to say I worship this fish, but my wife Constance still chuckles when I periodically express my fondness and respect for the creature.

It was the unanticipated and least expected in *Fellouzis v. United States* that brought me to my resting place on the water. After the trial, all seemed business as usual. David promptly filed a motion asking Alaimo to bypass the jury and enter judgment for the government on the issue of penalties. According to my opponent, that matter should never have gone to the jury in the first place. Shortly after I filed my response, the court denied the motion. With the government's options foreclosed at the trial level, now came the expected appeal. Before even addressing the penalty and other subsidiary issues, the Eleventh Circuit Court of Appeal would have to rule in our favor on statute of limitations. If the misaddressed envelope sank the case, there wouldn't be much left for the appellate court to decide.

In the meantime we were following our pre-trial stipulation to calculate the refund. My rough numbers showed the worst we could do was about $435,000, with the best just shy of $800,000.

David had agreed to send me I.R.S. computations as a starting point. This was a bear of an issue. Figuring out my clients' tax liability based on the jury's verdict was easy. What to do with the barred payment was another story.

As simply as can be put, when Manny and Mary first paid $300,000 to the government, that sum was just sufficient to cover all the taxes and interest they owed, as would later be calculated per the jury's decision. To our way of looking at it, all my clients' subsequent payments should therefore be fully refundable with interest. But the way the I.R.S. initially applied the $300,000 did not coincide with the subsequent jury determined liabilities. Thus, a good portion of what my clients first paid was allocated to liabilities they would not ultimately owe. Likewise, parts of their subsequent payments were used to pay taxes later found to be due per the verdict. And since we couldn't recover any of the $300,000, the government allocation resulted in initial overpayments lost to the statute of limitations and some of our non-barred payments lost to the satisfaction of valid tax liability.

If this is making any sense, you are way ahead of the curve. It barely made sense to David and me, and it was our case. I'm sure both of us had misgivings about trying to explain all this to the judge. You would think the prospect of re-entering Alaimo's courtroom for a mini-trial on this issue would provide us good incentive to work it out ourselves. But since when did good sense ever get us to settle on anything?

Again the government apparently had the best of the law. It seems the I.R.S. was entitled to allocate the $300,000 as it did because my clients' first attorney never objected. But was that initial allocation now binding? Who knows? Here's another new one for the law books. With the refund calculation yet to be tackled, and with the statute of limitations heading up to the appellate arenas for a very lengthy battle, we would have settled the case if the government had paid us $450,000 and let us go home. A quick phone call from David with an offer would have gladly sent us packing.

As July approached, we hunkered in for the long haul. Since appeals were not part of our contingency fee agreement, that meant more negotiating with Manny and Mary. I thought billing on an hourly basis was the fairest way to go. This idea seemed to send spasms of dread through my clients. Who knew how far the government might push? We could easily have more than one appeal to the Eleventh Circuit, and Manny was convinced the government would take this to the Supreme Court if it were unsuccessful with the intermediate appeals. Under that scenario, appellate fees could approach six figures, and there was, by far, no guarantee of winning. But then again, if we worked the appeals on a contingency, we might settle out on the short term, and the clients would end up paying much more in fees. That was the gamble, and I did my best to run through all the possibilities with my clients.

My choice was to start on the hourly payroll. I could use a little cash inflow from this case after all these years. Manny and Mary not only insisted on the contingency, but wanted the agreement to cover *all* appeals, even if the case made it up to Washington. With the prospect of years more work and an uncertain payday, I told my clients I needed an additional fifteen percent on top of the one-third contingency. This meant my total fee, if ever received, would be 48 1/3 % of the gross recovery. I suggested to Manny and Mary they consider a reduced contingency fee for just the Eleventh Circuit work, and I again alternatively extolled the benefits of paying on an hourly basis. Manny claimed peace of mind drove his decision. He needed to know that all legal work prompted by government appeals in this case would be accomplished without his out-of-pocket expense. So be it.

On July 5th we signed our new fee agreement, in which I extensively recounted all of my clients' options and specifically recited my rejected recommendations. Two days later I received a call from the Appellate Division of the United States Department of Justice. Bridget Rowan, the Division's attorney, politely informed me that the Solicitor General of the United States had decided to drop the appeal. What did that mean exactly? The United States would no longer contest the statute of limitations issue or the jury verdict. *Manna from heaven—my God!* Was this just a temporary shift in the political winds? If so, I needed to lock in Uncle Sam as best and as quickly as I could.

My next two or three weeks were consumed by sensitive discussions with the Appellate Division. This resulted in a stipulation for dismissal of the appeal and a semi-legally binding letter from the government agreeing never again to object to the jury's verdict. Our agreement didn't cover the refund calculation. The government reserved the right to appeal any order the trial court might enter on that issue.

Had we actually won? Was the major part of this war over? It seemed too simple. Why had the adversary all of a sudden reversed course? I felt like a battle-weary soldier who has been in war for so long he is frozen in shock when it finally ends. Manny and Mary, after their shock wore off, were initially suspicious and then, of course, delighted. When I had first told Manny about my conversations with Bridget Rowan and the possibility we wouldn't have to defend the appeals, he piped with relief that he was spared the added contingency fee. Did he really believe that, or was he being savvy? I reminded him our appellate contract was indeed still in effect, and we ended this go-round with my promise I would revisit the fee issue when the case finally concluded.

We still had the refund amount to work out. Even with the appeal gone, we easily would have settled had the government offered to split the difference in our numbers: $600,000 would have happily sent us to the showers. Within two weeks of the dismissal of the appeal, I received a letter from the Assistant Attorney General, probably authored by David, saying the government accepted our numbers and would be transmitting to me the refund checks as soon as the they got them from the I.R.S.

*Pinch me if I'm dreaming!* Had some heavy politico in the Justice Department ordered the troops to fall on their swords? Six weeks earlier we were working the long haul and would have delighted in a $400,000 settlement offer. Why hadn't the government simply initiated a compromise, rather than desert their case and hand us an extra $400k? After intense years of opposition, the United States of America suddenly and miraculously ended its case without a whimper.

Two months later I opened an envelope from the Justice Department and beheld the Statue of Liberty proudly emblemed on five United States Treasury checks totaling $813,343.52. I was overwhelmed. It is one thing knowing you have won; it's a quite another holding the fruits of your victory in your hand. I had never held so much money before in my life. The sight and feel and touch of these checks brought a greater and tangible reality to the victory. After some leaping about at the office, I called Manny and Mary, and we set a next day meeting to reckon our accounts.

Before facing my clients I needed my own reckoning. Starting with the numbers in our agreements, I was entitled to 48 1/3 % of $813,343, which translated into a $393,116 fee. Did that sound and look good! Without the appellate contingency, my original one-third totaled $271,114. My gosh, the fee for appeals that basically never happened, is over one hundred twenty-two thousand. That didn't seem too fair. On the other hand, I had spent close to a thousand hours on the case, which translates to a little less than $400 per hour. That's extremely reasonable for a contingency fee case. With the risk of never getting paid, courts commonly approve a resulting hourly rate two or three times the norm. The total fee looked reasonable when measured against the case as a whole, but standing alone, the appellate fee could raise eyebrows. Then again, our appellate agreement was crystal clear: "the clients acknowledge and understand that if the appeal filed by the United States is the only appeal taken by the United States, or that appeal is dismissed, the attorneys are still entitled to the entire 15% contingency fee." No wiggle room here. And wasn't it Mary who told me, when I pleaded for a fee adjustment in the darkest moments of the case, "a contract is a contract"?

On and on I went. Was I entitled to the fee; was it fair? Of course it was. I had worked miracles in this case. I earned it. I did get the better of the deal on the appellate contract, but my clients got the better deal on the trial agreement. But it still didn't sit right. As I continued to mull, Constance offered some clarity. As a partner in a large downtown Tampa firm for many years, she knew I had achieved a stellar result in this case. She also recognized that in most other firms, the effort I had expended would have been spread amongst a team of attorneys and would have cost the clients a fortune. The real question, she thought, was whether I believed I was *worthy* of the fee. Did I have some poverty consciousness to overcome? Did I truly value my efforts and abilities? Were there remnants of unworthiness lying around here?

After a pensive night, I met with Manny and Mary and told them how I felt and what I had decided. I believed I had provided exceptional service, obtained an extraordinary result, had well earned the fee, and did not choose to reduce the contractual amounts. I had difficulty saying this, and I'm sure it was not what my clients wanted to hear. They accepted my decision graciously and were predominantly relieved their fourteen-year struggle had finally ended. Of course, being handed a check for close to $420,000 helped brighten their morning.

It took Constance and me six months or so to find our 160 feet on the water. Had I not thought it possible, it never would have manifested for me. The same principle applied to the case. As the judge was deciding its fate, we began those fourteen months by intensively applying spiritual thought. We composed a spiritual mind "treatment," wrote it on index cards, put one in each pocket, and affixed the rest to bathroom mirrors, our car dashboards, the refrigerator, and other places in daily view. For a week or two we kept the treatment in our minds and firmly rooted in our consciousness. The applied spiritual thought was not just about obtaining an outcome; it also sought the manifestation of justice. So, in our minds, the result we held was a favorable, just, and equitable judicial ruling.

At that same time, I was defending a securities arbitration case for a major national brokerage. We had asked the arbitrators to dismiss the disgruntled customer's claim without conducting the customary trial. Such a decision would be unprecedented in arbitration proceedings of this nature. We wrote a spiritual mind treatment for that case on the same index cards. The panel was much quicker than Judge Nimmons, and a month or two later came the order of dismissal. Ironically, the basis for denying the claim was the customer's failure to present it within the time period required by the statute of limitations. In that case though—lest you think the law is completely arbitrary—the claimant had filed the action significantly and unquestionably beyond the time bar.

Other attorneys I knew, familiar with securities arbitration, were startled I got the case dismissed without having to go through trial.

We can become very proficient in shaping and creating our world through the use of mind. We discussed this before, using the analogy of the motion picture projector and screen. When we discover the relationship between thought and the play of our lives—when we see that the light of consciousness projects the stuff of our minds—then we can purposefully change our world by changing what we think.

Therefore, it is no surprise so many people in "new thought" (actually, there's nothing new about it), so many fundamental Christians, and countless others of no labeled persuasion are occupied and preoccupied with altering their mental landscape. They are expending great effort to align their minds with health, wealth, and whatever else they desire. For many it almost seems that "spiritual life" is just a means to prosperity, when in fact *real* prosperity is simply an ancillary effect of being spiritually centered. In any event, I'm sure most people begin to lead happier and more fulfilling lives when they discover the creative power of mind and start to consciously apply it.

When engaged in the process of using positive thought to create a better life, many people are not aware of the limitations found along this path. No matter how well we may watch and train our mind, for most of us it is unlikely we are aware of, let alone can control, the one-hundred-fifty thousand or so thoughts or "mind moments" we have each waking day.

Not only is our mind filled with much we don't notice, it is also subject to subconscious impulses significantly driven by a societal consciousness, which, at the moment is not particularly healthy. As our mental muscle increases, we can never be certain our power will not manifest an unconscious desire or fulfill an intended want that, through our lack of wisdom, doesn't serve us. Many practicing spiritual thought fail to realize this and therefore may become perplexed, disappointed, and discouraged by the unintended consequences of their practice. Even with our best of intentions and increasing prowess, at our stage of growth, we simply cannot master the entirety of our lives by controlling what we think.

This lesson, well known to the ancient Greeks, is magnificently taught in their greatest tragedies. The drama starts with someone, usually a king, on top of the world. He rules a vast empire with wisdom and kindness; his subjects and his family adore him; every facet of his life seems perfectly in place and in unassailable control. But some trivial incident exposes a minute character flaw, which, projected by the enormous power of our monarch, leads to his destruction. By the end of the play the king is either blind, or a beggar, or dead, and his realm and family are in utter ruin.

Those creatively applying thought, quickly come to appreciate the enormous projective power of mind. With a capable slide projector and a cavernous room, a one-inch slide can assume monumental proportion. Likewise, your mental projection may vividly assume considerable material proportion. This unfortunately leads many practitioners to become afraid of their thought and their speech, the latter being "verbal thought." I have often heard one person say with fear or concern to another, "Did you hear what you just said? You don't want that to happen. Better be careful what you say."

This fear is misplaced and results from attachment to thought. If you have changed the contents of your mind, the movie on the screen of your life may now be an uplifting tale rather than its former tragedy. But if you believe you *are* your new story, just as you once believed you were the old, you are still attached to the illusory drama of your life. You control the story line much more than you did before, but are still subject to suffer the unexpected script developments that are not to your liking. And if you're dynamically projecting your mind stuff on the *big* screen, the objects of your suffering can assume vast dimension.

Despite its limitations and pitfalls, recognizing the nature of thought and transitioning from negative to positive thinking is important and useful. But it is only a transition—just a stage along the path of Self-realization—not an end in itself. Ultimately, it doesn't make a bit of difference what you think. You heard me right. "As he thinketh . . . so is he" (Proverbs 23: 7). Scripture doesn't say a man is *what* he thinketh. We are *as* we think. This means that our thoughts, the contents of our minds, are irrelevant to who we are. It is our relationship to thought, our process of thinking, that determines our identity and self-experience. Our true nature is found when we disidentify ourself from the contents of mind, whether that content is unmanifested or projected into form. Self-realization occurs when we discover *we are the light* that projects our thoughts rather than the thoughts themselves, no matter how wonderful they may be. It is then we realize we are of Spirit and one with God.

Something tells me I've pretty much said this before, which I'll take as a good sign it's about time for me to finish this book. What does the future hold for me—or better yet, what do I choose to make of the next part of my life? What place will the law hold for me? There are many, many suffering men and woman in my profession today. Countless lawyers find their practice an emotional and spiritual desert that withers the soul. These days the real lawyer joke is: "What do you call a group of attorneys?" No, the answer is not "shark bait," it is "a seminar on career change." I do what I do well, yet I play in a very tough arena.

A little less than a year after the *Fellouzis* case, I took a trip to the Pacific Northwest. While visiting a friend in Seaside, on the Oregon coast, we were walloped that evening by an ocean storm. The next morning I headed south on the serpentine coastal highway. The road hugs the Pacific prominences and provides a bird's-eye view of the spectacularly rocky shore several hundred feet below. Although the sun and blue sky brightened the vistas, the storm's tailwinds made for rough seas and enormous waves crashing on the cliffs below.

I turned a sharp bend and decided to edge off onto a little rest area wedged between the road and the cliff. As I climbed out of the car with my leather bomber jacket collar turned up, the buffeting winds made me appreciate the little wooden fence separating me from the precipice. I hung on the rail, looked twenty stories below, and saw a horseshoe-shaped cove cut into the rock face. In dead center was a small sandy beach area, and on each long side were huge jagged rock outcrops. Massive waves thundered in, most of which exploded onto the rocks, shooting spray sixty or seventy feet into the air. A small portion of the surf ended more peaceably by washing onto the cloistered beach.

While marveling at nature's raw spectacle, I thought I spotted a group of sea lions riding the crests below. Wait—no blubbered mammals here, this was a bunch of surfers in wet suits. I didn't know if I was more shocked in disbelief or just aghast. Were those people insane down there? I stood mesmerized above the ten-or-so thrillseekers for close to an hour. Some hit enormous waves and had the ride of their lives; but the wipeouts were brutal. I saw incredible skill and agility, and major displays of fearlessness—or perhaps recklessness, depending upon your point of view. In this roaring cauldron, it seemed the slightest misplay could send one crashing into the rock sides instead of onto the narrow safety of the beach. Sometimes a surfer would disappear under a wave, and I found myself respirationally tense when the length of a good long breath passed without a reappearance.

After a while I realized there must be a method to this madness. All the surfers were still breathing, and no one had yet been pulped by the rocks. Too much was happening here just to attribute to good luck. Although I saw no carnage, I'm sure each of the hardies, despite his experience and skill, took a beating. As I drove down the coast, the wind lightened and the day warmed.

In the next week my experience and mental image of the surfers percolated, then reappeared in the cloak of metaphor. I saw in it my work. Mine, in its own way, was as exciting and also as rough and violent. One moment I could ride peaks of supreme exhilaration and at other times feel as if I'd been crashed to bits. Although I'm not always able to ride the wave, I've always seemed able to use the bottoms in some magical way to transport me to an even greater summit. At what point, if ever, does the surfer, after enduring the pummeling his venue provides, decide to move on to a more friendly stretch of beach? Would my spirit sweetly and gently soar to new realms if I played in a different sandbox?

Is the law my *dharma,* my path of life? For me it's a challenge to vision George apart from George the lawyer. In a way I feel legally inbred. But I do sense something; I do see something coming into clarity. As the page falls closing this chapter of my life, as I feel its breath of wind touch me, yes—yes, I do see how the next passage begins. . . .

# Appendix A

T HE YOGIC PATHS TO ACTUALIZATION are many, the primary being: *jnanayoga,* the path of knowledge, discrimination and renunciation; karmayoga, the path of action without attachment to result; *bhaktiyoga,* the path of devotion; and *hatha-yoga,* the path of the body. According to scripture, the aspirant chooses the form of yoga best suited to individual temperament and personality—different strokes for different folks. Hathayoga is particularly well suited to the intellectually overdeveloped, those who, because mind-fixed, are underdeveloped in their emotional, physical, or spiritual awareness. It uses body and breath, which are so tangible and grounding, as a means to self-awareness. This yogic path engaged me in the early 1970s and also is the one most commonly practiced in our mentally dominated society.

Hathayoga is not calisthenics. Various physical postures, called *asanas,* are assumed with mental focus upon body sensation and breath. Performing these asanas brings physical and health benefits that attract many participants to yoga. These benefits are of secondary value, however. The primary benefit is training the mind to become one-pointed. And what better way to concentrate attention in the face of our constant mental distraction than by using the direct experience of the body? Mental concentration is the gateway to meditation, and meditation the means to calm and still the mind, the latter recognized by almost all religions and spiritual disciplines as essential to God-realization. Be still and know that I am God (Psalms 46: 10).

315

In almost all yoga taught today, the physical postures are demonstrated and thus learned by students. According to the esoteric understanding of yoga, these asanas were not developed or invented, but discovered. It is believed that thousands of years ago in India, the *rishis,* who were God-realized seers, transmitted the ancient Vedic scriptures and the systems of yoga. The rishis' direct experience of Universal Energy, which they called *prana,* naturally and spontaneously moved their bodies into certain postures. These recurring body manifestations of Spirit were described and taught, and became the asanas of yoga. Thus, the yoga posture is an archetypal physical expression of God Energy. Esoterically then, entering an asana is a sacred invocation or prayer. Like working from the bottom up, or configuring an antenna, you become receptive to higher energy—you invite Spirit to descend into flesh by assuming the physical form that is the endpoint of Spiritual transmission.

# Appendix B

"DISCRIMINATION" is one of those words that has developed a bad rap. Our ability to distinguish and discern is necessary for survival and growth. Through our laws, we have chosen to organize our society in a manner that restricts us from making most public and some private choices based upon distinctions of race, religion, ethnicity, age, and gender. I am not permitted to consider race in hiring, but I may do so in choosing a tennis partner. I am prohibited from refusing you lodging in my hotel because of your religion.

Societal debate continues over the range and scope of choices we wish to restrict and the types of distinctions that will trigger the restriction. May I refuse to rent you a room in my single-family house due to your religious persuasion, or am I required to live with someone of contrary religious belief if I wish to rent at all? We have chosen to add "disability" to our list of impermissible distinctions, but are not sure whether to add sexual preference to the roll. As a general principle, we the majority feel that our dealings with others should be based upon individual factors such as character and ability, rather than upon perceived group distinction.

Somehow our well-intended battle against *illegal* discrimination and stereotypical treatment has spilled over and stigmatized the general meaning of the word. I remember a lecture given by a civil rights activist in which he decried, "all forms of discrimination must be eradicated," a refrain heard in many political stump speeches. By contrast, you don't hear too many people these days stand up and proclaim, "I encourage discrimination and promote it as an essential life skill"—though we're still allowed to have discriminating palates and tastes! I'm having some fun here, but the current use of the word does not reflect just a change in its common meaning; it also represents a less obvious rejection of the word's underlying meaning.

In our quest to eradicate unwanted discrimination, we have debased the power to distinguish and have discouraged its use. What suffers is clarity and perception. We complain that the media of news, art, politics, and entertainment reduce their message to the lowest common denominator, leaving us with homogenized and formulistic pablum. Has our power of discrimination waned so much we in fact can't digest more complex information? Or have the media purveyors perhaps lost their ability to provide it? Good citizenship and conduct require a child to differentiate between acceptable and prohibited behavior. Who will proclaim that cultivating this power of discernment in our young has been a priority in our society? Our ability to distinguish between right and wrong often requires recognition of subtlety and nuance. How is that perception developed through use of the broad-brushed vision approved of today?

# Index

To contact the author or arrange for an appearance or seminar, write to 2210 Harborview Drive, Dunedin, FL 34698, call 727 736-1402, or e-mail proofg@aol.com.